The Squeaky Wheel

The Squeaky Wheel

Complaining *the Right Way* to Get Results, Improve Your Relationships, and Enhance Self-Esteem

Guy Winch, PhD

library of congress cataloging-in-publication data

Winch, Guy.
The squeaky wheel : complaining the right way to get results, improve your relationships, and enhance self-esteem / Guy Winch.
p. cm.
Includes bibliographical references and index.
ISBN 978-0-8027-1798-6 (alk. paper hardcover)
1. Consumer complaints—Psychological aspects. 2. Complaints (Rhetoric)—Psychological aspects. 3. Criticism. 4. Interpersonal relations.
5. Self-esteem. I. Title.
HF5415.52.W56 2011
381.33—dc22
2010024506

First published by Walker & Company in 2011

Paperback ISBN: 978-1-9763-4213-4

1 9 7 6 3 4 2 1 3 9

Designed by Adam Bohannon

Typeset by Westchester Book Group
Printed in the United States of America by Quad/Graphics, Fairfield, Pennsylvania

Contents

Acknowledgments

I first pitched the idea for a book about the psychology of complaining to my agent, Michelle Tessler, whose immediate and emphatic response was "Write it!" Her professionalism and involvement were evident in every step, from proposal to finished manuscript. My editor, Jacqueline Johnson, at Walker & Company, provided me with expert advice and suggestions and wonderfully constructive editorial comments, not to mention support and encouragement, throughout my work.

I would also like to thank my readers for their time and efforts, all of which contributed to improving the manuscript: Jessica Rackman, Emily Epstein, Cara Brendler, Dr. Jennifer Hofert, Richard Leff, Roberto Fantauzzi, Ruti Cohen, Jean Ward, Rob Neiffer, Ron Rudolph, Louise Shimron, and especially Raquel D'Apice, whose detailed suggestions were truly invaluable.

My family has been incredibly supportive and eagerly tested out the techniques I suggest in this book whenever an occasion presented itself. Their feedback and encouragement has been extremely helpful. My brother, Dr. Gil Winch, has served as a sounding board for practically every thought, question, doubt, and idea I wrestled with throughout the writing. He was first to read every word and first to offer feedback and encouragement when doing so. I cannot thank him enough.

I owe a general debt of gratitude to my patients, especially the ones I discuss in this book. It requires both strength and bravery to open one's heart and expose one's deepest feelings to a therapist. They have taught me much and inspired me in many ways.

Several people were generous with their time, allowing me to ask many questions and sharing their thoughts and insights. Gil Chaimovitcz from CY, Professor Robin Kowalski, Beckie Williams, "Cari," "Bill," and especially John A. Goodman, who took time out from an extremely busy schedule to meet with me in New York City and share his decades of wisdom and experience.

Finally, I would like to thank three psychologists whose mentoring over various stages of my career helped shape my professional development: Dr. Thalma E. Lobel, Dr. Adelbert Jenkins, and Dr. Diana Fosha. Their influence and teachings infuse my work both as a therapist and as a writer to this day.

Author's Note

When discussing my patients, I made efforts to disguise their identifying information. Consequently, all their names have been changed. In addition, I have used pseudonyms for Bill (my friend from chapter 2) and Cari (the tree champion from chapter 8) to protect their privacy. All other names mentioned are real.

I have tried to back up my assertions with empirical scientific studies, with preference to those published in scientific journals with blind peer-review acceptance procedures. I provide full references in the chapter notes (although due to space considerations, the list is not as exhaustive as I would have liked). Admittedly, some of my ideas about complaints and their impact on our psychology and emotions (such as the merits of complaining therapy) have not yet been scientifically studied beyond my own observations and case studies, and I endeavored to mention such shortcomings in the text whenever it was relevant.

I have also included additional resources for several topics I touch upon in the book, such as consumer advocacy groups, resources for parents dealing with teen substance abuse, and where parents can find support and information about addressing excessive homework in their child's school. All such resources can be found in the notes to the appropriate chapters.

Introduction

The squeaky wheel gets the grease.
—American idiom

In many ways, life was simpler in the days of the horse and carriage. Wheels squeaked when they needed oiling and we responded with grease. The feedback system between wagons and their owners worked perfectly. Our day-to-day existence was far more physically demanding back then, yet we spent much less time complaining to one another.

Today, even the best of our grumbling elite, our kvetching prodigies, the cream of our moaning crop, all waste huge amounts of time and emotional resources on complaints that yield neither responses nor resolutions. We complain about everything, from the weightiest global issues to the smallest details of our daily lives. We complain with equal vigor about bad politicians and bad pedicures; about wars with the same frequency we complain about the weather (actually, the weather usually gets the edge on that one). We even complain about the actions of characters in our favorite TV shows with the same immediacy and personal investment as we do about the actions of our spouse or our friends.

Somehow, over the decades, complaints devolved from being a goal-directed and useful activity to a national pastime. We have become a nation of squeakers who face daily frustrations, resentments, and irritations without a clue as to how to address them effectively. Psychologically speaking, our complaining behaviors represent a waste of our limited emotional resources on a monumental scale.

True, most of our complaints are not significant to our mental health in and of themselves. Bacteria are tiny organisms but taken together their mass is greater than that of all other living things on Earth combined. Similarly, the vast majority of our complaints are also small (e.g., "It's hot!"; "You're late!"; "Again the aisle seat?"; "This needs salt"; "Now it's too salty!"), but their combined volume overshadows our positive utterances combined. Consequently, our complaints have become an important component in our daily lives. Businesses spend billions of dollars a year handling consumer complaints. And the giants of customer service are no longer the only players competing for our complaint dollars. The Internet is seeing a boom of complaint-related startups such as domycomplaining.com, which for a small fee will actually complain for you. Some of these ventures are now attracting millions in investor capital.

By their sheer cumulative weight, the impact of our complaining behaviors on our mood and psychology is striking. Ineffective complaining can damage our self-esteem, lead to depression and anxiety, and hinder our careers. It can cost us cold hard cash, ruin our marriages, affect our children's risk of drug use, and in some cases pose significant risks to our health and longevity.

Over the years, I've come to view complaints as opportunities rather than obstacles. I've encouraged scores of my patients to make meaningful complaints more effectively, to refuse to settle for venting alone, to get results. Speaking up about a complaint and attaining a resolution makes us feel empowered, assertive, effective, and resourceful. It can boost our self-esteem and enhance our feelings of efficacy. It can help us battle depression, improve our relationships, salvage partnerships, and deepen friendships.

Our complaints should be more than the mere airing of grievances; they can be tools we use to bring about significant improvements in many aspects of our lives. Effective complaints could lead to fundamental changes in our communities and better public services. When we complain to a company about a product and get it to fix or improve it, other consumers gain from our actions too. When seven-year-old Sydney Hotard wrote a complaint letter to Terrebonne Parish president Michel Claudet in Louisiana about equipment dangers in her local playground, her actions benefited every other child in the neighborhood, who shared safer equipment and an improved facility. Effective complainers can benefit whole communities and entire countries. Consider how much change we could bring to the world if more of us learned to complain effectively about the things that mattered.

Most of us are not opposed to becoming effective complainers—we simply don't know how to go about developing our skill set. I encountered the same problem when I began my own journey into the world of complaining. But over time and with much trial and error, I began to develop and improve my complaining skills. I did so first by handling personal and consumer complaints in my own life and, later, through counseling patients (when relevant to do so) on how to handle theirs.

This book is meant as a first step in that direction, a toolbox for the task ahead. It is time we reclaimed complaints as the functional communications they once were and ought to be again.

Chapter One
The Ineffective Squeaker Doesn't Get the Grease

Thank you, Lisa, for teaching kids everywhere a valuable lesson. If things don't go your way, just keep complaining until your dreams come true.

—"Bill Clinton," *The Simpsons* (2000)

After the turn of the millennium, the real estate boom in New York City that had started in the midnineties was not expected to last. The burst of the dot-com bubble, the looming recession, and the tragic events of September 11, 2001, soon took their cumulative toll on a city that yearned to return to quiet and stability. Yet something surprising happened. The building frenzy in New York did not subside—it expanded. The charge was led by real estate developers and private investors who were mesmerized by the market's seemingly endless upward trajectory.

The city's few remaining vacant lots and parking facilities were snapped up like bloody stumps in a shark tank. Seemingly overnight, massive rezoning turned run-down and decrepit industrial buildings into lavish new condominiums with unimaginative brick facades, cookie-cutter interior layouts, and doorpersons dressed like toy soldiers with a tassel fetish. Instead of quiet and stability, change was everywhere.

Indeed, it wasn't long before the apartment building I had been living in for over six years was sold to new owners, who promptly converted the building into corporate apartments, doubling the rental prices. I started searching for a new place to live. Most of the new construction was targeted toward the "luxury rental" market. I quickly learned that although most "luxury" rental apartments were no larger or more modern than the apartment I was living in, they were twice as expensive. As one especially haughty building manager put it, "Sir, we offer a twenty-four-hour uniformed doorman, a Viking six-range professional oven, and a bidet in every apartment," all items I had somehow managed to live without. Clearly, "luxury" was not for me.

I soon found a rare gem, a sun-drenched apartment on a high floor with unobstructed views in a newly constructed building that was happily doorman-free. I moved in the day the building opened. The moment the movers left, I made my way through columns of boxes and Bubble Wrap-encased furniture to my sunny windows. I threw them open, leaned out, and took in a deep breath of faintly fresh Manhattan air. I glanced down and saw the greatest danger unobstructed southern-Manhattan exposures could ever face—a vacant lot.

I knew right away that my view-filled and sun-brightened days were numbered. I looked out and imagined a brick beanstalk sprouting up to block the morning sun like a permanent concrete eclipse. My heart sank. I had a friend in construction. I called him right away.

"How tall are the buildings on either side?" he asked.

"One is fourteen floors, the other's a brownstone."

"It'll be fourteen floors then," he said definitively. "But the brownstone on the other side means the upper floors will probably be recessed so you'll still get direct sunlight in the morning and afternoon, not midday though."

"I can live with that," I responded, much relieved. My new apartment would continue to be bright after all.

The digging eventually began (albeit many months later) at six thirty on a Monday morning. And to be clear, I use the term *digging* loosely. One cannot simply "dig" into Manhattan bedrock. It is far too hard for a mere bulldozer or jackhammer. One of the reasons the island has so many skyscrapers is because it rests upon some of the hardest stone on the planet, known as Manhattan schist. The only way to bore into the stuff is with massive equipment. The thunderous drilling noise that woke me that morning was so deafening, I was at the window before I was even fully awake. I whipped open the blinds and saw a huge yellow machine shudder as it assaulted the bedrock beneath it. I clenched my fist and muttered, "Schist!"

The noise was unbearable despite the fact that my apartment's windows were made from thick glass and had more glazing than a box of Krispy Kremes. But double-glazed windows were no match for Manhattan schist. To add insult to injury, the furious vibrations that accompanied the drilling made my walls shudder, my dishes rattle, and my furniture migrate aimlessly around the living room.

"How long will this go on?" I asked my friend in construction later that day.

"The drilling part happens quickly," he assured me. "No more than six weeks."

Six weeks seemed like an eternity to me. But then I discovered the "luxury rental" building going up outside my window included an underground garage. The foundations would have to be deeper than my friend had anticipated.

"How much deeper, exactly?" I asked him the next day.

"A little over two months deeper," he replied.

"What?" I was dismayed at the news. "Are you telling me I'm going to have to live with this noise and those vibrations five days a week for over four months?"

"No, no," he quickly objected as if I were being ridiculous. "They work six days a week, not five." This was becoming a nightmare. "They'll drill on Saturdays too, but they're not allowed to start before eight a.m. on weekends, so you can sleep in." Clearly, my friend's definition of *sleeping in* was very different from mine.

My whole building was soon in an uproar. The deafening noise was the sole topic of conversation whenever neighbors met in the hallways, lobby, or elevator. Everyone with a southside apartment was miserable. My neighbors reported placing calls and writing letters to our management company to complain about the noise. Apparently, some of the exchanges were civil while others were more heated. But everyone reported getting the same response. Our property manager had nothing to do with the new construction and could do nothing about it.

Indeed, I wouldn't have expected the manager to. At that time in New York City, property owners had all the power. I knew of several other buildings that suffered through the noise and drilling of adjacent construction, and none of their tenants extracted any abatements or considerations from their management companies either. Eager as I was to vent my frustrations to my building management, I knew that doing so would serve absolutely no purpose. Rather than go through a pointless exercise in frustration, I decided to grimace and bear it.

I lasted two days. A miserable cold kept me up most of that Friday night, and the drilling started less than an hour after I finally fell into merciful sleep the next morning. I realized I could grimace but I could no longer bear it. My head was pounding, my sinuses were throbbing, and my kitchen dishes were doing the Macarena. The schist had finally hit the fan.

I was determined to write to my landlord and demand a reduction in my rent, ridiculous as that sounded even to my own ears. I wrote the best letter I could construct and mailed it the next day. I didn't necessarily expect to hear back from the management company; unless it was to tell me they had a good chuckle at my naïvéte. However, two days later, I received a call from the building manager himself.

"I wanted to get back to you because we've been getting lots of calls and letters about the noise. Lots of them. Of course, that construction has nothing to do with us," he hurried to add. "But you know … that was a very well written letter." He paused. "I'll tell you what I can do," he finally announced. "I'm going to give you a reduction on your rent, let's say for the duration of your lease.

We'll throw in a few extra months too since I have to draw up a new lease." I almost dropped the phone. The drilling would only last a few months. He was offering me a rent abatement that would extend almost six months past that!

"Thank you!" I said. "Thank you very much." My astonishment was profound. We arranged for me to stop by the office, and I signed an amended lease with the new lower rent that very afternoon.

The Mystery of Complaining Impotence

The episode left me feeling grateful but also extremely curious. Almost all affected tenants in the building said they complained about the situation, many of them asking for temporary reductions in rent, and every one of them reported being turned down. Some claimed they never even got a response. Why had my letter succeeded where theirs had failed? I analyzed the letter, trying to identify what had functioned as its "active ingredients" and whether they could be generalized to other situations.

First, I knew the situation was not the fault of my building's management company, so I took great pains not to sound angry or accusatory. However, I was not feeling especially calm or reasonable when I sat down to write my complaint letter, so "measured" wasn't necessarily easy to pull off. I also knew that it is harder for us to notice our sarcasm and anger when we read our words silently, so I made sure to read my letter aloud before mailing it.

Second, I knew that I was in no position to *demand* anything from my management company (no matter how infuriating I found the drilling situation) as they were not responsible for the construction noise. If I hoped for them to offer me a resolution, I had to provide them with an incentive to do so. Therefore, my letter conveyed an up-front pledge of appreciation if they offered me a rent reduction. I was asking them to do something out of the goodness of their hearts, and since sincere appreciation is the only real currency in such situations, guaranteeing my gratitude in advance was the best incentive I could provide them.

I deconstruct my letter fully in chapter 5 and lay out a simple and widely applicable formula for constructing effective complaints in any situation. At the time I wrote to the management company, I was still far from being well versed on the psychology behind our complaining behaviors. However, my curiosity was definitely piqued. I began to pay closer attention to how we complain—both as a psychologist in private practice and in my personal and social life. I also embarked upon an in-depth study of the literature on the psychology of complaining.

What I found was both surprising and confusing. Although we now complain more than ever about virtually every aspect of our lives, our complaints have become almost entirely unproductive! How is that possible? Prodigious amounts of complaining practice and experience should have honed our complaining skills to razor-sharp effectiveness, not caused them to become even duller. Why are we complaining so much yet resolving so little? Even more important, why haven't we noticed or done anything to stop the decline?

We've all been subject to poor service in a restaurant, unhelpful municipal workers, or tone-deaf health-service providers. We've all been kept on hold for too long or sat in dirty taxicabs. Each time we get the wrong information about a product we're purchasing or wait for the arrival of a tardy cable technician, our frustration grows and we have the urge to complain. And complain we do. We relate our tales of irritation and woe to our friends, family, and colleagues regularly. In a pinch, even a locker-room acquaintance or airport bartender will do.

But here's the strange part. We typically don't voice these complaints to the managers of the restaurants, the cabdrivers, the cable companies, or the corporate executives responsible for the bad products or services that are frustrating us. The very people empowered to resolve our complaints and address our grievances are often the *only* people who never get to hear them.

We do the same thing in our personal lives. When we're upset with a friend, a family member, or a colleague, that person is often the last to hear about our dissatisfactions, if he or she hears about them at all. Instead, we complain about the friend, the family member, or the colleague to our *other* friends, family members, and colleagues.

Happily communicating our complaints to everyone *except* the people who need to hear them most is profoundly ineffective, yet all of us are guilty of the practice to some degree. We expel our complaints in a huff of authentic irritation, but then seem perfectly content to watch them float up, stick to the ceiling, and deflate into nothing. Using complaints to create change when it matters, fix problems, or garner resolutions doesn't even enter our minds.

Perhaps the greatest illustration of our complaining impotence is the growing global phenomenon known as complaint choirs. They started when Finnish couple Oliver Kochta-Kalleinen and his wife, Tellervo Kalleinen, visual artists by trade, decided to harness the massive amounts of energy people expend complaining into something positive. The couple's idea of something "positive" was to have people sing their complaints aloud in public choirs, using music by actual composers. They tossed in matching shirts, choral arrangements, and of course synchronized whining—and they had a show!

The couple's debut kvetchapalooza was held in Birmingham, England, in 2005. Since then, complaint choirs have both formed and performed all over the world. Some complaint choirs' performances on YouTube have received over one million hits. As for the lyrics, they're exactly what one might expect—l aments about mobile-phone batteries, annoying bosses, and parking spaces. Based on the popularity of songs, the lack of toilet paper in public bathrooms is apparently a crisis of international proportions, one made even more poignant when punctuated with rousing choruses of "It's not fair! It's not fair!"

The Golden Age of Effective Complaining

The *squeaky wheel* expression was brought into American culture by Henry Wheeler Shaw of Lanesboro Massachusetts. He followed many callings as a young man, including stints as a coal miner and a farmer. In 1858, he settled in Poughkeepsie, New York, and soon began writing under the pen name Josh Billings. His first works reflected both his passions and his daily life, such as the contemplative *Essay on the Mule.* Alas, these early efforts were not well received. Exemplifying tenaciousness worthy of his subject matter, Billings decided to "reboot" his favorite piece by making it truer to his quirky linguistic sensibilities, which included a fondness for purposefully misspelled slang. The result was *An Essa on the Muel,* "bi Josh Billings." It was an instant hit.

Billings went on to author volumes of folksy witticisms and misspelled-slang-filled ditties such as *Josh Billings' Trump Kards.* Thus, Billings originated the kind of phonetic spelling that is today associated with urban culture and hip-hop. The man was clearly ahead of his time. Billings soon made a name for himself as a journalist and humorist in New York and quickly became a favorite on the lecture circuit. Some considered him the second-most famous writer and lecturer in the United States after Mark Twain. Billings was influential as well as popular. Many of his colorful expressions were adopted into the vernacular of the time. For example, the term *just joshing* was further popularized by his pen name and is still in popular use today (albeit mostly by octogenarians).

Alas, the majority of Billings's oeuvre did not survive into modern discourse. Gone are such pearls as *Error will slip through a crack, while truth will stick in a doorway* and *One-legged chickens are the least apt to scratch a garden.* As for the latter, we will never know whether Billings was stating a truism about disabled fowl or recommending a specific course of action to frustrated gardeners. "The Kicker" (which at the time was a term for "complainer") was his most famous piece of writing.

I hate to be a kicker,
I always long for peace,
But the wheel that does the squeaking,
Is the one that gets the grease.

The moral of "The Kicker" is that however much we hate to complain, doing so and doing so loudly enough to get attention is necessary at times. Billings's attitude conveys the sentiment of his era toward complaints. Back then, a complaint wasn't unleashed unless it had a job to do or a mission to accomplish. Back in Billings's day, life was *supposed* to be hard, which meant that our entire notion of what constituted a "complaint-worthy" situation was radically different. Complaining about the train running twenty minutes late when it only came through town once a week would have been perceived as silly and ridiculous.

When people did complain, their complaints were usually fired off as a last resort, and they were usually aimed at the correct target. If the horseshoe didn't fit, you took it to the blacksmith and he redid it (probably while shooting nasty glances at his apprentice, whose work was being corrected). If someone complained too frequently or unnecessarily, he or she would be labeled a *kicker*. The term was as unflattering then as it sounds today.

If Billings were alive today, he would no doubt consider the vast majority of us to be kickers. He would most likely be horrified to learn that instead of using complaints sparingly and productively, we now complain both with great frequency and with stunning ineffectiveness. But why has our entire concept of complaints and their function changed so radically? What has caused such a huge shift in our complaining psychology?

Gregg Easterbrook's *Progress Paradox* argues that as our lives have become better and more comfortable over the last century, many of us have actually become unhappier as a result. Our expectations have dramatically risen, leading to more opportunities for us to experience disappointment and frustration and consequently to complain. In addition, our lives have also become increasingly complex. We're regularly confronted with a huge variety of frustrations and aggravations that simply didn't exist before.

Josh Billings never had to confront problems with cable television, dishonest mechanics, or bad cell-phone reception. I doubt his wife ever asked him to discuss her dissatisfactions about their sex life, their parenting philosophies, or their communication issues. Of course, these assumptions about the simplicity of Billings's life are mere speculation, but then again, the man was moved to write an essay about his mule.

Along with modern progress came modern frustrations by the multitudes and the corresponding number of complaints. Once our complaints reached a critical mass, we became overwhelmed by them. They were too much for us to absorb, so we slowly became desensitized. As a result, we took other people's complaints less seriously, and our own complaints became less serious as well. In the United Kingdom, a recent Facebook group formed solely to complain about a discontinued candy bar (Cadbury's Wispa) and drew over a hundred thousand members. I sincerely doubt people got that worked up about a discontinued favorite snack in Billings's day.

The bottom line is that the *functional* aspects of our complaints have been neglected for so long that we now complain primarily for one reason, to vent our emotions. Venting is a way to release a buildup of negative emotions that can otherwise become pressing and stressful. Expressing such feelings can be healthy as long as we don't overdo it, serving an important psychological function—except these days, most of us don't even vent correctly.

Venting: A Quest for Emotional Validation

Rachel, a young patient of mine, was out at a bar with her boyfriend of several months when she caught him glancing repeatedly at another woman. She asked him to stop, they argued, and her boyfriend broke up with her on the spot. He then walked right over to talk with the other woman as Rachel stood there in dismay and disbelief. Rachel bravely held it together while she hurried to the ladies' lounge and allowed herself to burst into tears only once she was inside. A woman checking her makeup looked over as Rachel joined her at the mirror.

"God, men can be such douche bags!" Rachel sputtered as she dabbed at her eyes. While it would be fair to assume the vast majority of womankind would have responded with some degree of compassion in the situation, Rachel was not so fortunate. The woman responded, "Oh, yeah? How do I know you're not the douche bag?" She gave Rachel a nasty glare and walked out without another word. Rachel was too stunned to reply. Clearly, despite airing her feelings, Rachel did not experience much in the way of postventing visceral relief. She had voiced her complaint with the simple goal of venting her anguish. If the woman had walked out without responding at all, the encounter would have been equally unsatisfying but far less painful.

Rachel is hardly alone. Today most of us complain almost solely to vent our emotions. Venting used to be no more than a side benefit of tackling a complaint, an emotional perk we earned by taking the initiative to address a problem. But now venting has gone from garnish to main dish. Of course, venting is not without value. When we complain, we hope to purge the frustration, anger, or irritation that is generated by our dissatisfaction. Indeed, the expression *getting it off our chest* refers to the palpable lightness, the cathartic easing of internal tension, we hope to experience by speaking up about a troubling complaint.

But what creates the catharsis is not the voicing of our complaints aloud, but rather voicing them to *another person.* Complaining to an empty room offers little if any emotional relief, as most habitual mutterers can attest. Dog owners often vent frustrations to their tail-wagging friends when greeting them at the door at the end of a long day: "Daddy's boss made him crazy today, didn't he, boy? Yes, he did! Yes, he did!" Such complaints might reward us with a round of excited licks to the face, but not the deep visceral relief we associate with *good* venting. It would be equally unsatisfying to complain to a person who didn't speak our language.

To get true visceral relief, we need to feel the person "gets it." The quality of visceral relief we experience, the cathartic bang for our buck, depends on the extent to which the person listening to our complaint conveys an accurate understanding of our feelings and authentic compassion for our plight. In short, we need our feelings about the situation to be validated by the listener. The more sympathy and empathy the person hearing our complaint conveys, the more satisfying our unburdening feels.

Since we primarily complain to vent our feelings, deciding to whom we should address our complaint is extremely important. Rachel was clearly upset when she entered the lounge, yet the woman at the mirror did not react to her distress. Had she said, "Are you okay?" or "Here's a tissue," or even given Rachel a glance of sympathy as she burst into tears, the woman would also have been more likely to display a modicum of compassion moments later. But she did not give any such signals. The clues of her lack of empathy were there all along: Rachel had simply missed them. She reached the same realization herself in a later session:

"It took me a couple of seconds to step over to the mirror because I reached for a tissue first. She saw me bawling and said nothing to me. I should have realized she was a cold-hearted bitch right then. But all I wanted was for her to say something nice to me. 'Yes, honey, men can be douche bags!' was all I wanted. Or even just 'Let me help you with your makeup.' Why couldn't she just have said that?"

Rachel was correct, of course. If her complaint had received the simple response she was hoping for, she would have experienced some much needed emotional relief. But her encounter also highlights the many hidden dangers inherent in complaining (we will discuss these dangers in much further detail in chapter 4). The woman's heartless retort was almost as traumatic to Rachel as her boyfriend's hurtful behavior had been. Indeed, Rachel spent more time in our session discussing the encounter with the woman than the actual breakup.

The Safety Manual for Incident-Free Venting

We should always pause and ask ourselves three questions before we complain for the purpose of getting emotional validation (especially if we're feeling emotionally fragile or vulnerable). First, is the person we're targeting generally supportive and understanding? If we don't know the person well enough, we could always spend a moment to consider possible cues. For example, if we appear distressed in any way, does the person appear concerned, at least a little? If not, as happened in Rachel's case, we should abort the mission and acquire a new target.

Second, is the person in the right frame of mind to be supportive and understanding? If we're visiting someone in the hospital who is recovering from a car crash, we should probably keep complaints to ourselves about how difficult it was to find parking.

Third, is our target likely to relate to the topic? For example, most "starving graduate students" sweating out their comprehensive exams would not be at their most supportive if a working and successful old college roommate complained about the sunburn he suffered on a two-week winter vacation to the tropics.

Fortunately, Rachel's experience is more of an exception than the norm. Venting our feelings can be quite satisfying, especially when we choose the right listener and get authentic sympathy and understanding. The visceral rush of relief we experience can be quite powerful. We often remember such conversations vividly and think warmly of the people who shared them with us for years to come.

In numerous life situations, complaining purely to vent our emotions is not only an emotionally effective strategy, but also the most effective one we can take. People who minister to the elderly, the chronically ill, or the acutely sick; those of us who take care of children or sick animals; emergency responders and others—all risk an accumulation of angst and tension that comes from having to put our own emotions aside for the benefit of another. Mothers of newborns frequently spend entire sessions describing how depleted they feel from sleepless nights filled with soothing incessant crying, powdering diaper rashes, and cleaning up projectile vomiting. Unburdening themselves and receiving a dollop of emotional validation often creates a relief powerful enough to recharge their depleted emotional batteries, at least somewhat.

But such ideal venting experiences are relatively rare. Most of our complaints do not generate much in the way of emotional highs. Few of the numerous complaints we express every day garner us any sympathy at all, let alone the ultimate in emotional validation. Much as two-pack-a-day smokers report truly enjoying only one or two cigarettes of the forty-plus they inhale, our complaints provide us with similarly infrequent payoffs.

In fact, the opposite is usually more common. Our complaints can come with a price, one we often fail to anticipate. The effects of ineffective complaining can accumulate; they can damage our state of mind and our emotional well-being. We can find ourselves labeled as whiners, or office complainers. Some of us have been dropped as friends, sued, publicly ridiculed, and even killed, all for voicing a simple complaint.

Given these dangers and the elusiveness of emotional validation, our complaints must serve other functions as well, because they are simply too unproductive to exist solely for the rare event of a true emotional catharsis. Indeed, our grievances, gripes, and laments often have subtext, additional meanings or implications that go far beyond the surface content of the actual complaint and serve other purposes. Much like us, our complaints have become multitaskers.

Complaints as Social Communications

Robin Kowalski, professor of psychology at Clemson University, is recognized as a leading authority on the psychology of complaining. She's also researched bullying, teasing, vandalism, deceit, and betrayal. Kowalski defines complaining behavior as "an expression of dissatisfaction, whether subjectively experienced or not, for the purpose of venting emotions or achieving intrapsychic goals, interpersonal goals, or both."

Kowalski's definition of complaining clearly specifies the attainment of goals as one of the primary functions of complaining. However, when she studied why people actually complain, attaining concrete goals or measurable outcomes were rarely mentioned as primary motivators. Instead, Kowalski discovered that in addition to venting our emotions, our complaints serve four primary *social* functions.

The first motivation for complaining is that, much like alcohol, complaints are highly useful in lubricating social interactions. Think back to your first date with a significant other, past or present. While getting to know each other, you probably searched for common ground, likes and dislikes around which you could bond. Chances are your dislikes were expressed as complaints. For example, one person might say, "I hated that movie!" Prompting the other to respond, "You hated that movie too? Oh my God! We're like twins!"

Expressing complaints as icebreakers and commonality-seekers has many forms. Personally I've heard, "Hot enough for ya?" about as many times as I care to. And I find the winter version "It's freezing outside! And they say there's global warming!" to be equally annoying (although mostly because it displays a glaring misunderstanding about the impact of global warming on weather patterns). But whether or not we personally relate to specific complaints, they are often good conversation starters and allow us to seek common ground upon which to build our interactions.

Similarly, Kowalski found that our second motivation to complain is to convey a social image or to present ourselves in a specific light. Imagine you have been out of a job for many months and that you have passed the first few rounds of interviews at your dream company. You are then invited to have dinner with your potential employers, all of whom, you are dismayed to learn, are wine experts. A rare bottle is uncorked, the wine aired, and the bouquet sampled. Then the taste test. The first expert grimaces: "Not good!" The second sips and winces: "What a disappointment!" The third sputters, "They might as well serve this with fruit slices and a cherry!" Now it's your turn. You are not a wine expert, but you are desperate for the job. You taste the wine. It's delicious!

Do you say, "Love it! Pass me yours!" or do you bond with your potential employers and complain vehemently, "Terrible! Who made this, Kool-Aid?"

Our third motivation to complain is that doing so often provides us with social comparisons and allows us to evaluate our own standing in a variety of situations. For example, a stage actor might walk out of a final callback audition for a new production of the musical *Fiddler on the Roof* and bump into the person who had auditioned before him. Actor number one might try to elicit information about how actor number two fared by complaining, "Boy, it was hard to sing with all that fake hair in my mouth!"

If actor number two responds, "Lucky you, dude! I got cut before they gave out the beards," it could be good news for actor number one.

Lastly, Kowalski found that complaining is also a way of seeking explanations. For example, one of the complaints voiced most often by parents of adolescents as the parents walk by a messy living room is "Why am I the only one who cleans up around here?" These complaints often have a subtext. They are in essence requests for the teenagers to account for their behavior. They are also requests for the teenagers to help with cleaning up. Many parents complain in such ways while harboring hopes the recipients will hear not just their words but the subtext of their message as well. Of course, that we harbor those hopes does not mean our wishes are likely to be granted.

I doubt any teen has ever responded to such complaint drive-bys by exclaiming, "Gosh, Mom, you're right! Goodness, how could I have been so selfish? Now you sit right down and hand over the carpet shampoo!" The far more likely response to such parental laments is "You're blocking the television!"

The bottom line is that phrasing requests in the form of complaints is never an effective way to ask for help or accountability. "Please stop what you're doing and help me clean up" might get the parent a better response than muttering a series of complaints to an adolescent who isn't in all likelihood paying attention to begin with (more about how to complain to adolescents in chapter 6).

Using complaints as social communications rather than as calls for action is another reason we complain more today than ever before. Kowalski agrees with Gregg Easterbrook that our expectations have dramatically risen over the past fifty years. We expect better service, more immediate results, and more accommodations both from our service providers and from our friends, loved ones, and colleagues. When these higher expectations are not met, our dissatisfaction rises and we feel the urge to complain.

The Anti-Complaining Movement

Today we view complaints as just another form of social interaction, one devoid of any real or practical utility. In fact, complaining now suffers from a terrible image problem and our complaints are often viewed as societal nuisances, so much so that public discourse has lately centered on the need to drastically reduce the number of our complaints if not abolish them entirely. In recent years, community and religious leaders have begun issuing calls for us to go on a complaining diet. One of the chief advocates of the complaint slim-down is the Reverend Will Bowen, author of *A Complaint Free World.*

Bowen is convinced that complaining is not just bad for us but for our communities as well. In 2006, he challenged his congregation in Kansas City, Missouri, to go for twenty-one days without a single complaint. This is a much harder task than one might think. As the good reverend quickly discovered, most of us significantly underestimate how much we complain. To help his congregants, he gave them purple bracelets to use as a reminder to avoid complaining. When he caught himself complaining, he would switch the bracelet to his other hand and start the count over.

It took the reverend himself over three months to put together a string of twenty-one complaint-free days, and he believes he is a happier person for it. He is convinced the world too would be happier if there were fewer complaints. He established a foundation whose goal is to recruit 1 percent of the world's population (sixty million people) to become purple-loving complaint-free individuals.

Before anyone scoffs at his ambition, I must hasten to note that Bowen's Web site proudly reports that almost six million purple bracelets have already been sold or disseminated. His global initiative has caused millions of potential complaints to be squelched in their infancy, ridding the world of immeasurable quantities of emotional negativity.

The idea *sounds* terrific, but although the reverend is correct in assuming we complain too much, his solution is not one most psychologists would actually recommend. Voicing fewer complaints will not make us happier, nor will it necessarily make those around us happier (although with chronic complainers it actually might). Remember, Bowen does not suggest we can avoid experiencing feelings of dissatisfaction, disappointment, frustration, or any of the many other emotions that result in complaining. He merely advocates that we avoid verbalizing our complaints when we do feel these things. Yet, stopping ourselves from expressing such feelings when we have them, sweeping our emotions under the rug, is rarely a recipe for psychological health (or for that matter, world peace).

Actually, rather the opposite is true: squelching our complaints is far from advisable. Kowalski points out that stuffing our feelings down can make some people more prone to depression. In fact, depression might be the least of their problems as Kowalski explains, "People who inhibit expression of their emotions ... may lay themselves open to the consequences of a Type D personality style ... characterized by the inhibition of emotional expression."

Type D personalities have character traits that put them at significantly increased risk for coronary artery disease (we will examine an example of a type D personality, his complaining style and associated health risks, in chapter 3).

Bowen clearly has the best of intentions. In addition, he is an extraordinarily effective complainer in his own right (as evidenced by the millions of people who have responded to his complaint about complaining). However, the true problem inherent in our "culture of complaints" is not that we complain too much but that so many of our complaints are wasted and achieve absolutely nothing. The best way to reduce the number of our complaints is not to stop complaining cold turkey but rather to complain more *effectively*. If our complaints were generally more productive, all the things that cause us irritation and dissatisfaction would be more likely to change for the better (even if slowly), and eventually we would have fewer reasons to complain.

The Demise of Ye Olde Complaint Box

Although we no longer take our complaints seriously, businesses, corporations, and even government take them seriously indeed. Over the past three decades alone, customer service departments have gone from being corporate dumping grounds for failing and marginal employees to technologically advanced multibillion-dollar departments.

Corporations spend billions of dollars to handle our complaints and increase our consumer satisfaction. What makes this even more remarkable is that forty years ago, most companies' investments in customer service amounted to little more than springing for a new "complaint box" when someone sat on the old one by mistake. But in 1973, a strikingly forward-thinking secretary of health, education, and welfare, Elliot Richardson, came along. Richardson believed consumers should have control over their government programs, and he wanted to know whether such programs were doing a good job of serving their constituents' needs.

Satisfaction with customer service in governmental programs, a simple inquiry on the face of it, had never scientifically been investigated. Richardson turned to John A. Goodman, a graduate of the Harvard Business School, and his fledgling company, the Technical Assistance Research Program (TARP). He asked them to investigate complaint handling and other service aspects of government programs. Recognizing that Goodman and his team were young, brash, inexperienced, and idealistic, Richardson hired the RAND Corporation (the famed nonprofit institution specializing in research and policy analysis) to supervise their work.

But when the RAND Corporation issued their report claiming all was well and dandy in government programs, Goodman and his team did something only young, brash, inexperienced, and idealistic people do. They filed a minority report claiming all was neither well nor dandy with government programs as far as consumers were concerned. Their minority report reached the White House Office of Consumer Affairs, which responded to these unflattering claims in a manner highly uncharacteristic of politicians—it embraced them. Goodman and his team were promptly awarded a large contract to investigate complaint handling in both the public and private sectors.

In 1978, Goodman's group published their first report: "Increasing Customer Satisfaction through Effective Complaint Handling." Their findings represented a sharp slap on the wrist for both government and corporate America, whose philosophy of complaint handling had so far been to ignore complaints completely.

Complaint departments had traditionally been housed in the darkest bowels of corporate or government offices. They were usually referred to as "Siberia," representing a one-way trip to career obscurity for those sent to work there. Companies placed their poorest-performing employees there, the boss's eccentric but harmless nephew or those lacking the wherewithal to make it in the mailroom. But Goodman demonstrated to companies and government how drastically their ineffective complaint handling was affecting their customers' loyalty and how substantially it was harming their bottom lines, productivity, and program effectiveness. Their losses and missed opportunities were striking and undeniable. The ensuing gasps of corporate and governmental dismay represented the birthing cries of the modern customer service industry.

Goodman and his team were not asked to merely point out the problems with customer service, they were charged with coming up with solutions. One of their first big ideas was the creation of toll-free 800 numbers for consumers that would make it easier to communicate with government and corporations. Although the initiative seems like an obvious winner to us now, corporate executives and elected officials did not embrace it with open arms. Many corporations claimed the notion was flat-out stupid. The head of a giant telecommunications company who would have benefited most from the sales of such telephone services was a good example of the resistance the idea encountered. "Why would companies *ever* want to talk to their customers?" he exclaimed to Goodman.

But Goodman's team was not easily discouraged. They soon found willing partners and took their toll-free 800 number initiative to the Environmental Protection Agency, Highway Traffic & Safety, the Food and Drug Administration, General Electric, and other corporate entities.

The next step in their campaign to bring home the importance of customer service and complaint handling was to quantify previously nebulous concepts. They provided companies with the actual dollars-and-cents value of consumer "word of mouth" as well as "word of mouse" once the Internet era began.

In short, John Goodman and his colleagues single-handedly took our government and our businesses from being noncommunicative and often hostile entities and led them kicking and screaming into being the open, communicative, and user-friendly organizations they are (or aspire to be) today. His work paved the very highways today's effective complainers travel when pursuing resolutions to their consumer dissatisfactions. I think such major societal contributions should warrant some form of public recognition. Maybe not a ticker-tape parade, but a statue would be nice.

How Ineffective Have We Become?

It occurred to me that if anyone was qualified to comment on our current state of complaining effectiveness (or lack thereof), John Goodman was. So I met with him in New York City and popped the big question. "You've spent the last thirty-five years making it easier for people to complain," I said, resisting the urge to genuflect. "So how are we doing?"

"Oh!" Goodman immediately responded, his head shaking in dismay. "We're quite bad at complaining these days!" Goodman wasn't merely stating an opinion; scores of studies back him up. Think back to the last time you were dissatisfied with a packaged-goods purchase, a simple service, or any other small-ticket item of the kind we acquire regularly. You might have been disappointed with a new cell phone or MP3 player, a leaf-blower or humidifier, new software, a video game, or a fancy new gadget advertised on television that ended up looking as though it belonged at the bottom of a cereal box. Now, what did you do at the time? Did you complain to the store, call the company using their toll-free number, or write a strongly worded letter to the corporate headquarters?

Chances are you did none of those. One of the most consistent findings in Goodman's studies spanning many years and a large variety of industries is that in such situations a mind-boggling 95 percent of disgruntled consumers never complain to the corporate entity responsible for their dissatisfaction!

Goodman's findings are certainly bad news for us consumers, but they present even worse news for corporations. Consumer complaints convey hugely important information and provide vital feedback to companies about their products and services. If only a tiny fraction of us let corporations know when service failures occur or when we have problems with their products, it makes it extremely difficult for them to improve those services and products accordingly.

Goodman's research shows that 80 percent of customer problems are caused by a company's faulty procedures or bad systems, not by faulty products or inadequate sales or service personnel. This means that the majority of our complaints require remedies that can only be applied at the corporate level of a company, where decision makers have the authority to implement such changes. For example, complaining about technical support calls being answered by representatives who barely speak English is pointless, if we only voice the dissatisfaction to the representatives themselves. Only the company's most senior executives have the authority to change such practices. Yet, only 1-5 percent of our complaints ever get to these senior executives.

If the vast majority of our complaints never even reach corporate decision makers, they obviously cannot be addressed or fixed. Goodman also found that when service failures did occur, we not only refrained from complaining to company headquarters, we often simply took our business to their competition.

These findings might represent bad news for corporations, but they are especially dismaying from a psychological standpoint. We frequently walk out of establishments feeling frustrated, angry, or disappointed. We often find ourselves upset over a malfunctioning new coffeemaker, a hairstyle we paid too much for and dislike, or new software that keeps crashing our computer. The negative impact of these on our emotional well-being is small in and of themselves, but their cumulative impact and our habitual ineffectiveness in handling them can do significant psychological damage over time.

One of Goodman's earlier studies was on why so few of us complain effectively as consumers. If less than 5 percent of consumer complaints hit their corporate targets, what is preventing us from speaking up more productively? Goodman identified four primary reasons we fail to take action in such situations.

Our first and perhaps most frequent justification for not complaining is the belief that we lack the time or the energy to pursue our complaints effectively. Sure, we intend to take action when our daughter's dollhouse arrived with the roof missing, but life catches up with us and we never quite get to it.

Fair enough, we are indeed busy people. However, the "too busy" claim would be a far more compelling argument if we didn't actually spend a great deal of time and energy complaining about these very stores and businesses to a huge number of our friends and acquaintances. Goodman found that while we may refuse to write a single letter to corporate headquarters, we are willing to relate the exact same tale of consumer angst to an average of eight to sixteen of our nearest and dearest.

Surely, it takes far more time and effort to complain to sixteen people than it does to write one letter. But we no longer associate "complaining" with writing one well-phrased complaint letter. Instead, we imagine calling a hotline, being put on hold for hours at a time trapped into listening to nauseating music or bright and perky recorded sales pitches, at a time when we are feeling far from bright or perky. We envision getting the runaround, having to explain our problem over and over until we get to the correct person. Our fears and dread dissuade us from complaining before we even try.

The second main reason people do not complain is that they simply do not know where or to whom their complaint should be addressed. Do we march back to the store? Is it best to call a toll-free number? Should we write to the company headquarters, and if so, to whom exactly should we address our complaint? Not knowing where to address our grievances is a problem we all encounter. Recently, I was at a busy New York City restaurant for lunch with a colleague. A family from England was sitting at the table next to ours. The father was getting quite agitated at how long they had been waiting to order. Reaching his boiling point, the man twisted around in his seat and grabbed the next person he saw by the apron (literally).

"Oy!" he barked in a cockney accent. "We waited a good fifteen minutes for our table but it's been ten bloody minutes since then and we haven't even seen a waiter yet! Now, I expect you, lad, to take our order promptly, *waltz* into the kitchen, and make bloody sure our lunch gets made!"

The non-English-speaking busboy appeared both alarmed and confused as he stammered, "I no dancing!" and hurried away. Not knowing to whom our complaints should be addressed can stymie even the most assertive complainer.

The third reason we avoid complaining is a fear of counterattack. "High school and college students are the most disadvantaged in this regard," Goodman commented. Complaining to a professor or school administrator or even walking into a bank to challenge a late fee can be scary to some young adults. "They have a real fear of retribution. They have no experience with this stuff so they feel like children dealing in an adult world," Goodman explained. They worry that complaining will only get them poorer grades from a professor or that it will make a bank employee tamper with their account.

Such unfounded fears can inhibit many of us from complaining, not just high school or college students. For example, more than one person over the years has cautioned me never to send back a dish in a restaurant if it is not cooked to my satisfaction because doing so is bound to upset the chef. These people believe the cook will retaliate for the "insult" by enhancing the flavor profile of my dish with say … his saliva. Yet, few professional chefs would risk sabotaging their entire establishment by taking such childish retaliatory action, no matter how sensitive they were about their risotto.

The fourth and last reason we fail to complain is perhaps the most basic. We are convinced that doing so won't resolve our issue. We believe companies do not care enough about us to actually fix our problems or amend their policies. Many of us think most corporations actively avoid resolving consumer complaints as it costs them money to do so. We are certain they have no intentions whatsoever of providing us customers with real answers to our problems.

The irony is that John Goodman's efforts have actually created a huge sea change in that regard. Most of us have quite outdated perceptions of the customer-service edicts by which most companies and even governments conduct themselves today. We feel that way because of the dissatisfactions we experience personally and those we hear about from friends; the number of unresolved complaints we're exposed to is huge. It is easy to see how we might conclude that complaining never changes things.

After reading Goodman's studies, I was more convinced than ever that we were indeed woefully ineffective complainers, at least as consumers. What surprised me was not the *fact* that we were ineffective, but the *extent* to which our complaints had become entirely unproductive. I began to wonder about complaining in other areas of life. Were we saddled with the same complaining paralysis when it came to our personal and familial relationships as we were in our roles as consumers? Were we as hesitant to speak up to friends or co-workers?

I had only to reflect on my twenty years of experience as a psychologist to realize right away that the scourge of ineffective complaining was by no means limited to our behaviors as consumers. Rather, we use equally ineffective strategies when dealing with dissatisfactions and disappointments in almost every other aspect of our lives.

Ineffective Complaining in Our Personal Lives

Bob, the husband in a middle-aged couple I saw for a consultation session, gave a detailed and passionate history of their "communication" problems when I asked what had brought them to therapy. "It's not that we argue all the time, though," he concluded, "we just disagree a lot." Bob looked over at his wife, Shirley, and gave her an encouraging smile. "And we rarely raise our voices—right, honey?"

Shirley gave Bob a quick nod. I turned my attention to her and asked for her perspective on what had brought them to therapy. Shirley shifted away from her husband and addressed her answer directly to me.

"Bob's got a raging alcohol problem and he's in complete denial about it! I thought maybe he'd listen if it came from someone else."

Such surprise attacks or blindsides occur frequently in an initial couple-therapy consultation. One or both members of the couple may voice a complaint they had never voiced to their partner before. What usually alerts me to this blindsiding is the expression on the member's face as it's happening. The tip-off here was the mixture of shock, confusion, rage, and betrayal that contorted Bob's features. Although he struggled with several powerful emotions at once, rage won the day. Bob stood up, cursed Shirley like a sailor, and stormed out of the session.

I've seen all kinds of blindsides over the years, some minor and some, like Shirley's, rather huge. There was the wife who assumed her husband wanted to discuss financial issues only to discover his biggest gripe was her overinvolved parents. Or the husband who expected to discuss problems with their kids only to hear his wife lay out a graphic list of complaints about their sex life. Perhaps the most fortuitous blindside was when one young couple in their twenties each came to the session planning to surprise the other by announcing a desire for a divorce.

When I ask blindsiders to tell me why they have staged their ambush, their responses are varied. "I didn't think he would take the complaint seriously" or "I just assumed she wouldn't agree with me" are the most common rationales offered for their not having raised their concerns previously. "It would just start a fight" or "I didn't feel like talking about it for hours on end" are also frequent explanations. People also say, "Whenever I bring up a complaint, I just get attacked, so I don't even try anymore" or "Somehow I always end up being the bad guy, even when I'm the one whose feelings got hurt."

My observations about couples' blindsides by no means constitute a scientific study. Nonetheless, the anecdotal trends are so strong it is fair to assume we use precisely the same logic to justify our ineffective complaining habits within our relationships as we do for our ineffective complaining habits as consumers (other than Goodman's second reason of not knowing where to address our complaints). Couples assume that complaining to their spouse will not elicit change. They think such conversations will be more trouble than they are worth, and they fear that bringing up their dissatisfactions will only result in their partner's retaliating.

Both as consumers and in our personal lives, we are aware that keeping silent about our complaints will do little to bring about a resolution. We desperately want change, but somehow we convince ourselves that inaction is our best option even when we know it achieves absolutely nothing. Companies won't change if we don't learn to complain effectively, and the same holds true in our relationships. Our loved ones will never change if we avoid telling them our complaints as so many of us do (although, as we shall see in chapter 6, complaining effectively within a relationship is far more complicated than dashing off a complaint letter about a loose wheel on our daughter's new tricycle).

The Rise of Cyber-Squeaking

Over the past few years, our busiest complaining arenas have relocated. Watercoolers, locker rooms, and beauty salons have been replaced by newer and fresher complaining venues. The richest venting grounds and popular kvetching water holes are now just a computer screen away. There, in the wide and vast reaches of cyberspace, complainers gather by the thousands. Complete strangers can complain around the clock on virtual soapboxes. Other Web sites disseminate complaint-inspired manifestos and revenge-driven agendas. A few have even inspired multimillion-dollar complaint-oriented businesses.

The number of Web sites devoted entirely to complaining is now legion. But the earliest versions of these enterprises hoped to do little more than provide a place for us to vent our frustrations by offering message boards to post our complaints for all (and at times, for none) to see. One of those pioneers was Neal Larry, whose Web site whatseatinya.com (now defunct) offered its visitors a place to post their complaints and the simple promise that we can experience the joy of venting. Larry was convinced his site served a great public need. So much so that he referred to it as the "chicken soup of the Internet." "Be truthful," he admonished on his home page, "do we really get anywhere complaining to our spouses or significant others? I know I don't!"

Putting aside Larry's appalling lack of marital tact, he was serious in his efforts to provide relief to herds of pent-up complainers. His home page ended with the sincere and hearty invitation "Tell me what's eatin' ya!" Larry's style and vernacular were so reminiscent of a certain Josh Billings I wonder if his garden had ever been ravished by one-legged chickens.

Such sites (amusing as they may be) are actually tantamount to flying white flags of effective-complaining defeat. Larry offered no advice or suggestions about how to get responses from the entities about whom we are invited to vent our frustrations. He assumed that not only would corporate America ignore our complaints but also our loved ones. Although charming and well-intentioned, Larry's Web site actually represented how the majority of us perceive complaints in the twenty-first century and thereby symbolized practically everything that is wrong with our current individual and societal attitudes about complaining.

Chapter Two
The Trouble with Bill
The Hidden Costs of Ineffective Squeaking

I'm tired of my own complaints. I gotta get some new thoughts.
—Melvin Udall, *As Good As It Gets* (1997)

A few days after the drilling outside my apartment was completed, I met my friend Bill for a lunch to congratulate him for being promoted to partner in his company. By all accounts his rise through the ranks had been rapid, and his advancement was no doubt fueled by his ambition, competence, and strong work ethic. A bright and capable young man in his thirties, he had a long and promising career ahead of him. After we chatted about his job and his new responsibilities, I asked Bill whether he was enjoying the new fifty-inch plasma television he had purchased to reward himself for the promotion.

The change in his mood was instantaneous. His brow furrowed, his jaw clenched, and his grip on the silverware made his knuckles go white. The hair on the back of my neck stood up. I had never before seen Bill angry, let alone so enraged. I asked him what was wrong.

"The cable company sucks!" Bill spat. "Their new high-def cable box keeps malfunctioning and screws everything up!" Bill's voice was not loud, but his tone was so intense, a waiter approaching our table with a pitcher of water pivoted like Baryshnikov and headed straight back into the kitchen.

"Every few days, I get locked out of the system and I have to call the cable company to authorize the service," Bill explained. "You know how long that takes with those automated menus and hold times and having to verify who I am and where I live. Then they send out a technician, and you have to stay home for that. So they came and they tinkered, but they never fixed it. Sure, it worked fine when they left, but an hour later the glitch kicked in and I had to call them all over again! They've been over twice already and it keeps happening!"

"So what did you do?"

"There's nothing I can do! I barely watch TV anymore, it's too annoying!"

I remembered how thrilled Bill had been only months ago when he first got his new television. He had paid thousands of dollars for the set and then hundreds more to have it hung on the wall like a movie screen. I signaled the waiter to bring us some water and turned back to my friend. I tried to suggest he persist in his complaint.

"I'm telling you, there's nothing more I can do!" Bill insisted. "There's no point in calling their tech department if they obviously don't know how to fix it!" The waiter stepped hesitatingly toward our table, hurriedly poured me half a glass of water, and dashed away.

"They haven't been able to fix it *so far*," I interjected, "but you can ask to speak to a supervisor in the tech department, and they usually know much more about—"

"The technicians were out twice! There's no point! Those people don't care!"

The last statement was issued with a real edge, as if Bill were daring me to challenge his assertion that the situation was hopeless. I decided to follow the waiter's lead and retreat, at least from the topic of conversation.

Bill was clearly an ineffective complainer, but worse, he was so convinced of his basic inability to complain productively, he believed doing so could only cost him further aggravation. Of course, Bill's inaction came with costs of its own. First, his passivity was costing him the pleasure of enjoying his large-screen television. I had seen his entertainment system in action when it was first installed, during happier pre-glitch times. The clarity of the picture and the sound quality, not to mention the size of the thing, were indeed a pleasure. But on the rare occasion Bill still watched his television, the experience was so fraught with worry the glitch would act up, it was far from pleasurable. Bill used to be perfectly happy with his old, far smaller, glitch-free LCD screen. His lack of complaining effectiveness meant the several thousand dollars he had invested in buying and installing the new but unwatchable set were completely wasted.

The Internet Complaint Industry

These days, many of us feel so overwhelmed and incompetent about handling our own complaints that we've actually begun outsourcing our grievances to strangers. Over the past decade, a menagerie of complaint-oriented businesses has sprouted up on the Internet to address our new and growing complaining needs. Entirely new professions have emerged from these cyber-initiatives. One of them is the "complainer for hire," self-proclaimed experts eager to help us resolve our most annoying complaints for a modest (and at times immodest) fee.

For example, Carl Shoolman, founder of consumerxchange.com, charges a flat fee of $43 per complaint as well as an additional 5-10 percent commission of whatever they recover. Interestingly, they list their maximum commission as a whopping $1,000. Apparently, they're hoping NASA tries returning a defective satellite to RadioShack.

However, at least psychologically speaking, there is something to be said for such services (as long as their fees are reasonable). Our unresolved complaints often nag at us obsessively, and some of us experience repeated pinches of irritation whenever we're reminded of them, no matter how frequently. Bill probably felt a tightening in his stomach whenever he passed by the living room and glanced at his television with longing and regret. For people like Bill, complainers for hire can be like dog walkers for our minds. They pick up the complaint droppings, open the windows, and air the place out so it doesn't stink.

However, the complainer for hire is only one amid an entire ecology of Internet complaint start-ups both large and small. As might be expected in such a Darwinian environment, many ventures never make it to profitability. Historically, new Internet frontiers always spawn new ideas, fads, and oddities, most of which are extremely short-lived. Some, such as Microsoft UK's horrifically misconceived iLoo (their idea for a Wi-Fi enabled Porta Potti, because who doesn't relish the idea of sitting in one of those for a good long read), never even make it to market.

But the strongest ideas do survive. Some of the new complaint start-ups have even attracted multimillion-dollar investments. One of the complaint business models that appear to be thriving is a deceptively simple idea with a twist. It is a similar approach to Neal Larry's complaint message boards, but the new big boys of consumer message boards promise something far more valuable to consumers than a simple venting session; they offer the promise of an actual dialogue with the very corporations to whom our complaints are addressed. Theoretically speaking, Bill could post his complaint about his cable box on a message board and have his cable company respond directly.

It sounds like a wonderful solution, except that when this new genre of complaint start-ups burst on the scene, no corporations had yet agreed to participate in any such dialogue with consumers. Nonetheless, numerous complaint start-ups *assumed* corporations would embrace the idea of communicating with their customers and were even willing to gamble significant amounts of investor capital on it. What allowed these investors to sleep at night was a series of studies conducted by John A. Goodman and his colleagues.

Among the concepts Goodman and his group first quantified was how much it cost companies to acquire new customers through advertising, marketing, and other means. This crucially important concept had never before been translated into real dollars and cents. When we get annoyed at a product or a service and walk out in a huff vowing never to return (or hang up in a huff after calling a customer-service hotline), how much does our potential defection cost the company in question? Goodman found that acquiring new customers could cost a business *five times* as much as holding on to existing customers through improved customer service (and dehuffing).

For corporations, the conclusion was (or should have been) obvious. It was in a company's best financial interest to repair any service failures that caused them to lose existing customers. If trolling message boards could help them mollify disgruntled customers, restore customers' faith in a product or service, and thereby retain their loyalty, "a-trolling they should go."

A second set of studies Goodman conducted was even more compelling in this regard. They found that when complaints are handled to our satisfaction, we actually become more loyal as customers than we were before we had the problem. When it came to fostering positive word of mouth for a product or company, a successful "service recovery" had *twenty times* the impact of regular advertising.

We should not find this surprising. Relationships that are tested but are able to repair whatever ruptures are created are often stronger than untested relationships. This is true of almost any kind of relationship in our human repertoire, whether it's a romantic relationship, a friendship, or a business partnership.

I often caution patients who are entering into new romantic entanglements that it can be tricky to assess the long-term prospects of their romance accurately until they have their first big fight. Only once they've seen how their partner handles an argument can they feel confident about their capacity to resolve issues and problems as a couple when these arise in the future. Similarly, when a company manages our disputes or dissatisfactions well, we naturally feel more loyal to it as we're also more confident that should further dissatisfactions arise, they too will be well-handled.

While many of the Internet complaint-message-board sites promise companies might respond to posts on their boards, companies do actually respond to complaints posted on Thor Muller's complaint start-up, getsatisfaction.com. Thor Muller believes Get Satisfaction represents a game-changer, the next step in the evolution of consumer complaining and customer service. According to the Web site, Get Satisfaction has already helped "thousands of companies and employees as well as millions of customers work together to improve tens of thousands of products and services." Clearly, something about their business model is working. But what is making them stand out in such a crowded field? One of the elements Muller emphasizes most is that he wants the tone and dialogue of discourse on the site to be as civil as possible. He goes so far as to call his site a "Switzerland" between companies and customers, and by all accounts civility does reign there.

The Dark Side of Internet Complaint Sites

While the "professional" complainers and the "Let's hold hands and dialogue" message boards are numerous, they are vastly outnumbered by another genre of Internet complaint destinations, the "Boy, am I furious" Web sites. Those sites offer similar kinds of message boards and discussion threads as getsatisfaction.com, but they do not share Thor Muller's fondness for civility. In fact, the "Boy, am I furious" Web sites are used primarily for "flaming" corporations, their products, and their services.

For those readers who, like myself, had previously associated "flaming" solely with outdoor grill settings and spontaneously combusting charcoal briquettes, let me explain. *Flaming* refers to the practice of leaving messages online, either via boards or e-mail, that are purposely hostile or insulting to the recipient or subject of the missive. Flames are irate and often derogatory posts left by people (flamers) on topics about which they have strong feelings, often of the simmering hateful kind.

However, these days, flamers are no longer content with sending angry e-mails or leaving nasty posts on message boards. Many of them have resorted to financing, creating, and obsessively maintaining entire Web sites devoted solely to expressing their loathing toward the companies that have wronged them. There are so many of these "dark passion projects" that in 2005 *Forbes* magazine ran a story rating the "Top Corporate Hate Websites." The list included sites devoted to despising and maligning such giants as Microsoft (apparently, a flamer favorite), Verizon, American Express, and others.

Psychologically speaking, these obsessions are not exactly healthy expressions of normal consumer angst. At first, I assumed complaints posted to these sites related tales of terrible injustices, exotic stories of corporate heartlessness or unusual atrocities perpetrated on innocent consumers. But I was gravely disappointed. Most of the complaints I read were remarkable solely for the irritation they conveyed, not for the egregious nature of the complaints themselves. The majority of them tended to be run-of-the-mill stories of the "Dammit, I got overcharged" and the "Sucks that I have no cell-phone reception" sort.

If an erroneous cell-phone bill can create an emotional wound so deep that it drives someone to build an entire Web site just to express his persistent rage, one might suggest his phone bill is the least of his problems. Perhaps an hour or two with a skilled mental health professional would be time and money better spent. Although I have a sneaky suspicion their treatment might yield nothing more than inspiration for their next Internet venture, Shrinks-I-love-to-hate.com.

Some complaint Web sites straddle the middle ground between flaming and consumer advocacy. For example, pissedconsumer.com lists the number of hits each complaint category generates, making it more convenient for the casual reader to assess the exact level of repugnance a given company engenders in the general public. I was surprised to find that one of the site's higher-rated complaint categories is the enterprise known as Girls Gone Wild Videos. Its bestselling jiggle-fests have already recorded thousands of hits by angry ex-customers who felt cheated in some way. How ironic that videotapes of drunken girls exposing their breasts can create almost as much pent-up tension in some customers as they release in others.

Denying Our Inner Effective Complainer

As plentiful as the options to outsource our complaints to the Internet are, as far as my friend Bill and most others are concerned, these online complaint busters all share one small but fatal flaw. To utilize their services Bill would have to write up the details of his complaint and provide the professional complainer with dates, numbers, and documentation. However, those are exactly the tasks Bill finds most annoying about the complaint process, as do most of us. Indeed, the most common hurdle we have to overcome when pursuing a complaint is the aggravation of sitting at our desk, gathering receipts or correspondence (which can often require a bit of a search through drawers and piles of paper), and writing everything down in detail. Therein lay the deal breaker for Bill when it came to outsourcing his complaint to a professional complainer. A similar effort on his part would also be required simply to post a coherent account of his problem on a message board.

Yet, millions of us are doing exactly that: we are posting our trials and tribulations on consumer message boards and hiring others to complain for us after providing them with all the necessary details. But once we've gone to the trouble of writing out all the details of our complaint, we could simply look up the company's e-mail address online, add a "Dear Executive," and send off the complaint ourselves!

The Better Business Bureau Web site (www.bbb.org) allows us to look up any business and get the names, addresses, and phone numbers of the company's senior executives. After gathering all the information and details of the incident, knowing where to send our letter is often the only obstacle standing in the way of an effective complaint.

Do you see the paradox of using complainers for hire? We pay good money for them to handle our complaints because we feel too ineffective to do so ourselves. But by compiling all the information these "professionals" require, we're basically completing 90 percent of the work for them. Further, by preparing our cases for the professionals to handle, we are actually demonstrating that we're perfectly capable of being effective complainers ourselves. Yet, the mere *idea* of complaining remains so overwhelming to us, we fail to realize that we have what it takes to do it alone! Potentially, we are all perfectly effective complainers, but the vast majority of us are somehow in complete denial about our abilities.

Denial is an interesting phenomenon. We typically deny ideas, facts, feelings, or beliefs that we experience as threatening to our egos. But here, we're denying something positive—that we are capable of being effective as complainers. This raises an important question. Why would someone as bright and competent as Bill so readily embrace his inner ineffective complainer and all the frustrations that go with it? Unfortunately, Bill's attitude toward complaining hinted at a deeper and potentially far more damaging mental process, one that operates far beneath the surface and poses a danger to ineffective complainers everywhere.

Complaint Avoidance as Self-fulfilling Prophecy

Bill was absolutely convinced his cable problem was unsolvable. But in reality, his mind had been deceived by a sneaky psychological mechanism of his own making—a self-fulfilling prophecy. Each time Bill passed by his television, he felt upset about not being able to use the set properly, and he felt helpless to do anything about it. Two failed technician visits had convinced him the problem was unsolvable. He was so certain any attempt to remedy the situation would fail (the prophecy), he never even bothered to try calling a third time (the self-fulfillment thereof). With Bill taking no action to resolve the problem, it indeed never got fixed. Bill's faulty assumption about the hopelessness of the situation and his ensuing inaction were the only reasons the prophecy came true.

Failure-oriented thinking of the "It won't work so why bother?" variety strongly reinforces whatever feelings of helplessness and disempowerment we already have about a situation. In Bill's case, such defeatist thinking made him even less likely to attempt a proactive solution whenever he faced his massive nonfunctional wall adornment. Bill became angry over lunch not because he was reminded of the cable glitch, but because he was reminded of his powerlessness and helplessness to do anything about it. It was that reminder, those feelings of passivity and victimhood, Bill found so irritating and distasteful.

Indeed, such defeatist thoughts should be distasteful to us. Experiencing strong feelings of passivity or helplessness can easily threaten our sense of general well-being. Psychological wounds hurt when they are exposed, just as physical wounds do. Feeling incompetent in any domain, no matter how trivial, can affect our mood and our self-esteem for the worse. This is especially true when we're reminded of our ineffectiveness regularly, as Bill was whenever he had the urge to watch television.

With complaints, our *self-fulfilling* prophecies are always *self-defeating*. Our fears of confronting endless automated menus, pop quizzes about our mother's maiden name, the last four digits of our Social Security number, or our favorite childhood pets become hugely exaggerated in our minds as a result.

A quick look around any home is usually sufficient to reveal a number of broken or unused newly purchased products, items we remain convinced we cannot fix or be reimbursed for. Ironically, most of us do not discard such objects. Perhaps we still hope to pursue our complaints about them in the future, or maybe we're simply not ready to admit how frustrated and helpless they make us feel. In the meantime, they remain in the back of our closets or on shelves in our garage, forgotten monuments to our complaining impotence and the self-defeating prophecies that created them.

Both self-fulfilling and self-defeating prophecies have repeatedly been studied for many decades. Sadly, the lessons learned are too often forgotten or ignored. One well-known self-fulfilling prophecy is the Pygmalion effect, first suggested by Robert Rosenthal and Lenore Jacobson in 1968. The Pygmalion effect refers to how students' performances conform to the expectations of their teachers. When teachers are exposed to information about which students are more gifted, they unconsciously behave in ways that encourage these students' success. The opposite is true as well. Teachers who expect less from certain students behave in ways that encourage them to perform below their capacity. This dynamic is tricky to correct because the influence teachers have on their students occurs in ways that are largely unconscious on both the teachers' as well as the students' part.

The damaging aspect of the Pygmalion effect is that students who are poorly regarded often internalize this negative message about their potential. They start to believe the lower expectations of them are justified, and they begin to behave accordingly. They start thinking of themselves as less capable than they would have had the teacher thought better of them. Indeed, the danger inherent in self-fulfilling prophecies is their power to make us conform to their expectations of our character, perceptions, and behavior. A recent study by psychologists Allison Smith of Rutgers University and her colleagues Lee Jussim and Jacquelynne Eccles discovered that the negative impacts of the Pygmalion effect on schoolchildren could last for up to six years!

Self-fulfilling Prophecies That Defeat Entire Communities

Self-defeating prophecies are detrimental to individuals (such as Bill or poorly regarded students), but they can also emerge in groups and can even engulf entire communities. One of the most common ways community self-defeating prophecies are formed is by ineffective complaining. I watched the birth of one such prophecy just a few weeks ago at my local drugstore.

The employees of this establishment are notoriously unpleasant. So much so that it wouldn't surprise me to learn they were hired based solely on their ability to scowl and look annoyed. They must at least have passed rigorous interview tests such as "We'd like to see how long you can stare disinterestedly into space while slouching." Although the store's employees were rarely friendly themselves, they had clearly been instructed to greet customers with friendly *phrases*. The results would have been comical if they weren't incredibly annoying. For example, their checkout greeting, "Did you find everything you were looking for?" came across as "Oh, are *you* still here?" Their rendition of "Thank you, now have a nice day" was eerily reminiscent of "Thank you, now go walk into traffic."

On this particular day, an older woman stood at the checkout counter struggling to open her purse (arthritis can make such endeavors challenging), and the cashier was blatantly rude to her. The store manager was out of earshot but standing nearby. Several people on the checkout line began grumbling, "Someone should complain." However, while some customers agreed the manager should be alerted, others voiced arguments against complaining. "They know the employees are always rude here, but the management just doesn't care" and "Complaining never helps" were mumbled by more than one person.

Nonetheless, given the manager was only a few feet away, a couple of people did talk themselves into alerting him to the incident. To his credit, the manager seemed truly dismayed to hear their report. He immediately called the employee off the register and into his office. The customers waiting to check out were so pleased they almost did the wave.

However, when I visited the drugstore again a few days later, I was greeted by the same ill-mannered employee staring into space disinterestedly while slouching behind the register. It might seem that the store's management could not care less about their employees' attitudes toward customers, but the truth is slightly more complicated. Even had he wanted to, the manager could not probably have fired the rude, slouchy scowler on the spot.

Many franchises and corporate retail stores have rigid procedures for terminating employees. It often requires two or three formal warnings before a dismissal. The problem is, once employees have been issued a warning, they usually make efforts to be polite when their manager is present, then go back to being rude otherwise. Unless we complain, managers have no further grounds upon which to advance toward the rude employee's exit. Since most ensuing rude behavior happens only when the manager is absent, when an incident occurs, we have to take the proactive step of seeking the manager out in person or calling the store to complain later.

However, in the interim, customers get a faulty impression when they see the employee still radiating apathy from behind the register. They conclude that complaining to the manager doesn't help and refrain from doing so the next time the employee is rude. This leaves the manager no "ammunition" with which to sanction the employee, who then stays in position. This convinces us even more that complaining is pointless, which leads the entire community to perpetuate a self-defeating prophecy that only reinforces our inaction and helplessness. The ongoing reign of rude employees in any establishment is just another example of the price we pay for our collective ineffective complaining skills.

Learning Learned Helplessness

Self-defeating prophecies, whether individual or collective, often create and then reinforce feelings of helplessness. For example, Bill "learned" to be helpless after only two unsuccessful technician visits. Dr. Martin Seligman, the preeminent psychologist, began his career investigating the powers of learned helplessness as a psychological construct and the many ways it affects all areas of our lives.

In the early 1960s, Seligman was a psychology graduate student at the University of Pennsylvania. Although a newcomer to the field, he had the good fortune to be working on the recently discovered phenomenon of learned helplessness with psychologists Steve Maier and Bruce Overmier while studying learning behavior in dogs.

Dogs were placed in a metal cage with a barrier in the middle. A mild electrical shock was sent to the part of the cage where the dog stood. The dog could avoid the shock by simply jumping over the barrier. If the dogs did not jump over the barrier themselves, they were shown how to do so. Consequently, the next time the cage was shocked, the dogs jumped over the barrier right away.

In stage two, the dogs were then placed into a restraining harness. When the electrical shock was sent to the cage, the dogs tried desperately to jump over the barrier but were unable to escape the harness. The harness was then removed and the dogs were free to jump over the barrier as they had in the earlier rounds of the experiment. But when the cage was shocked, the dogs made no efforts to jump over the barrier and escape. Instead, they stayed in the shocked side of the cage, whimpering helplessly. The dogs had learned helplessness so well they behaved as though they were helpless even once they were not.

Consider the parallels in Bill's experience. He had a glitch in his cable system that caused him distress when watching his television (the unpleasant "shock"). Twice he called in technicians to escape the problem (jumping over the barrier). At first, the problem seemed solved (the shock was avoided), but then the glitch returned (the shock seemed inescapable). After only two attempts to fix his cable glitch, Bill gave up trying and learned to be helpless. Just like the dogs, he became convinced that nothing he did could solve the problem, this even though a senior technician would likely have figured out a solution in minutes. Bill not only acquired learned helplessness, but it took only two "exposures" for helplessness to take root. Bill and the dogs were miserable about their situation and perfectly capable of taking action to relieve themselves. However, so convinced were they of their helplessness, they took no action at all and, unfortunately, remained miserable.

We know today that when people find themselves in situations in which they perceive frustrating or challenging events to be out of their control, they often enter a spiral of negative thinking. They become convinced nothing they do can better their situation, and they believe any effort to escape their predicament is doomed to fail. We saw the same mechanism at play with the customers in the drugstore.

We can all fall prey to learned helplessness in various areas of our lives at one time or another. But with complaints, we do so with alarming frequency. Little else can explain Goodman's findings that 95 percent of us fail to complain effectively about certain consumer dissatisfactions. One can only conclude that we have already succumbed to a societal learned helplessness, at least as consumers.

John A. Goodman agrees. He feels that many of today's consumers already believe complaining changes nothing and that doing so may even carry negative consequences. He calls this phenomenon trained hopelessness. If trained hopelessness and learned helplessness sound similar, it is because the two concepts have much in common. In both cases, we end up with distorted perceptions of a situation that convince us we are powerless when in fact we are not.

The hidden psychological danger inherent in the situation is that feeling powerless, helpless, or hopeless regularly can have serious implications for our mental health and place us at high risk for clinical depression. In fact, it was observing how depressed the dogs in his experiments appeared after learning helplessness that affected Martin Seligman the most. He knew depression was known to be dangerous, for our mood and quality of life as well as for our physical health. Studies at that time had already demonstrated that depressed individuals were susceptible to a variety of serious illnesses, were more prone to heart attacks and obesity, and were even condemned to shorter life spans than those who were not depressed.

Bill's complaint-related learned helplessness was by no means a guaranteed one-way ticket to depression. But today, our complaints are so ubiquitous and operate throughout so many spheres of our lives, the accumulation of helplessness and passivity we feel can easily add up. Our ineffective complaining skills as consumers are just the tip of the iceberg. We avoid voicing complaints to our loved ones, friends, work colleagues, and bosses just as often as we avoid voicing our dissatisfactions with products or services. While not all complaints *should* be voiced (more about those dangers in chapter 4), what prevents us from speaking up when we should is the same thing that prevented Bill from pursuing his complaint—a false belief that doing so will not help. Indeed, learned helplessness is by definition a reaction to an *unreal* constraint. It is a cognitive distortion, a problem in our *perceptions.* Once we are in the grips of it, even the most unreal constraint can feel very real to us indeed.

Effective Complaining: An Essential Life Skill

Dennis was a twenty-five-year-old, bright man from New England who moved to New York City to start law school. He had come to therapy a few weeks before school began to deal with the challenges and adjustments of moving from a small town to the big city (his mother, a therapist, had urged him to do so). Dennis's first couple of days in law school went poorly. First, he had problems with his financial aid (which required additional paperwork but were resolvable). He had also moved in with a roommate who turned out to be fond of watching slasher and horror movies after midnight, whereas Dennis couldn't stand them at any hour. He then went to the bookstore and discovered the bank had set his credit-card limit too low, making it impossible for him to purchase all his books. To top it all off, the laptop he ordered two weeks previously had not yet arrived.

Incredibly frustrated and annoyed, Dennis first went to the financial aid office where the "impatient and overworked" staff told him to produce documentation that should already have been in his file and of which he had no copies with him. From there he went to the bank, where he was told they could fix his credit limit but that doing so required information from his local bank back home, which he didn't have with him either.

Later that night, Dennis was awoken by bloodcurdling screams. He leaped out of bed and rushed into the living room, where his roommate was engrossed in yet another viewing of *Nightmare on Elm Street.* It was all a little too much for Dennis. He began yelling at his roommate for being incredibly inconsiderate and selfish. This did not go down well with the bewildered roommate, who had no idea Dennis was already sleeping. According to Dennis, their arguing was loud enough to drown out even the death screams of Freddy Krueger's victims. The next morning, Dennis's new laptop finally arrived, but something made it crash whenever he opened the Web browser. Nothing he tried seemed to remedy the problem, and already late for class, he had to give up and run to school.

By the time he showed up to his therapy appointment that afternoon, Dennis was utterly despondent. First, he burst into tears. Then he informed me he could not handle the pressures of law school and that he had decided to go back to New England. I was shocked. I tried reassuring Dennis that none of the problems he had encountered had anything to do with his actual studies. But by then, Dennis felt so disempowered, he felt unable to resolve even the smallest of his complaints.

I realized Dennis was well on his way to becoming depressed as he sounded completely beaten down and hopeless. What was shocking was that it had happened so quickly. The week before, Dennis had appeared a little anxious about starting school, but his entire posture, manner, and speech were generally positive and confident. I gave it my best effort in the session, but nothing I did could make Dennis reconsider his decision. He simply felt too overwhelmed to consider staying. He left New York the following week.

Dennis provides us with an unfortunate illustration of the real hidden dangers in complaint-oriented learned helplessness—their ability to generalize across situations. The learned helplessness Dennis acquired after his initial failures to resolve run-of-the-mill complaints generalized to a broad feeling of powerlessness and ineffectiveness that caused him to reach a rash and premature decision. He became convinced he could not manage the demands of law school, even though he had never experienced problems with his classes and subject matter or with his professors.

In numerous experiments Martin Seligman and other researchers demonstrated how learned helplessness generalized from one task to another. But upon further reflection, a major problem with their logic became apparent to Seligman. We all run into frustrating complaints regularly, much as Dennis did. If learned helplessness was indeed so easy to trigger and if depression was so often the result, why aren't we all walking around feeling helpless and depressed? Seligman went over the data again and came up with a vitally important insight:

> Not all the rats and dogs become helpless after inescapable shock, nor do all the people after being presented with unsolvable problems or inescapable noise. One out of three never gives up, no matter what we do. Moreover, one out of eight is helpless to begin with ... What is it about some people that imparts buffering strength, making them invulnerable to helplessness? What is it about other people that makes them collapse at the first inkling of trouble?

Seligman's questions were profound when he voiced them thirty years ago. Did some qualities or characteristics make some people immune to learned helplessness and by extension more *resilient* to depression? Conversely, what made other people *less* resilient and *more* prone to depression and learned helplessness? What could such qualities teach us about how complaint-related learned helplessness might be avoided?

The answer to these questions has everything to do with how we understand our predicament in the first place. It boils down to one crucial factor—exactly whom or what we think is responsible for our problems.

To Blame or Not to Blame

When we find ourselves in an unpleasant situation and believe no action we take will change our circumstances, we do the most human of things—we attempt to understand *why* we are in the situation. In other words, we feel compelled to place the blame somewhere (which is why we often accuse furniture of "being in the way!"). Seligman and others found that how we make these attributions, whom and what we blame for our perceived lack of control, has a huge impact on whether we're likely to feel helpless and consequently on our overall mental health.

So where did Bill place the blame for his cable woes? Whom did he blame for his predicament? Bill saw the glitch as resulting from the incompetence of the cable company (an external factor), not from his own actions or inactions (an internal factor). Martin Seligman's studies, as well as those of other researchers, demonstrate that if we believe the cause of our failure is external, we assume it is not in our control, and that very attribution places us at risk for learned helplessness.

Also important is whether we perceive our lack of control as temporary or permanent. Bill believed that since two technicians failed to fix the cable box, all the technicians at the cable company were therefore incompetent. He saw the problem as fixed and stable, not temporary. Perceiving our lack of control to be permanent also implies we are not in control and increases our likelihood of becoming helpless. Lastly, Bill believed complaining further would not work because generally "Those people don't care." If we perceive our lack of control as resulting from general factors that we have no ability to impact, rather than specific factors that we can influence, we also put ourselves at risk for learned helplessness.

The same was true for Dennis, who saw his problems as stemming from his own inability to manage the "system" and the "big city." Therefore, he did not attribute his failures to circumstances or lack of effort or persistence. Rather he felt all the crucial elements were out of his control, thereby rendering him helpless to change things and manage his complaints effectively.

Let's examine how we might react if we were in Bill's situation but had a more positive attribution style. First, we would believe that since the cable box was new and since new technology often has glitches that can be fixed, persisting in our complaint would eventually lead to our resolving the matter. We would see the situation as requiring persistence, and we would see persistence as within our control.

Second, we would also see the problem as temporary rather than permanent. For example, we might believe that even if most of the company's technicians were award-winning incompetents, someone in the company had to be capable of either fixing the glitch or switching us to a cable box that worked more reliably. Therefore, a third technician might be able to resolve the issue. Finally, we would assume that although our prior two complaints had not resolved the issue, and even if the technical-support department was largely incompetent, someone from a different department and higher up in the company would respond if we addressed our complaint to them personally.

Thus, two different people might face the exact same situation, fail in their initial efforts to resolve it, but attribute their failures to entirely different factors. Bill perceived the problem as not in his control, as unfixable by technicians, and as unimportant to the company. But a positive Bill would perceive numerous ways to continue pursuing his complaint (e.g., by requesting to speak with a supervisor, insisting on a more senior technician, or switching the cable box himself). He would also see past failures as related to the competence of the two specific technicians rather than to the company as a whole.

Lastly, positive Bill would assume that persisting in his complaint (for example by speaking to higher-ups in the company) would eventually lead to the issue's being resolved. Positive Bill might get just as aggravated about the cable glitch and the inept technicians as Bill did, but he would not fall into the same self-fulfilling prophecy of passivity and helplessness.

Seeing Our Complaints as Half-Full

What in their fundamental psychological makeup makes Bill and positive Bill so different? What set of characteristics determines which people are prone to learned helplessness and depression and which are not? Seligman summed up these differences with one word—pessimism. We all run into hurdles in life, but pessimists tend to understand these hurdles as personal, stable, and global. "This always happens to me," "Just my luck," and "It never rains, it pours" are all "pessimisms." Pessimists attribute their failures to causes that make things seem out of their control, and by doing so they set themselves up for helplessness. On the other hand, optimists tend to see setbacks as manageable, temporary, or circumstantial.

The difference between optimists and pessimists is hugely significant. Seligman's team found that when life challenges occurred, pessimists were eight times more likely to become depressed than optimists were. Indeed, we saw how easily Dennis became depressed when dealing with his simple obstacles. Pessimists were also shown to do more poorly at school, had less successful careers than optimists of equal ability did, and had more turbulent friendships.

Fortunately, Seligman's later work showed that things were not as dire for pessimists as they first seemed. He found that optimism was a skill set, one that could be learned. He then tried teaching optimism to others, and the results were extremely encouraging. When ten-year-old children were taught how to change their attributions to think and act optimistically, it reduced their later rate of adolescent depression by half.

Can our attributions about the causes of our failures and successes make that much of a difference? How much do they affect our mental health, our tendency toward depression, or how we perform tasks of daily living? Yes, such attributions can make a critical difference, and not just to depression. Attributions affect our performance on a large variety of everyday tasks. To illustrate this, one study took the research out of the lab and placed it firmly into an arena of daily life in which the impact of such attributions could easily and objectively be quantifiable—the basketball court.

A high school varsity team was evenly split into two groups comparable in ability. One group had regular coaching in which they received standard feedback based on their technique during practice. The second group received similar coaching, but in addition they received feedback that specifically attributed successful plays to their ability (which puts things in their control) and bad plays to lack of effort (which leaves things in their control as well). These two coaching styles were administered for only fifteen minutes in a given practice session. Players were evaluated before and after a one-month training period on their success at twenty-five shots from the free-throw line (fifteen feet from the basket).

Before the training period, the two training groups showed no differences as they had been distributed equally according to player ability. As expected, the regularly trained group did not show a significant improvement in their scores after the training period. However, the group trained using attributions improved by an average of almost three baskets—a result that could easily change the outcome of a game in a team's favor. Focusing the players' attributions of successes and failures on factors that were within their control (having good basic ability or making efforts) made a major difference in their performance.

But what can those of us who are more pessimistic do to change our outlook? How might we apply this remedy to the complaint-related situations we face in our daily lives?

Unlearning Learned Helplessness

Let's revisit those poor dogs. Researchers, after teaching the dogs to be helpless, were curious if they could get them to unlearn that lesson. Dogs that had already become helpless were released from the harnesses and shocked. Then they were dragged over the barrier by a research assistant, thereby helping the dogs escape the shock. The previously helpless dogs eventually learned to jump over the barricade when shocked. Once people (or animals) believed that they had options for action, that they were not actually helpless, they could begin to overcome their helplessness.

That is one of the primary messages of this book. Our complaints *can* be resolved, they *do* matter, and taking action to pursue them is always better than falling into passivity and helplessness. This is especially true when our complaints are significant to us or when we encounter them regularly (such as Bill missing the joys of his giant television).

To complain effectively, we must first change our attributions, our understanding of past failures. If we complained ineffectively in the past, it was not because we lacked the basic ability to be effective, but because we lacked the skills and expertise to do so. The information in this book (especially the formulas laid out in chapter 5) should close that skill-set gap. We can teach ourselves that the harness of trained hopelessness we feel envelops us when we consider complaining is only illusory. We can discover we are not tethered to an electrified cage. We can indeed jump over the barrier if we just keep trying to do so.

In addition, when acquiring our effective complaining skills, we should start by pursuing small or easier complaints at first. Doing so will allow us to regain our sense of confidence and agency and demonstrate that we are indeed capable of complaining productively. A success under our belt will then fuel our optimism when we tackle trickier or more complicated complaints later on. From a psychological perspective, all it really takes is one incident of assuming control, and by doing so having a positive impact, to jump-start us into believing we are not helpless. One well-handled proof-of-concept complaint, no matter how small, is enough to open our eyes that we can *make* things happen in our lives as opposed to just *letting* them happen.

For example, before going ballistic and accusing his roommate of selfishness, Dennis should have asked him if he minded turning down the volume. If his roommate responded reasonably, Dennis might then have felt empowered enough to tackle his next complaint more proactively. He could have called the bank's customer-service line to request an increase in his credit-card limit without going back to his home branch, as credit-card companies often authorize such requests over the phone. Asking his mother to send copies of financial documentation should have solved his financial-aid woes, and a session on the phone with tech support (which was free with his new laptop) should have resolved his crashing Web browser.

When working on our complaining skills, we should always go from the easiest complaint to the hardest (or from the least to the most complicated or annoying). For consumer complaints, I suggest first finding the address of the business and the phone numbers of their headquarters. Having such information at our disposal is always a motivational pick-me-up. Even if we plan to call a customer-service hotline, knowing we can escalate our complaints directly to the highest rungs of a company if necessary can inoculate us from giving up at the first sign of getting the runaround or when dealing with less than helpful customer-service representatives.

When our complaints are directed to our loved ones, our colleagues, our roommates, or our friends, we can always ask to reopen discussions or revisit issues if they were unsatisfactorily resolved in the past. Acquiring effective complaining skills and changing our perceptions from pessimistic to optimistic will not only help us avoid feelings of helplessness or depression, but it will enrich us personally and psychologically as well.

However, being mindful and putting in the effort to switch from a pessimistic to an optimistic perspective is by no means a simple endeavor. Such cognitive retraining can require a huge investment of time and emotional energy.

Martin Seligman knows this well as he himself undertook that very challenge. Doing so allowed him to change the direction of his life as well as the future of psychology as a science in dramatic ways.

In 1998, Martin Seligman was elected president of the American Psychological Association by the largest margin in the history of the organization. He had spent thirty years researching learned helplessness, pessimism, and depression, but despite his incredible success and stunning international recognition, he realized in the days following his election that psychology as a science and especially as a practice was still focused entirely on the disease model of mental health—the study of what makes us sick. The questions of what makes people happy, what makes us virtuous, what gives our lives meaning, and what builds our character strengths had all been profoundly neglected.

Thus, he decided to embark on his grandest initiative of all and the science of positive psychology was born. Days afterward, the study of human strengths and the science of happiness and meaning was launched by the person most singularly positioned to establish this new quadrant of psychology, giving it both scientific legitimacy as well as professional and public acceptance. Martin Seligman's journey from the dark side of learned helplessness, depression, and human suffering to the bright side of happiness and positive psychology constitutes one of the most remarkable professional tours of duty in the history of any science.

Not everyone is open to such radical reevaluations of our basic perceptions and beliefs. For example, my friend Bill was not. But fortunately, life intervened on Bill's behalf (as it sometimes does). Several months after our lunch, his building switched cable providers, and the new company's high-definition cable box worked just fine.

In many ways, our complaints always straddle these two extremes. While ineffective complaining could ultimately lead to learned helplessness, depression, aborted law degrees, and unwatchable giant televisions, learning how to complain effectively could be as invigorating to our psychology as learned helplessness is numbing. Pursuing small complaints effectively could lend us a general emotional resiliency to protect us from the pull of helplessness and depression. Martin Seligman is currently working with the U.S. army on the new and cutting-edge Comprehensive Soldier Fitness Program, which in part uses Seligman's optimism research to create emotional resilience in soldiers. The hope is that their resilience will reduce the incidence and severity of problems such as post-traumatic stress disorder.

As we shall see in the next chapter, complaining effectively can be instrumental far beyond building emotional resiliency to consumer trained hopelessness. It can improve our self-esteem, our relationships, and our happiness as well. In some cases, it can even save our lives.

Chapter Three
Complaining Therapy
Squeaking Our Way to Self-esteem

It is better to light a single candle than curse the darkness.
—Chinese proverb

I kept thinking about my last session with Dennis and his decision to leave law school. I had just spent the better part of a year investigating complaining psychology, yet Dennis had quit law school as a direct result of his inability to manage an unfortunate series of regular complaints (albeit at a time of significant life transition and elevated stress). Although I could have coached him through them, doing so would have been both unwise and inappropriate. Dennis had come to the session to talk about how terrible he felt, to get support and empathy from someone who could understand what he was going through. For me to shunt his feelings aside and commandeer the session for an effective-complaining tutorial (especially one he had never requested) could have been perceived by Dennis as dismissive and insulting if not downright infantilizing. Further, he could also have taken my initiative as verification that he was unable to handle life in the big city by himself. Ignoring Dennis's fragile state of mind and insisting we tackle his complaints would have risked doing more psychological harm than good.

However, the experience with Dennis left me pondering a tantalizing question. If complaining helplessness could affect someone so negatively, could *successful* complaining have an equally positive effect? Could resolving a meaningful complaint actually *boost* someone's confidence or self-esteem? Most successful complaint resolutions elicited initial surges of relief and satisfaction, no matter what the complaint entailed. But if the matter we resolved was meaningful to us, could our emotional and psychological gains extend beyond that first rush of success?

I believed that pursuing complaints that caused us feelings of helplessness or powerlessness and resolving them successfully would yield therapeutic benefits. But I was not sure how deep any such benefits would go or how long they would last. Of course, my assumptions were still just that, assumptions. The psychological effects of "complaining therapy" have not yet been investigated scientifically. However, I was in a position to examine them anecdotally, and the best way to do so was through case studies in my practice and the prism of psychotherapy.

My patients frequently discuss their most personally meaningful complaints in their sessions. Most of those complaints involve numerous people or are too complicated and messy to tease out one single complaint from. However, occasionally simple dissatisfactions about a specific person or situation do come up, and those are the ones best suited to evaluate the potential of complaining therapy. I decided to wait for just the right complaint to present itself in my practice. A few short weeks later, one did.

A Heartbreaking Dating Service

Sarah was forty, single, and not happy about it. She was an attractive, athletic small-business owner with a great sense of humor, so it was not immediately apparent why she was struggling to find a life partner. But Sarah's design business meant she spent virtually all her time at work or at work-related functions, leaving little opportunity to meet potential mates. As Sarah put it during one of our earlier sessions, "As for meeting men through work, there aren't any. I'm surrounded by estrogen. It's me and twenty middle-aged seamstresses. The only time I even sniff testosterone at work is if one of the women goes menopausal and shows up with a hormone-replacement patch."

Like many hardworking New Yorkers over forty, Sarah had little time or energy for the "bar scene," and she had already explored most of the obvious alternatives such as continuing-education cooking classes, hiking and biking groups, book clubs, yoga retreats, lectures at numerous New York City institutions, speed dating, singles events, and various others.

"And none of them had eligible single men in their thirties and forties?" I asked when I first heard Sarah's long list of venues.

"Very few of them did. And men in their forties are not looking for female business owners in their forties. They're looking for trophies."

"Trophy wives?"

"Trophy hookups," Sarah responded.

Sarah tried online dating sites. But it took far too much time to go through people's profiles, and few of the men she considered interesting (and age appropriate) responded to hers. She was beginning to lose hope. Then she saw an ad for a dating service that focused exclusively on "marriage-minded people." All clients went through an extensive background check that included a "unique" personality test. Clients were also assigned a personal matchmaker who recommended potential mates based both on a personality test and on his or her personal acquaintanceship with clients. The only hitch was that the service cost thousands of dollars, way out of Sarah's price range. But when Eileen, the service's senior salesperson, promised Sarah they could have her in their system and out on dates within days, Sarah took a chance and signed up.

She came into our next session smiling and happier than I had seen her in weeks. "I had to dip into savings in a big way," she admitted a little nervously, "but my last date was over a year ago. I'm not getting anywhere. I guess this is my last shot. I had my hair done and I did their photo session this morning. Eileen said my profile should be up on their site by Monday." Excitement crept into Sarah's voice. She smiled. "Let the dating begin!"

But the dating did not begin. Three weeks and numerous phone calls later, Sarah finally got through to Eileen. The sales adviser denied having promised Sarah she would be in the system that quickly. "Besides, Sarah, I just called you a few hours ago with a message about your first match."

"I was here all day, there was no call," Sarah insisted.

"No? I think Tina was supposed to call. Tina's your personal matchmaker. Let me look for her and she'll call you right back."

Tina indeed called back with Sarah's first match a few moments later. "I guess when she described him he sounded okay," Sarah reported to me in a session. "But when I asked Tina why she chose this specific person for me, she couldn't mention one thing that indicated why this man might be good husband material for me, not one thing we had in common."

"That doesn't sound good," I said as warning bells rang loudly in my ears. This service was beginning to sound like nothing more than a poorly run racket.

"It was awful!" Sarah groaned. "Tina kept confusing me with her other clients. My personal matchmaker, who is supposed to know me well enough to find me a husband, didn't know a thing about me. And my file was right in front of her!"

I did not have to encourage Sarah to speak up about her concerns as she had already done so. Tina had quickly reassured Sarah that she was not yet up to speed because of glitches in their computer system. Sure enough, a few days later Tina called with Sarah's "proper" matches.

Contender number one was fifty-four years old. Sarah declined an introduction, having specified a ten-year age limit (i.e., no one over fifty) as well as a maximum eight-inch height differential when she first signed up (Sarah is five feet four). Contender number two was forty-seven but six feet six. Sarah declined again. Contender number three sounded okay and even had decent pictures, except

Sarah noticed his listing said "married." Sarah was not persuaded by Tina's reassurance that "his divorce is imminent," and she declined that one as well.

Contender number four seemed to have no items of obvious disqualification. Sarah was not too hopeful at that point, but she did try to keep an open mind. The man called Sarah the next day, but he was not calling for a date. He told Sarah he was suing the company in small-claims court. He had called simply to extend a warning about them. Sarah was astonished.

"Then why are you still in their system?" she asked, dumbfounded the company would set her up on a date with someone who was suing them.

"I've been trying to get out of their system for months, but that's how incompetent they are, they haven't taken me out yet," the man explained. "It's fine with me. Every time they match me with someone, I call them and warn them to get a full refund."

Sarah called the company the next day and asked for her money back. Tina refused to give Sarah a refund of any kind. She would, however, be happy to "keep providing you with carefully selected personalized matches." Sarah was not without effective complaining skills (often a must for small-business owners). She marched over to the company offices and voiced her complaints to Eileen in person. After a loud and nasty confrontation, Eileen would not refund a single penny.

Sarah did not give up. She wrote a letter of complaint to her credit-card company and asked to dispute the charges. The dating service responded by providing Sarah's credit-card company with copies of their sales contract, which clearly indicated Sarah had missed the refund window, albeit by only a few days. Sarah wrote to the credit-card company again, arguing the dating service purposefully delayed entering her into the system until the refund window had expired. The credit-card company was apologetic but denied Sarah's claim.

Sarah arrived at our next session devastated. She had spent a huge amount of money as a last resort to find love and happiness.

But all she had to show for it was a significant financial loss, heartache, and disappointment. "I just feel like crap," Sarah moaned. "I've tried so many things and ... nothing works! Why is it so impossible to find someone?"

My heart went out to Sarah. She was smart, attractive, and creative, but her devotion to her work and her consequent sparse dating history had slowly eroded her confidence. True, she still felt good about herself as a designer and as a business owner. But as a woman in the dating world, as a potential mate, she felt worse about herself than ever. "I know it's not logical, but it feels as though I've been rejected by every man in that database," Sarah explained while dabbing at her eyes with a tissue. "I just *feel* like somehow I wasn't good enough, like there's something wrong with *me*! Why do I feel so terrible about myself?"

I realized that helping Sarah pursue her appeal to the credit-card company was exactly the kind of opportunity I had been waiting for. Not only was Sarah's complaint entirely justified, her experiences with the dating service had left a huge mark on her mood and state of mind. Helping Sarah get her money back was something she deserved, and doing so (if she was successful) would allow me to observe the longer-term impact of complaining therapy on Sarah's feelings of despair and powerlessness as well as on her overall self-esteem.

Sarah's question about her self-esteem was a good one. Remember, Sarah had rejected three men for being inappropriate matches, and she was given valuable advice by a fourth. She herself had been rejected by no one, not one single person. So why was she experiencing such powerful feelings of rejection? Why was her self-esteem taking such a hit as a result?

I thought about the overlap between Sarah's and Bill's complaints. Both she and Bill had invested thousands of dollars on a consumer purchase (a dating service and a huge-screen television) and both of them felt frustrated, disappointed, and angry at the result (faulty mate selection and faulty cable reception). Both Sarah and Bill had complained repeatedly in efforts to remedy their situation, and both of them were unsuccessful. Finally, they both felt powerless and unable to pursue their complaints any further, Bill because of learned helplessness, and Sarah because she had seemingly exhausted her options.

But while Bill's mood had been affected by the incident, his overall self-esteem had not been. He still felt competent, capable, and good about himself as a person. However, Sarah's self-esteem had suffered a veritable body blow. How can we make sense of the vastly different impacts these two complaint experiences had on Bill and Sarah? To do so, we must ask ourselves a question, the answer to which might seem obvious at first but actually isn't:

What exactly *is* self-esteem?

Self-esteem's Identity Crisis

Back in my graduate school days, self-esteem was known to be a complex psychological entity about which researchers had raging and fundamental disagreements. Needing to catch up with the last fifteen years of research into this hugely important construct, I spent several hours at the library. I discovered that self-esteem was known to be a complex psychological entity about which researchers had raging and fundamental disagreements. Hooray for progress!

To be fair, there had been some forward movement, with several new and promising theories. Many of the specific points of contention were different from what they had been. But overall, the field was still a mess. Perhaps in part because the primary arena for discourse about self-esteem had shifted over the past decades and was no longer our psychology departments; it was our town squares, our schools, and even our halls of government.

In the 1980s, books, television shows, celebrities, and "informed" politicians all began touting self-esteem's great powers. High self-esteem was said to improve children's academic performances, reduce teenage pregnancy rates, and decrease crime and gang violence. Millions were spent on self-esteem programs. Books and workshops promised miracles, and a host of less conventional self-esteem "boosters" competed for our attention on late-night TV. Self-esteem soon became the most coveted psychological accessory of the day. Sure, having intelligence, creativity, common sense, kindness, and other such traits was nice if you could get them. But the *must have* item for any season was good shiny self-esteem. In popular culture, self-esteem became synonymous with overall mental health, even though they were entirely different constructs.

The only problem with the self-esteem "gold rush" was that none of the books, programs, or workshops actually panned out. They were all fool's gold. Even if people supposedly improved their self-esteem, doing so had no impact on their lives. Undeterred, the State of California commissioned an entire task force to investigate self-esteem's seemingly magical powers. The task force found that self-esteem was actually *not* related to academic performance, teenage pregnancy, drug use, or gang violence. Self-esteem, at least as we measured it at the time, seemed to be related to little. The State of California responded to this report by their own task force by promptly implementing self-esteem programs in California schools.

The folly of lawmakers aside, the question remains, what is self-esteem exactly and how is it impacted by our complaining behaviors?

Self-esteem refers to our general and specific positive or negative attitudes toward our "self." We usually establish such self-views by observing how people around us respond to our actions and behaviors, and by comparing ourselves to the actions and behaviors of others. Most experts agree on that much. But here's where it gets tricky. People have attitudes about themselves that are both *global* (am I a good person, am I intelligent, am I creative?) as well as *specific* (am I a good mother, a competent pianist, or a loyal friend?), and these two separate facets of our self-esteem (global feelings of self-worth and our self-worth in specific domains) are largely independent of each other.

For example, the star of a high school football team who struggles academically might have low academic self-esteem even as his global self-esteem, his general sense of self-worth, is high. Someone whose general feelings of self-worth are quite low could still be an amazing cook and have great specific self-esteem about her abilities in the kitchen. Hits to our global self-esteem have more dramatic emotional consequences than hits to areas of specific self-esteem. Drops in global self-esteem are related to depression and anxiety, while drops in specific self-esteem, less so. Specific self-esteem is far more related to our behaviors, our efforts, and our persistence at tasks than to a global sense of well-being.

Let's examine Sarah's experience with that knowledge in mind. Her complaint about the dating service made her feel powerlessness as a consumer, not as a woman, and thus was in the domain of her specific self-esteem. Why she might have felt incredibly disappointed by or angry at having been sold a poor service and been through a highly frustrating experience was easy to understand. But her general self-esteem was suffering in addition; her global self-worth had dropped precipitously. Why?

Global and specific self-esteem are distinct entities, but they still interact and affect one another. The more meaningful a domain of specific self-esteem is to us, the bigger the role it plays in our lives, the more influence it exerts on our global self-esteem. The high school jock invests hours a day on his football skills and gains many social advantages from his success. But he does not spend nearly as much time studying, nor would he gain any incremental regard from his peers for doing so (which, although unfortunate, is true in most school settings). Because football is far more meaningful to him than academics, any hits to his self-esteem as a football player would have a far greater impact on his global self-esteem than would changes in his self-esteem as an academic student.

Bill loved his television dearly, but it did not significantly reflect upon who Bill was as a person or upon his general self-worth. But for Sarah, failure in the realm of dating, even if it was as a consumer, was of huge personal meaning and of significant consequence. Therefore, it was of immense relevance to her global self-esteem and general sense of self-worth. This is true for all of us. *When our complaints are related to an aspect of our lives that is highly meaningful or important to us, our ability to complain effectively can have a significant impact on our sense of self-worth.*

The other aspect of self-esteem that can be tricky is that, unlike basic intelligence, creativity, or common sense, many aspects of our self-esteem do not remain static throughout our adult lives. They fluctuate up and down in response to our experiences. Consequently, we can gain or lose self-esteem at any age. For example, as retirees, we might find our self-esteem drops when we least expect it to. If we had derived large portions of our self-esteem from our professional status or successes in our careers, life might suddenly seem empty and lacking in meaning. We must then take time to find new sources of satisfaction and, by doing so, redefine how we view ourselves and rebuild our self-esteem.

Fluctuations in self-esteem can occur in response to any significant event in our personal or professional lives. What matters in such situations is our own interpretation of the events and the subjective meaning they carry for us. Receiving a good grade on an exam, having a meaningful and productive talk with our kids, or getting a kind word from our boss can all have small but positive impacts on our self-esteem, just as the opposite experiences can have negative impacts. Such vacillations are the psychological equivalents of having good and bad hair days.

Sarah's global feelings of self-worth had suffered because even though her unresolved complaint related to a specific domain of consumer self-esteem, it touched upon an area that had huge personal meaning for her—the dating world. But something else contributed to Sarah's drop in her general self-worth as well, something even more damaging—a sense of victimization.

Effective Complaining: The Antidote for Victimization

Unresolved meaningful complaints make us feel powerless and helpless, but they make us feel victimized as well. Anyone who drives off a car lot in a lemon, or assembles a complicated piece of furniture only to find a crucial piece is missing, or is bumped from a flight for no apparent reason, feels victimized to some degree. It is also natural to ruminate on how unfair the situation is, on why the passenger next to us has a pillow and we don't, or on why the technician always shows up five minutes before the end of a six-hour window. The combination of these two perceptions and feelings—powerlessness and lack of fairness—often results in lingering feelings of victimization.

Feelings of victimization (as well as humiliation and shame) are extremely damaging to our global self-esteem. However, complaining, speaking up, and proactively following through can reverse the effects of victimization, especially if we are successful in doing so. Taking appropriate action and complaining can literally *undo* lingering feelings of helplessness and hopelessness more effectively than years of psychotherapy. However, the only thing that can undo feelings of victimization is to make sure our complaints get *resolved.* Complaining effectively and resolving meaningful dissatisfactions or grievances can reverse feelings of victimization and rebuild our self-esteem.

Complaining effectively can be a powerful therapy, one that requires only the will and the skill set to get results. Sarah needed my help in both those departments, as her will and determination were already in decline and she had exhausted the limits of her own complaining abilities. Luckily, by our next session I had an idea I thought might work. I took the plunge and pitched my suggestion to Sarah: to complain to the credit-card company again. Not surprisingly, she was not eager to do so. Her state of mind was still fragile and she was reluctant to set herself up for another disappointment.

I explained my reasoning about why her complaint should work. Sarah's appeal to the credit-card company was dismissed because the refund window had closed. But the true rationale for her complaint was not the refund window, but that the dating service had reneged on every one of the guarantees in their contract. To me her situation was similar to our purchasing a refrigerator at the store but discovering its cooling system is faulty once we get home. It looks like a fridge but it doesn't keep things cold.

Sarah had purchased a dating service but wasn't provided appropriate dates. The service had made Sarah numerous promises, such as the number of eligible men they would introduce to her. I suspected that if she went over their contract, she'd find quite a few promises that were never fulfilled. From what she'd told me, it might even be all of them. I suggested to Sarah that she enumerate the guarantees the dating service had made in their contract and structure her letter with point-by-point examples of how they'd failed to deliver.

Sarah agreed to write to her credit-card company one last time. Her mood began to improve the moment she did because she was taking action she thought might be effective. Her mood improved further when a few weeks later the credit-card company ruled in her favor and placed the full amount she had paid the dating service right back into her account. "And unlike bachelor number four, I didn't even have to sue them for it!" Sarah announced triumphantly in our session.

Most gratifying of all was that Sarah's self-esteem began to recover as well. Fighting the dating service and winning made her feel stronger and more confident than she had in years. She felt as though her resolve and character had been tested by these events, and that she had come through the ordeal feeling stronger and more empowered. She felt like a fighter instead of a victim.

I wondered whether Sarah's global self-esteem had improved at its baseline or whether she was just feeling the temporary effects of her victory and the satisfaction of seeing thousands of dollars flow back into her savings account. If her much improved disposition was merely a result of her improved finances, the positive effects on her self-esteem should only be temporary. Research on lottery winners shows that although they reap huge gains in happiness and life satisfaction after winning millions of dollars, their moods and dispositions usually return to their pre-win baselines within months.

But Sarah continued to thrive many months later. She began to entertain thoughts of putting herself into the dating world again.

She seemed eager to find new venues in which she might meet men with whom she shared common interests. But she had trouble coming up with options that excited her. We were discussing this dilemma in a session when I thought of Martin Seligman.

One of Seligman's major conclusions from the science of positive psychology is the importance of identifying our "signature strengths." Signature strengths are those parts of ourselves that are unique, that we connect with, and that we find extremely fulfilling. They are usually stable traits, talents we can choose either to exercise or to ignore. Examples of such strengths are valor and bravery, perseverance, honesty, and kindness. Seligman recommends we identify the signature strengths with which we feel most comfortable and incorporate them into our lives however and whenever we can. Doing so is one of the keys to experiencing authentic happiness.

Sarah had numerous strengths. She was already using her originality, creativity, and leadership as an owner of a design company. But Sarah had one strength she had not yet employed—her terrific sense of humor. I suggested that as a vehicle to meet people and explore something new, she try an improvisational-comedy class. Sarah decided to up the ante. The next week she signed up for a class in stand-up comedy. Two months later, she took the stage for the first time at a major New York comedy club. She brought the tape of her performance to our next session. It was a real treat to watch. Sarah took the mic like a real professional and had incredible stage presence.

Sarah had effectively complained her way back to good self-esteem and even better spirits, and she had discovered a new passion. Even more gratifying, Sarah kept her best news for last. One of the comics asked her out after her show. Other than having an obvious sense of humor, the man was single, in his early forties, and five foot ten. They had a date that weekend. "We laughed the whole time!" Sarah reported the following week, radiating a glow that reflected her bright mood, her newfound confidence, and her fully restored self-esteem.

Saving Steve from a Broken Heart

Learned-helplessness research teaches us that people are not equally susceptible to depression or drops in self-esteem when they experience powerlessness. Consequently, not everyone would see gains in global self-esteem if he or she complained effectively. But by resolving a meaningful grievance, many people could still benefit emotionally, psychologically, and in some cases materially. I was encouraged by the results of Sarah's complaining therapy and therefore eager to explore these possibilities with another patient.

The day after Sarah told me her good news, I had a session scheduled with Steve, a fifty-two-year-old paralegal with whom I had just started working the previous week. Steve was what I call a Reluctant. Reluctants are men who came to therapy not because they feel the necessity themselves but because their wives force them to do so. In the majority of couple-therapy cases, one member of the couple is more motivated than the other, and this difference can be stark. But Reluctants are men who are sent to therapy *by* their spouses, not coming *with* them. Reluctants are usually browbeaten into making an appointment after weeks, months, and sometimes years of spousal pressure, the wife's urging often continuing relentlessly until the husband finally cracks.

Reluctants usually show up at their first session already resentful about being there and with no intention of engaging in therapy. While that might be all fair and well from the Reluctant's point of view, I typically know nothing of the fighting and drama that have gone on. Consequently, I'll start what I think is a regular first session only to be immediately ambushed by a colorful array of passive-aggressive behaviors fueled by years of unspoken marital resentments. Unpleasant as such beginnings are to sit through, they do make it easy to tell when a patient is a Reluctant.

Steve listened to my opening question about what brought him to therapy without looking me in the eye even once. When I finished speaking, he glanced up at me, scowled, looked away, and mumbled, "*Some people* think I'm irritable and selfish." It was a disowning-of-responsibility classic.

"Which people?" I inquired.

"My wife, I guess." Steve's entire manner radiated resentment.

"Does anyone else think you might be irritable and selfish beside your wife?"

"Nah."

"And do you agree with your wife's assessment?"

Steve shrugged but said nothing. Since I assumed Steve's wife did most of the talking in their relationship (which is usually the case with Reluctants), it was important that I not exceed his verbal output and play into his marital dynamic. Instead, I cocked my head sideways like a dog listening to bad karaoke and waited.

Steve shrugged again. I continued to wait. "I guess," Steve finally said.

"Actually, that sounds like a no."

"What do you mean?"

"I mean it sounds as though you don't agree with your wife's assessment."

Steve shrugged again. I waited. "Everyone gets irritable," he finally replied.

"Like I said, Steve, you don't seem to agree that it's an issue. And since you're my patient and not your wife, maybe you can tell me what *you* think is the issue."

"I dunno. I guess there isn't one."

"Well, no, there's at least one. You seem reluctant to tell your wife when you disagree with her. Like about your irritability."

"I told her I disagreed about that."

"And yet here you are," I said gently. "Steve, you're not the first husband to sit in my office because his wife insisted on it. Your wife thinks you're too irritable and selfish and she sent you here to get fixed. I understand that and I applaud your effort to follow through. But you've done your job. You've conveyed what you had agreed to convey."

"So now what?" Steve challenged me.

"So perhaps in the time we have left we can discuss things from your perspective, not hers. Would that be okay?" Steve nodded. "Great. Now tell me about your home life. But try to stick only to your point of view. I really want your perspective." Steve nodded. "Good. So tell me about your marriage, the good, the bad, and the ugly."

In his halting manner, Steve did. As I suspected, there wasn't a ton of good to go with the fair amount of bad and the serious dollop of ugly. Steve had stored up fifteen years' worth of grievances and frustrations, most of which I was certain he had never voiced to his wife even once. He sounded depressed, anxious, insecure, and self-deprecatory. He was also significantly overweight and his appearance was markedly unkempt. Steve was neglecting himself both physically and emotionally.

He also reported having been diagnosed with a mild form of cardiovascular disease the previous year. His doctor told him he was at risk for a heart attack and advised lifestyle changes. But Steve had been unable to modify his eating habits and sedentary lifestyle. I was alarmed when I heard that. He was more at risk for coronary heart disease than he realized.

Steve was a classic example of what health psychologists call a type D personality. Type D's (the *D* stands for "distressed") experience a significant amount of negative emotion but are emotionally *un*expressive. Type D personalities bottle up their abundant bad feelings inside so thoroughly, they have *four times* the risk of cardiovascular disease than non-type-D personalities with similar basic risk factors. In Steve's case, teaching him to express his complaints (which are negative emotions) could do more than improve his mood or self-esteem; it could possibly save his life.

Heart-Attack-Prone Personalities

The type D personality is a relatively recent construct. In the 1950s, coronary heart disease emerged as the number one killer in the country, prompting a massive research effort to narrow down its causes and develop potential preventions. In 1964, cardiologists Meyer Friedman and Ray Rosenman discovered that people who had a cluster of specific traits—such as always feeling hurried and rushed—were at much larger risk for coronary heart disease. They called these people type A personalities. They also found that people who had a seemingly opposite style, those more relaxed, slower-paced individuals, were at much lower risk for coronary heart disease. They called these type B personalities. Type B personalities actively took steps to avoid stress in their lives and minimized situations that might cause it. As the research evolved (I was briefly involved in such research at the time), type A personalities were found not only to have a sense of time urgency but also to be highly competitive and impatient. Most important, they could be aggressive and hostile. Over the years it began to seem as though the aggression and hostility of type A's constituted their biggest risk for coronary heart disease.

But in the 1990s, categorizing by general and overarching character traits such as those represented by type A and type B personalities became controversial and slowly fell out of scientific favor. Then in the middle nineties, Dr. Johan Denollet of the Netherlands found something interesting. People who experienced a lot of hostility and anger like type A's but who had trouble expressing these negative feelings were also extremely vulnerable to hypertension and chronic distress. They even had far higher mortality rates than other high-risk cardiac patients. It seemed as though the combination of low self-esteem, a surplus of negative emotions, and an inhibition about expressing those emotions put these people at significant risk. Denollet demonstrated that their levels of stress and distress were potentially *fatal risk factors* for their cardiac health.

Steve fit the profile for a type D personality perfectly. Since holding in abundant negative emotions places these people at risk for coronary heart disease, learning to complain effectively could be extremely helpful for type D's, such as Steve, in learning to be more emotionally expressive. Acquiring an effective complaining skill set could theoretically reduce their stress levels and perhaps even their risk for cardiac events.

Steve was miserable and angry but unable to speak up about it. Steve grumbled a lot, mumbled, and even whined on occasion, but he rarely complained. I told Steve about the research findings for type D personalities and that it might be important for him to learn how to express his emotions in a safe way. I suggested we start by working on how Steve could voice complaints to his wife. Steve was with me throughout the type D personality review, but he looked alarmed when I mentioned the possibility of complaining to his wife. I reassured him that I did not mean for him to go home and unleash a torrent of previously unspoken resentments. "There's a river of dissatisfactions flowing inside you," I explained, "but I'm not suggesting we smash Hoover Dam." Instead, I proposed letting out only a small stream of dissatisfaction, enough to reduce the levels in the reservoir. Any small complaint would do to start, even something tiny.

Steve was hesitant at first. But after a few more lulls of silence, he mentioned that his wife mocked him when he watched reruns of his favorite science-fiction television show. She called him "Trekkie nerd boy," he explained, wincing as he said it.

"Do you respond when she does that?" I asked.

"What's the point? She knows I hate it but she does it anyway."

"In part she does it because you don't object. You don't complain and that gives her the message that it's okay to mock you about it. I wonder what would happen if you spoke up calmly, respectfully, but firmly and voiced a complaint about wanting to enjoy your favorite television show in peace."

"I do complain sometimes," Steve insisted. "But it doesn't help."

"I see. How exactly do you complain to your wife about it?"

"I tell her to shut the hell up and leave me alone."

"Ah, well, that might feel fair, but it's not especially effective. Let's see if we can come up with something that would get you the result you want."

We spent the rest of the session discussing how Steve could best voice his complaint to his wife. Steve was so unsure of his complaining abilities that he took notes throughout (which I always encourage). By the end of our session, I had persuaded him to give effective complaining a try. Steve's marriage had much bigger problems than his television-watching habits or his wife's impatience with them. But while the characters in Steve's favorite show all lived long and prospered, unless Steve learned to speak up effectively, he himself would not.

Choosing Our Complaints Wisely

Steve's predicament was not a result of his being a Reluctant. Rather, all cohabitating couples must make decisions about what complaints to voice and which to forgo. Otherwise, couples would spend their entire relationships voicing small annoyances and irritations to one another (as some chronically bickering couples do). Professor Robin Kowalski, the psychologist who researches complaining behaviors, once asked her students to list pet peeves from romantic relationships past and present. The number of pet peeves her students listed was so staggering she had to arrange them into categories to make any sense of them. The complaints ranged from serious (refusing to communicate, feeling lack of trust, receiving irrational guilt trips) to mundane (borrowing too many things, not replacing toilet-paper roll, talking through movies) to slightly disgusting (nasty body odor and nose picking were the standouts).

Choosing which complaints to voice and making wise decisions when doing so is one of the most important aspects of effective complaining. To be truly effective, *we should never voice more than one complaint at a time.* Therefore, we often need to consider which of our dissatisfactions we should focus on. Complaints that are meaningful to us are far more important to address as they have the biggest impact on our lives and our self-esteem.

However, for Steve and for those just beginning to develop their complaining skills, it is more important to start with a complaint that is both simple and specific. For purposes of practice, we should always choose easier complaints. The more simple and specific our complaint, the easier it will be for us to assess if voicing it had the impact we were seeking. Steve could tell if his complaint was effective simply by noting whether his wife reduced the frequency of her "Trekkie nerd boy" insults or ceased them altogether. If she continued to mock him regularly even after he complained, he would know that his efforts were not sufficiently effective.

I was looking forward to Steve's next session, eager to hear whether he had summoned up the courage to complain to his wife. Men like Steve were usually so hesitant to voice their emotions they often came up with numerous excuses to avoid doing so. A part of me expected to hear Steve present a litany of reasons for why he had not followed through with his assignment, but my gut instinct told me that he had taken my suggestions to heart.

Surprisingly, however, Steve did not show up for the session at all. At first, I wondered if the complaining assignment I had proposed was too much for him. His absence might merely also be another display of passive-aggressive resistance. I called Steve at home and his wife answered. She told me he was in the hospital. He had suffered a heart attack the night before.

The immediate surge of guilt I felt was so powerful, I almost suffered one myself. I had encouraged Steve to complain to his wife and boldly go where no Reluctant had gone before. I would have been devastated if doing so had tipped his fragile ticker into a full-blown heart attack.

I asked Steve's wife for details about his status, but she was rushing to get back to the hospital with some toiletries and a change of clothes. She did say she would tell Steve I called, which was reassuring as it meant he was at least alert and communicative. Steve called me himself a few hours later. Luckily, the heart attack was mild and he was going to be discharged once his doctors finished running tests.

"I'm very relieved to hear that, Steve," I said. "Maybe we should put the complaining on hold for a little while until you feel better and your doctor indicates you can tolerate stress well."

"Nah," Steve responded. "I did that already. I spoke to her last week after our session. It went okay. We actually talked. It was good. I told the cardiologist I came to see you. He was all for it."

Steve said he would call to set up another session once he was back on his feet. I was extremely relieved to hear Steve was doing well and thrilled he had followed through with his assignment. He came in for a session a month later. His heart attack had shaken him (and his wife) to the core, but in a good way. It had shifted something fundamental about his perception of his marriage and life as a whole. Heart attacks are often powerful wake-up calls to those who survive them.

Steve was still the same person with all the same issues and problems with emotional expressiveness. But he now knew that holding back his complaints could literally cost him his life. He reported having a more open dialogue with his wife. He also mentioned that she seemed more responsive to his complaints, and in his month of convalescence at home, she did not insult him even once.

Steve's initial foray into effective complaining and his heart attack days later were a case of perfect timing. Our session and Steve's following up by making his *Star Trek* complaint were a kind of proof of concept for him. The experience demonstrated an approach Steve could take when expressing small complaints that mattered to him, and his heart attack had given him every incentive and motivation to continue being more emotionally expressive.

I realized as we were talking that Steve had really come to the session to say good-bye. For a moment, I was touched that Steve felt strongly enough about our brief work together to do so. However, my inner glow of satisfaction was short-lived as Steve soon mentioned that scheduling the session had been his wife's idea, not his own. However, he did add, "But I didn't mind … that much." Coming from Steve, the statement was practically endearing. Steve was still a Reluctant (in that he was still doing his wife's bidding), but at least he was no longer complacent when it came to his type D tendencies. Steve had decided to fight for his health. He fully understood that working with his wife on becoming more emotionally expressive (by expressing his complaints) was the best way to do so.

Complaining therapy can be a powerful tool when used correctly, but it is not a cure-all or panacea. Whether effective complaining will rid us of depression, increase our global or specific self-esteem, improve our relationships, or benefit our communities depends on many variables. The details of the situation, the nature and personal meaning of our complaint, the personality of the recipient, our delivery, and even the cohesion of our community efforts can all combine to determine the outcome of complaining battles.

However, in theory, complaining therapy represents a new alternative for achieving stress reduction for type D personalities like Steve. Of course, until such assumptions are scientifically investigated, they are nothing more than intriguing hypotheses.

Complaining Therapy Does Not Require a Therapist

Among all my patients, the one whose life was most altered by complaining therapy was Rose, and she achieved the results entirely on her own. She was born between the two Great Wars and raised in a middle-class Jewish family. Rose went to college, married, and divorced. In her late twenties, she married her second husband, Irving, and quickly introduced him to her second-greatest passion—Latin ballroom dancing. Irving's spirit soared when he danced with Rose, even though by all accounts his feet often did not. But over their years together, and there were many of them, Irving became a decent and competent hoofer. Rose's true love was singing, but her chances of a career as a chanteuse were sidelined by a lifelong struggle with severe and crippling depression.

Unfortunately, when Rose was younger, such depressions had few effective treatments. She first tried the talk therapy of the day,

Freudian psychoanalysis. The treatment consisted of four sessions a week of laborious and often pointless introspection. Rose was instructed to discuss whatever came to mind, recount fragments of her dreams, follow random associations, and explore every nuance of her childhood memories, however inaccurate her recollections (today we know our memories are often extremely inaccurate). All this was typically done to unearth the patient's hidden oedipal complexes, shameful death instincts, and a host of other mythical psychological entities. While such work can at times be fascinating, it did little for Rose's depression.

Rose and her husband moved to a lovely apartment near New York City's Central Park. They had two children together, they traveled, and they went Latin ballroom dancing every single week without fail. However, over the years, Rose's depression became progressively worse. By the time she ended up in a psychiatric hospital in the 1960s, the only real treatment option she had left was electroconvulsive therapy—ECT.

ECT has been around for many years and is extremely effective for treating severe depressions (including bipolar depression and psychotic depression). But the treatment remains a highly misunderstood procedure to this day. Its frightening reputation is primarily a result of its depictions in film and television. ECT scenes usually start with a "desperate inmate" being wrestled to a gurney by stocky male nurses. The "victim" (they are usually portrayed as such) bucks and writhes in terror, only to be eventually strapped down and secured. Then "evil" doctors step in and jolt the victim's brain with so much electricity, sparks fly as if it were happy hour at Frankenstein's laboratory.

Anyone seeing these scenes would be appalled at the idea of submitting to such a barbaric treatment. However, in reality ECT is a far less exciting affair—for everyone involved. Patients are put to sleep by an attending anesthesiologist, just as they might be for a surgical procedure. They are administered muscle relaxants (to prevent convulsing and flopping about), then given a short electrical impulse to the brain (measured in seconds).

The first time I saw ECT performed on a patient of mine, I stood in the procedure room, mask on my face, not quite sure what was supposed to happen. Then I saw the person's fingers and toes move slightly. And ... that was it. The doctor announced they were done. If I blinked, I would have missed it.

Not surprisingly, Rose was extremely reluctant to submit to ECT. However, as is often the case with medication-resistant depressions, the treatment did wonders for her. She returned home and did well for several months. But her depression always returned (ECT is effective but relapse is common without maintenance outpatient treatment). Rose spent her years in and out of the hospital as well as in and out of depression, with brief respites brought about by her continued shock treatments. Rose hated having to go to the hospital "to get zapped in my brain," but nothing else seemed to work for her depression.

Unfortunately, Rose's self-esteem generally recovered far less quickly than her depression did. She gradually felt unable to manage basic aspects of her life and left all financial decisions, travel planning, and other complicated tasks for her husband. As the years progressed, Rose's feelings of self-worth continued to drop until she felt too incompetent and too intimidated to write even a simple check.

When I met Rose, she was seventy years old and had just come out of another lengthy hospitalization. She and her husband had been referred to me for couple therapy. Her psychiatrist hoped it would augment her individual therapy and the maintenance ECT treatments she received every few weeks as an outpatient (which is a common practice for older patients with a lifelong history of severe depression such as Rose). In our first session together, Rose appeared hesitant, unconfident, and tired. She glanced at Irving each time she answered a question, to verify her answers were accurate. Toward the end of the session, I asked Rose about the longest she had gone without a hospitalization. Rose thought for a moment, glanced at Irving, thought again, and then suddenly her eyes lit up.

"The methadone clinic!" she exclaimed, her voice twice as strong as it had been a moment earlier. "It was the methadone clinic!"

Irving nodded. "She's right, it was the methadone clinic."

"Methadone clinic, Rose?" I asked jokingly. "Shooting up heroin, were we?"

Rose smiled for the first time. She sat forward in her seat and began telling me the story. Her speech was slow as she started (slow rate of speech is one of the symptoms of severe depression), but by the end of her tale, she was speaking at a normal rate. For a period in her life Rose had gone years without being hospitalized, and her mental health was the strongest she and Irving could recall. Rose had been occupied during those years with one thing—pursuing a complaint.

Some years earlier, Rose and Irving lived on a lovely, quiet street in Manhattan during a time when most streets in the city were neither quiet nor lovely. Heavy drug use was rampant, and in response the city began opening methadone clinics for recovering heroin addicts. One of these clinics was scheduled to open right on Rose and Irving's block.

Residents on the street were outraged as soon as they heard of the plan. They envisioned their upscale neighborhood block becoming overrun with recovering heroin addicts. Some methadone users sold their methadone for drug money, and this attracted other addicts to the areas surrounding methadone clinics. The image of junkies dealing drugs and shooting up outside their homes caused a panic that drove residents on the block to gather and discuss opposing the city's initiative. But the task was daunting. They would literally have to fight city hall. They would need a strong leader, someone who could speak up, organize, and strategize. They needed a general. And their general was Rose.

Rose turned her apartment into a war room. She organized letter-writing campaigns, protests, and a slew of other measures. The block association's fight with the city was protracted. Rose faced pressures, stresses, and organizational challenges she would have never imagined herself withstanding. Yet, she not only weathered these storms, she won the battle! The city eventually knuckled under the pressure and canceled the methadone clinic. Other than her beautiful daughters and granddaughters, whom she and Irving loved dearly, Rose's methadone-clinic complaint was the biggest accomplishment of her life. Rose's depression continued to recede even after the fight with the city was over. Her involvement with her children and husband increased and her life became fuller. Most important, Rose's depression remained much milder and more stable for many years.

The effects of Rose's complaining self-therapy did not last forever. But the changes both she and her husband attributed to pursuing her complaint were truly remarkable, especially given the severity of her lifelong depression. Amazingly, the potency of the experience had not entirely faded. The mere recounting of the events in our session had a significant impact on Rose's recovery. She seemed to bounce back from her hospitalization much quicker than she usually did.

Over the next months and years, I made sure we discussed her battle with the city in full detail, and I referred to her experience as a "rabble-rouser" as often as I could. A substantial part of the therapy centered on Rose's experience with the complaint, as she was able to recall and even reconnect to the feelings of empowerment and competence she experienced at the time. We also explored other ways in which she could revive such feelings in her daily life.

Rose wished to become more involved in her and Irving's personal financial decisions and others she had shied away from for many years. She continued seeing her psychiatrist and receiving periodic outpatient ECT, and she and Irving continued to see me for couple therapy every few weeks. Her complaint against the city was never far from our discussions, and Rose did not require another hospitalization for almost ten years.

Steps for Complaining Therapy at Home

Rose demonstrates a crucial point about complaining therapy—it does not require a therapist. Rather we need only good intentions, a valid and meaningful complaint, and an effective complaining toolbox. To that end, chapter 5 discusses specific formulas for constructing effective complaints, and chapter 6 discusses considerations and useful techniques for voicing and receiving complaints from loved ones.

When starting complaining therapy, it is best to gain some practice with effective complaining skills by choosing a simple and comparatively easy-to-resolve complaint, either consumer or interpersonal. With interpersonal complaints, successful resolutions are those in which *both* parties feel relieved and satisfied by the outcome. Therefore, while the payoffs of such breakthroughs can be substantial, the hurt feelings responsible for creating the ruptures in the first place can make resolving them more difficult. When choosing an interpersonal complaint for practice, make sure it is a low-stakes, non-personally-meaningful issue for you as well as for the complaint recipient. For example, a complaint about a spouse ignoring housework should be easier for both parties to tackle than a complaint about avoiding intimacy.

Second, it is best to choose complaints that allow us to assess our success with ease. A single, simple consumer complaint is often well suited for practice sessions. Either the product or service in question is fixed, replaced, or reimbursed or it is not. On the other hand, a complaint about a teenager's making insufficient efforts in school is much harder to gauge. Increased efforts may not always be visible as teens often study in their rooms and out of our sight, and such efforts might not be immediately apparent in their grades, as improved academic efforts often take a while to pay off.

Once we have practiced our effective-complaining skill set and we feel more confident in our abilities, we can move on to a more meaningful complaint. However, we should be careful to think through all aspects of our complaint, as well as all possible eventualities before making our choices. When Rachel (from chapter 1) complained about her boyfriend's flirting with another woman, she might have anticipated an argument, but she definitely did not expect to be dumped on the spot.

Successfully acquiring effective complaining skills can be empowering, uplifting, and even exciting, but we should resist the temptation of becoming too "complaint happy." Packing our bags and embarking on a cross-country complaining spree to settle scores with every company or person who ever wronged us is probably unwise.

Chapter Four
When to Squeak
How to Avoid Complaining Dangers

Many complain of their memory, few of their judgment.
—François Duc de La Rochefoucauld

Joanna was a thirty-year-old corporate-event planner, which meant both personal and professional pride were at stake when it came to planning her own $100,000 wedding. Joanna agonized over every detail, such as the exact height of the tabletop flower arrangements at the reception dinner. She wanted them to be large enough to be impressive but not so tall as to be obstructive to the people at the table. Joanna's attention to detail and her tendency to micromanage had been frequent topics in our sessions as she was aware she had the potential to lose the forest for the trees. Therefore, she agreed that once the big day was upon her, she would let go of all the meticulous details she had spent months agonizing over and focus on simply having the best day of her life.

After the ceremony, Joanna arrived with her new husband at her reception once it was in full swing. She noticed the tabletop flower arrangements immediately. They were twice as high as they should have been and obstructed the free flow of conversation around the tables. Although she had vowed to remain calm in such a scenario, Joanna's best intentions were forgotten the instant she laid eyes on the "freakish man-eating orchid topiaries." She marched from table to table examining the extent of the "debacle." Then she tracked down the caterer and chastised him in front of several guests. Next, she laced into the wedding planner, creating a minor scene—mostly because the man did not take kindly to being yelled at in front of people he considered potential clients. Joanna became so worked up, she ran out of the reception in tears.

Unfortunate as it was, Joanna's experience teaches us several lessons about the dangers of complaining. First, we should always make sure to identify exactly what we hope to gain by complaining before we voice our dissatisfactions. Joanna's wedding had otherwise been a wonderful affair; even she acknowledged that much. However aggravating she found the flower arrangements, she had nothing to gain by complaining so vigorously in that moment and ruining her wedding day. Had Joanna paused long enough to consider what complaining might accomplish, she would probably have saved herself considerable heartache and embarrassment.

Second, some complaints are simply not worth pursuing, while others are not worth pursuing at that specific time but could and should be addressed later. It might be best to postpone our complaints about weddings, other celebrations, vacations, and special events until something can be done about them. Yes, it's incredibly annoying when the wrong cake is delivered to the surprise birthday party, when the last available "sea-view" hotel room faces the parking lot, or when our new T-shirts arrive at the bowling championship with team bowel printed on them. But just because we have good cause to complain does not mean it is always wise to do so at that very moment.

If, despite our better judgment, our frustration is too strong and our urge to vent too powerful, we could take a few minutes to vent our emotions discreetly and then move on. For example, Joanna should have grabbed her husband, her mother, or her bridesmaid and privately vented about the "freakish topiaries" for two minutes (no longer). She should have asked for an emotional-validation quickie (a sympathetic ooh, a cluck, and a hug), then used her post-venting relief (small as it might be) to shake off her irritability and refocus on celebrating her wedding day.

The third and most general lesson we can learn from Joanna is that complaints always come with dangers. While some of these can be anticipated, many cannot. Unfortunately, we usually find out about the latter group the hard way. In 2008, Lauren Newton was having her hair done in her stylist's kitchen in Washington County, Pennsylvania. Alas, she did not love the new do and complained about it to her stylist. The stylist left the kitchen, came back with a loaded gun, and fired a warning shot *into her own ceiling.* Newton wisely heeded the warning shot by fleeing. The stylist, demonstrating an appalling misunderstanding of how warning shots actually work, proceeded to shoot her fleeing client in the lower back. Luckily, Newton recovered from her wounds. No word on her hair.

Complaint Boomerangs

We launch many complaints into the air, and as Newton discovered, some of them come back to bite us in the ... lower back. We read and hear about victims of complaining-related violence all the time and in every media, and although sporting events are often the venue of choice for such encounters, they can happen anywhere. In 2007 in Australia, Joseph Durrant, a forty-seven-year-old man, was stabbed to death by a woman for complaining about her barking dog. In May 2009, Crystal Samuel was shot in the arm at a South Carolina Waffle House by her waitress after she complained about the service. Closest to home for me, both geographically and topically, in 2006 actress-director Adrienne Shelly was murdered in her New York City apartment. The suspect then claimed he did it because she *complained about construction noise.*

Of course, most of our complaints do not result in physical harm at all. But we do risk bruising our feelings and self-esteem, our pride and dignity.

The only way for us to prevent our complaints from boomeranging is to use common sense and consider the consequences of our actions. Most of us believe our common sense is sound, and in many areas of our lives perhaps it is. But when it comes to complaining, even the smartest of us often forget to pause and consider the consequences of our actions. When we fail to employ good judgment, even common and simple complaints can boomerang on us. Of course, those are usually the ones we don't see coming until it is too late.

In the summer of 2001, Jean-Claude Baker, the owner of Chez Josephine, a top New York City restaurant, received a letter of complaint from Francis Flynn, a professor at Columbia University. Professor Flynn had become ill after celebrating his first wedding anniversary with his wife at the restaurant. Professor Flynn wrote:

> I am writing this letter to you Mr. Baker because I am outraged about a recent experience I had at your restaurant. Not long ago my wife and I celebrated our first anniversary. To commemorate the event we made plans to dine at your restaurant.
>
> ... The evening became soured when the symptoms began to appear about four hours after eating. Extended nausea, vomiting, diarrhea and abdominal cramps all pointed to one thing: Food poisoning. It makes me furious just thinking that our special romantic evening became reduced to my wife watching me curl up in a fetal position on the tiled floor of our bathroom between rounds of throwing up.
>
> ... I am furious about this entire ordeal. Although it is not my intention to file any reports with the Better Business Bureau or the Department of Health, I want you, Mr. Baker to understand what I went through in anticipation that you will respond accordingly.

Mr. Baker did respond accordingly. He panicked. Food poisoning scares could ruin a restaurant. He confronted his cooks, threw out vast quantities of food, contacted vendors, and sent Professor Flynn an immediate letter of apology. Such complaints could spell disaster for any establishment, but coming from such a prestigious source as a professor at an Ivy League business school, and given the severity of the letter, the damage to the restaurant's reputation could be immense.

Mr. Baker was no doubt equally concerned by Professor Flynn's dramatic (and thinly veiled) threats to pursue legal action. For example, "Although it is not my intention to file any reports with the Better Business Bureau or the Department of Health, I want you, Mr. Baker to understand what I went through in anticipation that you will respond accordingly" conveyed the message "Your response to my complaint had better be good. I already have the Better Business Bureau and the Department of Health on speed dial and I have restless-finger syndrome."

Mr. Baker knew the situation was serious. What he did not know was that he was not alone. Two hundred and forty of the best restaurants in New York City had received similar letters by the same Professor Flynn. And the professor had dined in none of them. Nor had he spent his anniversary curled up in a fetal position on the tiled floor of his bathroom between rounds of throwing up. Professor Flynn had never become ill at all. Rather, he was conducting a stunningly ill-advised consumer-behavior study about vendor responses to restaurant complaints.

Restaurateurs talk. The story of the hoax quickly hit the media. The hapless Professor Flynn was humiliated in newspapers and Web reports all over the world, and the Columbia University Business School was left scrambling. It tried a variety of damage-control measures including having the professor as well as the dean of the Business School issue immediate letters of apology to all 240 restaurants.

Despite those efforts and to no one's surprise, Professor Flynn was promptly sued by several of the restaurateurs, as was the Columbia University Business School. The professor's experiment unraveled quickly and disastrously. I imagine his wife spent the night watching him curl up in a fetal position on the tiled floor of their bathroom between rounds of throwing up.

We each have individual patterns, preferences, and quirks that dictate our complaining behavior. Some of us complain regularly to our colleagues at work but do so rarely in our homes. Others have the patience of a saint at their jobs, but whine about the smallest things with their families. We also tend to have *complaining favorites,* our go-to people for complaining. Those are usually selected based on their past skill at providing emotional validation for our venting. Our complaints might even have seasonality, increasing in the winter or the summer, or peaking during the holiday season.

Given the ebb and flow of our complaining behaviors, we can all become blind on occasion to the unexpected consequences of our complaints for any variety of reasons. Few studies have examined the psychological and emotional dangers inherent in our individual or even collective complaining behavior patterns. But the findings of those that did were rather straightforward. The most common danger inherent in our complaining behavior and the one that often carries the harshest consequences is simply doing too much of it.

Chronic Complainers Start Young

Psychologist Amanda Rose from the University of Missouri followed students in the third, fifth, seventh, and ninth grades for six months. She wanted to explore the impact of excessive discussions about complaints and problems on the tweens' and teens' friendships as well as on their individual mental health. Teens and tweens often spend many hours discussing the same issue and tackling it from every possible angle. These marathons could start during morning recess, continue throughout the day, and go on in person or via phone, text messages, social networks, and e-mails well into the evening. Friendships are ordinarily considered to have positive influences on teens' and tweens' mental health. But Professor Rose was curious to see whether an excessive focus on complaining would have a detrimental impact. She called the intense complaining marathons co-rumination.

The results were stark and rather surprising. Over the six months, girls who spent too much time co-ruminating with friends deepened those friendships (which was good), but they also became significantly more depressed and anxious (which was obviously not good). Interestingly, the same finding was not true for boys, who spent less time talking to their friends about complaints and problems than the girls did. Like the girls, boys who co-ruminated with friends also had increases in their friendship scores over time, but they did not have the same increase in anxiety and depression.

Why would excessive complaining with a friend make girls feel more depressed and more anxious over time? The researchers hypothesized that because co-rumination involves an intense focus on the details of complaints or problems, "it also may cause problems to seem more significant and harder to resolve. This could lead to more worries and concerns about problems and associated anxiety symptoms."

This explanation seems plausible to me, yet one can understand why the girls in the study had become depressed and anxious in another way. I believe co-ruminating affects something far more fundamental—how we construct our identities. By devoting so much time to discussing their problems and complaints, the girls were allowing the cumulative mass of their dissatisfactions *to define who they are.* By complaining excessively, by having dissatisfactions become such an integral part of their actions, thoughts, and feelings, they were defining their social roles and public personas and influencing the very nature of their identities.

However we prefer to define ourselves, in many ways we are what we do. We might like to think of ourselves as artists, but if we spend forty hours a week waiting tables and only get around to painting one afternoon or two a year, we are hardly painters, we are waiters. We're certainly much closer to getting a managerial position at Applebee's than an exhibition at the Guggenheim. Of course, if we resume painting regularly, the story will be different.

If we are defined, at least in part, by the dominant activities in our lives, what does it make us if the thing we spend all day doing is complaining?

We Are the Yarns We Spin

According to some psychological schools of thought, our identities are shaped by the stories we construct, the narratives we develop to understand the multitude of experiences that make up our lives. Where we chose to place ourselves in these narratives in large part is up to us. Imagine the *lone* survivor of a horrible train crash who lost a limb in the accident while everyone else died. Was his a story of miraculous survival and stunning good fortune or a story of tragedy, disability, and loss? Interestingly enough, how the survivors of such horrific accidents construct their narrative of the events can have a huge impact on their physical recovery and on their long-term mental health. Those who suffer such events but see themselves as incredibly lucky survivors do much better than those who see themselves as unfortunate victims.

The specific roles we give ourselves in our stories as well as those we give others, and the functions and abilities we attribute to ourselves and others in our narratives, all shape our perceptions of who we are. By complaining excessively we construct a narrative of our lives in which we inhabit the role of someone who is hurt, helpless, or victimized. The more dominant we allow complaints to become in our lives, the more we cast ourselves in victim roles. The longer we stay in these roles, the more they become our identities.

The implication here is that complaining, certainly for teenage girls, should have clear dosing guidelines. An overdose of complaining can cause an increase in both depression and anxiety. Therefore, it would be wise to counsel teenage girls to be aware of the amount of time they spend co-ruminating. Setting a specific portion of time to complain (no more than an hour), then moving to a more problem-solving approach, might be the best mix to allow girls to benefit from venting, getting emotional validation, and deepening their friendships, without falling into depression and anxiety.

Of course, teenage girls are hardly the only group who tend to overcomplain. Adults too are in danger of crossing the line between casual kvetching and complaining overload. Limiting the length of our complaining sessions is wise at any age. The goal should be to strike a balance between venting our emotions and securing a cathartic relief (by having our feelings emotionally validated), and making purposeful efforts to put the complaint behind us until we can take productive action. When our well of dissatisfactions is especially deep, we should make concerted efforts to avoid falling into it and drowning.

However, for some of us this advice comes too late, as we have already fallen down the well and become drunk on our dissatisfactions. Some of us have nurtured feelings of victimhood with a steady diet of complaints for too long, and by doing so we may already have reached a complaining point of no return—we may have gone chronic. Of course, it can be difficult for us to know if we've gone that far, as chronic complainers rarely recognize themselves as such, even when it is as clear as day to every single person around them.

None Are So Blind as Chronic Complainers

Chronic complainers are made, not born. Some of us are created in our early years by parents who constantly gave in to our whining and by doing so taught us that "poor me" is a strategy worth sticking with. Some are created in our adulthood, forged by difficult lives and unfortunate circumstances, and some are hatched in our old age, spurred on by an avalanche of aches, pains, and loss. But regardless of when or how our obsessive complaining begins, most of us are entirely blind to it.

We do not become chronic complainers overnight. At first, we might merely seek sympathy and compassion from others for an authentically distressing event. We might have lost a parent, been fired from our job, or seen our marriage dissolve before our eyes.

We might have lost a promotion, discovered a betrayal by our best friend, or lost our pension in a financial collapse. All such incidents are worthy of a sense of loss, mourning, and perhaps even depression. Eventually, time moves on, only in some cases, we do not. We continue to complain about our sadness, our loss, and our lot in life, unwilling to give up the compassion we elicit from those around us, the support upon which we have come to depend.

But there is a crucial moment, a point of no return, for which we must always remain vigilant. The corner is turned the instant our friends' support turns from compassion to pity. It is turned the moment those around us began to think of us as victims.

We must catch this transition when it happens because we must refuse their pity. We must reject it as if it is contaminated, because psychologically speaking, it is. Unless we are survivors of truly tragic circumstances or we have gone through authentic and terrible hardships, it is always extremely detrimental to accept pity from others and embrace victimhood. By succumbing to the special attention pity offers us, the convenience of lowered expectations, and other secondary gains associated with being objects of others' sorrow, we become victims in our own eyes as well as those of others.

This transformation is often sudden but subtle enough that we fail to realize the changes in the attitudes of those around us. Despite our being unaware of it, our identities go through a shift in their eyes. Our friends no longer refer to us as Kevin, Paula, or Kyle; instead they think of us as that-poor-Kevin, terrible-what-happened-to-Paula, or feel-so-bad-for-him-Kyle. Pity is extremely toxic to our mental health. Accepting someone's pity in other than truly tragic circumstances is allowing them to grab our self-esteem and trample it underfoot. Pity is pure psychological poison, and chronic complainers consume it by the bucketload.

Chronic complainers are often completely oblivious of how extreme their complaining has become, even when everyone around them already regards them as walking complaint emitters. How is this possible? It happens because chronic complainers have a very different view of things. In their eyes, they are not complaining at all, they're merely pointing out the obvious, that the boss is too demanding or the workday is too long, or that the hot water from the cooler really isn't hot enough to make tea properly. They believe they speak for everyone when they complain about the conference-room door that still squeaks annoyingly, the unfairness of not landing the new account, the paperwork being stuck in procurement, or Christmas falling on a Sunday.

Chronic complainers never see themselves as negative; they see the world as negative and themselves as merely reacting to it appropriately. Much as is the case with learned helplessness, chronic complaining is a distortion in our perceptions. Once we begin to think of ourselves as victims, our minds do the rest by automatically seeking validation for our feelings of victimhood. At any hint of our being treated wrongly or unfairly, however insignificant the incident, we immediately note it as further evidence the world is against us. But whenever we encounter something positive or encouraging that might contradict our victimhood mentality, it is swiftly (and often unconsciously) marginalized and neglected.

The interesting question about chronic complainers is, do they complain so much because they are unhappy, or are they unhappy because they complain too much? Psychologist Amanda Rose believes it is a little of both. She concluded that in teenage girls, depression and co-rumination formed a vicious cycle in which the more depressed the girls became, the more they complained, and the more they complained, the more depressed and anxious they became. I believe that our complaints and victimhood reinforce each other in similar ways. The more we complain, the more victimized we feel.

And the more victimized we feel, the more dissatisfactions we perceive and the more material we have to complain about.

The Reverend Will Bowen and his purple-bracelet crusade against overcomplaining struck a deep chord with his congregation and many others because he correctly identified the personal and communal price we pay for this vicious cycle of negativity. However, his solution—avoiding expressing our complaints entirely—is really only substituting one problem for another. Such avoidance can actually have a negative psychological, emotional, and physical impact, as Steve's coronary scare demonstrated in the previous chapter. Overcomplaining is a real problem, but forgoing complaints entirely and becoming less emotionally expressive is akin to tossing out the baby with the bathwater.

The only true solution to our overcomplaining and certainly that of chronic complainers is to learn how to use our complaints as emotional tools, ones that can better our state of mind and general sense of well-being. This means being able to identify which complaints are worth pursuing and which are not. This crucial step, evaluating the merits of our complaints before we voice them, is one many of us need to spend more time considering. It is also one most chronic complainers avoid altogether.

For Whom the Bell Complains

Although much of the mental anguish and suffering of chronic complainers is self-imposed, they rarely suffer alone. Their constant negativity often has a hugely detrimental impact on the other members of their households. The Bells were referred to me for family therapy after Tommy, their eldest son, had threatened to kill himself only a few days earlier. Tommy had spent the night in a psychiatric emergency room, and family therapy was suggested upon discharge (in addition to individual therapy for Tommy). I met the Bell family in my office when the scare and drama of the past days was still fresh in everyone's mind.

Tommy was a tall and lanky fourteen-year-old. It's hard to describe his face because he had long, oily hair that covered his forehead completely and fell over his eyes and even his cheeks. I could make out so little of him, he might as well have been wearing Groucho Marx glasses and a fake mustache. His younger brother, Brad, was seven and fidgety.

It took the family thirty seconds to come into my office and take their positions. Mr. and Mrs. Bell sat down on the couch, leaving two chairs for the boys. Brad took one chair, but Tommy decided to sit on the floor in front of the couch, with his back to his parents. During those thirty seconds, Mr. Bell amassed the following complaints: "Tommy, don't sit on the floor." "Brad, sit up." "Tommy, must you sit with your back to me?" "Brad, stop fidgeting. And don't slouch!" "Tommy! It's not polite to sit on the floor." And to his wife while glancing at Tommy: "Why can't you say something to him? Why is it always my job?"

The chronic-complainer detector in my head went "Ding!" and shot to code red. With eight complaints in thirty seconds, Mr. Bell seemed to be the real deal.

Mr. Bell briefed me on their issues. Tommy had started having problems at the beginning of the academic year. His grades slipped further throughout the semester and he became noncommunicative at home. Arguments between Tommy and Mr. Bell began to increase in frequency and intensity. Finally, in the midst of one of their arguments, Tommy threatened to jump out the window. Mr. Bell was terribly alarmed but quickly (and correctly) called emergency services. It was completely appropriate for him to do so because one should never take chances in such situations. Tommy was taken to the emergency room and hospitalized for observation. He was discharged the next day but had refused to go to school since.

"There's just no communicating with Tommy," Mr. Bell sighed. "He won't even look at us. Brad! Stop playing with your shirt!" Mr. Bell turned his frown back to Tommy. "He doesn't listen to a thing we say anymore." Mr. Bell shot his wife a glare. "Honey! You're allowed to say something, you know, I'm always the bad guy." He then turned back to me without giving his wife a chance to respond. "Maybe the hospital discharged him too soon. Look at that, he won't even ... Tommy, when's the last time you washed your hair?" Tommy leaned forward and away from the couch. "You see"—Mr. Bell shrugged—"he's completely shut down."

A quick glance at Tommy reminded me he probably found his father's constant stream of complaints far less exciting than I did. His suicidal threat was a classic cry for help. Tommy felt smothered by his father's constant criticisms and control. He was already fourteen, yet his life seemed to be completely lacking in autonomy. That was why he had chosen to sit on the floor. He knew his father would complain about it, and that was exactly what Tommy wanted to demonstrate for all to see, that he wasn't even allowed to *sit* the way he wanted.

I had to get Tommy's parents to allow him more autonomy or there could be more suicide threats. Boys who have already made one suicide threat have a thirty fold risk of committing suicide compared to boys without such a history. Once a suicidal threat has been made, the situation is serious. I didn't know if Tommy would speak to me at all, but I had to bring his perspective into the session, whether he agreed to give it to me or not. "What do *you* think the problem is, Tommy?" I asked. Tommy shrugged but said nothing. After seeing more mental health professionals over the past week than he could probably count, Tommy had no reason to think he could trust me just yet. But I wasn't concerned. I didn't need Tommy's input.

One reason family therapists always prefer younger children to join the session, even if they are not the focus of the family problems, is that they are a wonderful source of information. If you want to know what is really going on in a family, a seven-year-old will always tell you. So I turned to Brad. "What's wrong with Tommy, Brad?"

"Dad gets on his case all the time so he gets mad," Brad said without hesitation.

"Is that right, Tommy?" I asked gently.

Tommy shrugged.

"Tommy, that's rude!" Mr. Bell exclaimed. "Really, just answer the doctor!"

"It's okay," I reassured Mr. Bell, "I speak fluent 'shrug.' " Tommy's lip twitched. "One shrug usually means yes, and two shrugs usually mean no. And that was one shrug, right, Tommy?"

Tommy shrugged. Brad giggled.

I asked Brad a few more questions and got some further background on Mr. Bell's chronic complaining. If I wanted to address it, I would clearly have to do so directly but also respectfully. The atmosphere was tense, which also made it necessary to get the entire family to lighten up a little. Time was running out in the session so I decided to take the plunge. "Mr. Bell, I noticed when you all first came in and sat down, you voiced a lot of complaints."

He looked at me guardedly. "I did? I didn't notice. I don't complain that much."

Brad rolled his eyes.

"Mrs. Bell, is that true?" I asked, smiling innocently.

"Oh, honey, you complain all the time," she said to her husband. I glanced at Brad. Brad nodded. I looked down at Tommy. Tommy shrugged.

"Mrs. Bell, do you complain about the kids as much as your husband does?"

"I *never* complain about them," she responded defensively.

"Oh. Perhaps that's why your husband complains so much," I said as if the thought had just occurred to me. "You don't complain at all so he feels he has to do it for both of you."

"That's exactly right!" Mr. Bell agreed. Mrs. Bell said nothing.

"Here's what I think the problem is," I said to all of them in a more serious tone. "What happens if you put too much water in a glass, Brad?"

"It spills over," he responded right on cue.

"Exactly," I said. "We're like the glass and complaints are like water. We only have room for so many before things spill over. The tricky thing is, our glasses are different sizes, so it can be difficult for the person doing the complaining to see that someone's glass might already be too full." I looked at Mr. Bell. "Tommy's glass has been full for a while. He doesn't have room for any more complaints. But it was hard for you to see that on his face." I glanced down at Tommy, who was following my words closely. "Maybe because of the hair." I gave Tommy a quick wink.

I turned to Mr. Bell. "The bottom line is that you should only complain so much. Complaining focuses us on everything that's lacking in our lives and causes us to miss the good things we already have. You have to work on being less critical of your sons. You have to complain less."

I turned to Mrs. Bell. "But unless you take over some of the parenting responsibilities from your husband, he won't be able to. He can only stop complaining once you start."

I then addressed them both. "And unless you both find a way to communicate more positively with each other and with your sons, Tommy's glass will remain full and Brad's will spill over next. You've had a scare, but you were given another chance as a family. A chance to work hard together, to change the way you operate as a unit. I think you should embrace that chance with both arms, all four of you. Today should be your new beginning."

Mrs. Bell nodded vigorously. Brad sat with his mouth agape, completely still. Tommy actually parted his hair and looked up at me. I felt like smacking my armrest and crying, *The defense rests!*

Mr. Bell was not impressed by my closing argument. "He's refusing to go to school and I'm supposed to say nothing?"

I looked over at Mrs. Bell. She met my gaze expectantly, waiting for me to answer her husband. "You missed your cue," I said to her. She looked confused. "Mrs. Bell, you were supposed to take over, remember? You should have said, 'Honey, if Tommy refuses to go to school, you won't need to say anything to him because I will.' "

"Yes, right." Mrs. Bell nodded. "I just didn't know we started yet."

"Then let's start now. Are we game?" Mrs. Bell slowly nodded. Mr. Bell nodded as well, then Brad. Tommy shrugged. "Good," I said. "Time for your homework." I reached into a drawer and took out a deck of cards. "It's family homework of course." I ignored the Bells' puzzled stares and took out twelve cards: four kings, four jacks, and four queens. I gave the cards to Mr. Bell.

"You get twelve complaints a day, Mr. Bell. Each one costs you a card. You can only complain *after handing over a card* to the person—kings for Tommy, jacks for Brad, and queens for your wife. Once you run out of cards, you run out of complaints. At the end of every day, all cards go back to you, and you start fresh the next day. The cards are nontransferable. You can't give Tommy five and Brad three. It's four each, max." I then handed Mr. Bell a blank card. "Keep a record of what time you ran out of cards for each person every day. Let's track the learning curve and see if you can push the time back so eventually you have cards left at the end of the day." I looked at each of them. "Is everyone clear on the homework?"

The Bells stared at me, slightly bewildered, except Brad, who squirmed with delight at the prospect of this new family game. Indeed, the cards were a game. I wanted the Bells to have fun with it, be silly with each other, and banish the dark cloud of chronic complaints and negativity that hovered over their lives and home. The cards were just the beginning. As the therapy progressed, Mr. Bell would also need to complain effectively, including learning how to distinguish which of his many complaints he should voice and which he should let go. I did not yet know how Mr. Bell's chronic complaining began, but learning to manage his complaints effectively would give Mr. Bell a sense of competence and empowerment that could help undo his lingering and habitual sense of victimization, whatever its origin.

Fraudulent Chronic Complainers

Mr. Bell is an example of the classic chronic complainer in that he is unaware of the extent of his excessive complaining as well as of its impact on those around him. But some chronic complainers not only recognize their propensity to overcomplain, they delight in it. For them, complaining is only a means to a fraudulent end. They purchase outfits they cannot afford, wear them to special occasions, then fabricate a complaint so they can return them the next day (a practice known as deshopping or retail borrowing). They buy items at discount outlets and return them at regular stores for the full price, pocketing the difference. They eat at restaurants or check into hotels that advertise "satisfaction guaranteed or money back" with complaints already in place. Their schemes are endless and at times quite sophisticated, and they typically give no thought whatsoever to the impact of their practices on the businesses in question or other consumers.

So who are these people? Most businesses assume such "consumer deviants" are only a tiny percent of the population and therefore, from a business standpoint, worth ignoring. But are their assumptions correct? Exactly how common is fraudulent complaining behavior? After all, such behavior verges on the criminal, if not qualifying as such outright.

Apparently, it is not as rare as many assume. In 2005, researchers Kate Reynolds and Lloyd Harris recruited over one hundred illegitimate complainers from shopping malls in nine different cities, simply by asking people to recall if, as consumers, they had ever complained unfairly for gain. Just like that, over a hundred people happily admitted to lying through their teeth about a consumer complaint. Of course, those were just the people who *admitted* to illegitimate complaining. It would be fair to assume that at least some of those queried had indeed done so but denied it nonetheless.

Those that did confess to false complaining were then asked to describe those incidents fully and specify the motives for their actions.

One of the most striking findings was that many illegitimate complainers were not actually financially challenged. They could well have afforded the items or the services for which they requested full refunds. They made fraudulent returns for the sheer sport of doing so. While most of them would never dream of stealing from a friend or cheating an acquaintance out of fair payment, they rationalized their illegitimate complaining as a match of wits with huge and impersonal corporations and therefore saw their behavior as "beating the system." They considered their actions to be victimless crimes.

Another indication that subjects in the study were untroubled by guilt or ethics was apparent in that they confessed to using illegitimate complaining as a "pick-me-up," a "mood enhancer" to get them out of a funk. This was surprising because the researchers had not stumbled onto a psychopath convention or the local antisocial club's annual outing. Rather, their subjects were regular people, shoppers in a mall. That made the findings rather extraordinary.

Some subjects in the study admitted to complaining behaviors that skated dangerously close to the thin ice of true antisocial behavior. These people were well aware their actions had real implications for sales and services employees because they used illegitimate complaining as a form of interpersonal bullying and harassment. Such subjects went about getting refunds, returns, and free services by voicing unjust and sometimes harsh personal complaints against the sales and service employees themselves rather than the product. Some of them admitted to manufacturing their accusations entirely out of thin air, even though doing so could jeopardize the service employees' jobs and livelihood. These subjects expressed sentiments such as:

"I like going into a shop and just complaining for the sake of it ... it's amazing how much havoc one person can cause."

"I think some of those shop assistants need to be put in their place."

"It's a laugh to wind up [annoy] the waiters and waitresses by making a few unreal complaints when you are on a night out with the boys, it gets the night going."

That such "laughs" could get someone fired, that they disrupted the employees' lives tremendously and caused them potential emotional and financial hardship, were completely ignored by the illegitimate complainers. Their behavior qualifies as bullying because the sales and service employees were severely disadvantaged in these encounters. Their responsibility to "please the customer" strictly limits their ability to respond to the false accusations.

Many illegitimate complainers admitted to engaging in such behaviors habitually, leading researchers to realize such practices might be far more common than originally thought. The researchers concluded, "The prevalence and pervasiveness of fraudulent complaint behaviors reported suggests that organizations may be enduring vast financial costs by way of compensating customers for problems and faults for which they are not legally liable."

The subjects in the study were likely willing to confess their nefarious consumer activities because the researchers did not require them to give their names. Obviously, most illegitimate complainers do not advertise their fraudulent shopping or their mistreatment of service employees.

Even though other consumers end up "paying" for this illegitimate complaining, such behaviors are still tolerated if not actually encouraged, especially here in the United States. How else might we explain the audacious pride some fraudulent complainers take in their cheating and stealing that leads them to self-publish books about their antisocial consumer activities? Many such chronicles describe how to finagle countless expensive products: Super Bowl tickets, first-class flights, rooms at five-star hotels, and even thousands of dollars in cash. These authors proudly document their lack of honesty and of civic responsibility. Some even endeavor to make their living by touting their "reign" of shamelessness in "how I did it" tomes, selling them to other budding social parasites so they too can become noncontributing members of society.

Chronic complainers and fraudulent ones illustrate the dangers of overcomplaining to the people themselves, their families, and their communities at large. However, in some circumstances *under*complaining can be just as dangerous and problematic as overcomplaining.

The Dangers of Undercomplaining at the Doctor's Office

Not complaining when we should can be extremely psychologically damaging. In extreme cases, it can even be life-threatening, largely because we typically most fail to speak up when our complaints are directed toward our health and mental-health providers.

Few professionals command the same authority and natural respect as do physicians. In the United States, doctors are usually considered experts whose opinions we of the general public have insufficient knowledge or understanding to challenge. Despite WebMD.com and other such Websites' efforts to educate and inform the public, few of us feel comfortable questioning the decisions of our doctors.

In some cultures, questioning a doctor's authority and judgment is completely unacceptable. In highly authoritative cultures, developing countries, or rural areas where medical resources are scarce, it would be both incredibly rude and incredibly ungrateful to complain about the available medical care or the manner in which it is delivered. Similarly, in economically disadvantaged towns or neighborhoods, when our options for medical treatment are strictly limited, we might be equally hesitant to bite the only hand that treats us.

But here in the United States, things are only marginally better as many of us are fearful about expressing complaints about our treatment to our health-care providers. Some signs of change do exist, as more and more of us are demanding to be active partners in our health-care decisions. Still, the majority of us feel extremely hesitant to demand or even request more of a say in our own care. Many physicians balk at such collaboration and refuse to view patients as partners. Many of us have had physicians order a procedure or test they thought was important and we thought was unnecessary. Few of us speak up in such situations, and even fewer do so adamantly.

Some of our complaints are shared by the vast majority of patients, yet even those are rarely expressed. Complaints about a physician's bedside manner or waiting times for appointments are extremely common, yet we rarely voice them at all, at least to those who could actually do something about them. (We will revisit the issue of waiting times in doctors' offices when we discuss complaints as community activism in chapter 8.)

Mere inconveniences aside, undercomplaining to our health providers can be the most damaging to the health of our children. Children are unable to advocate for themselves. Unless we are vigilant and proactive about our children's health needs, serious conditions can be missed. While most parents do a great job regarding their children's physical health, our children's mental health is often another matter entirely.

Mental disorders are still highly stigmatized in every culture, even ours. I've witnessed many parents minimize their child's psychological and emotional problems even when such problems are stark and even when their child is suffering profoundly as a result. In many cases, parents are simply unaware their child's behavior lies outside the norm. But in some cases, the problems are far more obvious. Teachers and other parents might even point out that something is amiss, and often despite those warnings, some parents still feel too anxious or ashamed to investigate the concern.

Thus some parents seek treatment for their child's mental disorders only once the condition has so deteriorated that it literally cannot be ignored. The tragedy here is that many psychological and cognitive problems can be fully remedied if the child begins the right therapies in time. When parents fail to complain to their child's pediatrician, school, or health provider if they sense something might be psychologically wrong, it can cost the child untold and unnecessary mental distress. Such was the case for five-year-old Sheena.

Sheena and her parents were referred for family therapy by her mother's individual psychologist. The therapist had become concerned after Sheena's mother described behavioral problems Sheena had at home and in school. When we spoke on the phone, Sheena's mother described her as a delightful but rambunctious little girl who was shy around adults. When I asked about her peer relations, her mother admitted Sheena had "few friends or play dates" and added, "We had her evaluated when she was two, so we know she's not autistic or anything."

When I asked what had prompted the evaluation, Sheena's mother reported that she had been concerned something was wrong with Sheena but felt reluctant to bring it up with their doctor. The pediatrician had not noticed anything was amiss during

Sheena's checkups, and her mother didn't want to "question the doctor's judgment." Instead, a family friend who was also a school psychologist did a brief "unofficial" evaluation of Sheena at twenty-four months and concluded Sheena "did not seem autistic." It put the mother's fears to rest, and the issue had not been revisited despite Sheena's deteriorating behavior.

I met the family later that week. Something was clearly wrong with Sheena from the first glance. She was an adorable little girl, but her teeth were extremely crooked and she had terrible vision (the lenses in her glasses were thick). Sheena also had obvious delays in expressive-language skills, as her speech was more appropriate for a three-year-old than a five-year-old. However, the biggest tip-off to the parents' denial was that Sheena was still in Pull-Ups. Her lack of toilet training was never mentioned either on the phone or once they were in the office, yet Sheena's trousers barely covered her diapers. They were as visible to me as they must have been to every other child in her class. Her classmates' response to her wearing diapers could not have been pleasant for Sheena or good for her self-esteem.

Sheena's behavior problems, the original reason for the referral, were also unusual. She did not seem to have trouble following direction and responding to her parents' or my requests, as some children do. But then a few minutes into the session, Sheena climbed onto her father's lap and sat there playing with her shirt. Her father's cell phone started ringing, and he shifted position slightly so he could reach it in his jacket pocket. Sheena's face immediately contorted with frustration and annoyance, and she twisted around and punched him squarely (and hard) in the face.

I was shocked and alarmed by the suddenness of it. Sheena's father exclaimed, "Ow!" and quickly placed her beside him as he rubbed his nose. Sheena did not seem alarmed by her actions or repentant. Her father gave her a chagrined glance. "She hates that ringtone," he explained. Sheena's mother went on talking as if nothing had happened. In part, what makes denial so fascinating is how hugely visible it is to everyone except those embroiled in it (such as the denial of chronic complainers of the excessiveness of their complaints).

I am not a specialist in child testing or in developmental assessments, but I found it abundantly obvious that Sheena required a thorough learning evaluation and full psychological assessment. When I suggested it, both parents seemed confused as to why such a procedure was necessary. After all, Sheena had been evaluated at twenty-four months and was given the all clear. I had Sheena join her babysitter in the waiting room so I could explain my concerns about her language skills, toilet training, and impulse control to her parents. Unfortunately, the "delicate" approach rarely works with parents who are in denial about their child's problems. Denial is a powerful psychological defense and is extremely difficult to pierce, even at the best of times. I knew I might have to be blunt.

Once alone with the parents, I told them flat out I believed Sheena was a delightful little girl, but I suspected she had a larger issue that had not yet been diagnosed. I was especially concerned with her impulse control. Her father immediately became defensive. "Sheena's not a criminal!" he sputtered. "She doesn't have problems with 'impulse control,' she just gets frustrated!"

"All five-year-olds get frustrated," I explained. "But they don't usually sock daddy in the kisser when his phone goes off, no matter how much they hate the ringtone." I discussed the benefits of early diagnosis, including the possibility of their learning tools to manage Sheena's temperament, to help her improve her behavior, and to help her reach her maximum potential. Her mother softened but her father remained adamantly against it.

Over the years I've met several families in which a child with obvious special needs remained undiagnosed and untreated because the parents were reluctant to complain to mental-health or even health professionals. Some parents hope their child catches up over time (despite clear learning or developmental deficits). Others are reluctant to label or stigmatize the child by inviting formal evaluation. Parents sometimes allow their own shame and denial to prevent them from getting their child needed help.

Fear of being stigmatized or labeled is only one factor that leads to undercomplaining regarding our mental health. A far larger problem is our general lack of knowledge and understanding about the psychotherapy process itself and the ways different treatments are supposed to work. Despite all the therapists and psychotherapy around us, few of us know what to expect when we see a therapist for the first time.

So Many Therapists, So Few Complaints

We usually think of psychotherapy as a realm in which we feel comfortable, free to express our feelings, thoughts, and complaints to an objective party. However, when something our therapist says or does upsets us, precious few of us feel comfortable or free expressing our dissatisfactions.

In a 1999 study, Professor John Hunsley of the University of Ottawa in Canada asked college students who had recently left psychotherapy at a university psychology clinic their reasons for stopping treatment. Only a minority of patients stated they terminated therapy because they had accomplished their goals (personal finances were not a consideration since this was a university-run clinic). Instead, patients indicated they dropped out of psychotherapy because it was going nowhere (34%), or because they were not confident in the therapists' ability (30%), or because they thought therapy was making things worse (9%).

But here's the kicker. When the researchers asked the therapists to indicate what percentage of their patients dropped out because of dissatisfaction with the services, the therapists all said—zero percent! The therapists believed none of the terminations had anything to do with their performance or skills, when in fact a large percentage of patients ended therapy for those exact reasons. Indeed, much as in Hunsley's study, most dissatisfied psychotherapy patients do not complain when a problem arises with their therapist. Instead, they simply drop out before achieving their treatment goals, often without intending to seek out another therapist and continue the work. And they have good reason for avoiding such following up.

When our complaint is about a physician or a medical provider, a simple phone call and release form transfer our medical records, and a new doctor will be up to speed on our cases in days. But we spend weeks, months, and even years seeing therapists. Our therapists know much more about us than could ever be conveyed in medical records or session notes. For most of us, the thought of transferring to a new therapist who doesn't know the details of our lives is tantamount to starting the entire process over. Thus most of us are extremely reluctant to switch therapists even after a significant "service failure."

Complicating matters, as shown in almost every psychotherapy-outcome study, is that the "active ingredient" that matters is the quality of the relationship between the therapist and the patient. The nature of that bond most determines how effective the therapy will be. Other variables, such as the therapist's years of experience, theoretical orientation, age, or gender, have about as much impact on treatment outcomes as the therapist's choice of fabric softener does.

Of course, this rule has some exceptions when it comes to specific conditions, such as panic disorder, for which treatment protocols are usually effective regardless of who administers them. But overall, the relationship between patient and therapist (often called the working alliance) is of paramount importance. For most of us, expressing dissatisfactions to our therapist is extremely uncomfortable, and doing so can disrupt the very thing that makes psychotherapy work.

Another "fear factor" is that confronting our therapist also means confronting someone who knows all our weak spots while we know none of his or hers. True, therapists *should* respond to complaints the way any service provider should, by being grateful they have been expressed. It allows the patient's concern to be addressed and any ruptures in the crucial working alliance to be mended. Indeed, when we voice complaints to our therapists, we should expect them to be met with calm and empathy, not with irritation or impatience. Alas, this is not always the case.

An even more fundamental problem is we often have no idea how to determine acceptable standards of practice. Psychotherapies, by definition, all have one thing in common—two people talking (or more in the case of family or group therapies). Beyond that basic tenet, it is an eclectic and mixed bag of experiences. Psychotherapy has many forms and therapists do things so differently that it's often impossible for a nonprofessional to know whether something that was said or done in a session is in line with professional standards.

Many years ago, an acquaintance of mine, an Ivy League college graduate, called to ask my opinion about a technique her male therapist had recommended. They had been working on issues related to sexuality and sexual inhibition, and her therapist suggested it would move things along quicker if she (my acquaintance) was nude during the sessions. This young woman called me to ask not how to report her therapist to the American Psychological Association for an ethics violation, but rather whether I agreed that nudity would help her work through her issues more expeditiously. I told her never to go back and to report the man to the New York State licensing board.

Patients face another hurdle when wishing to lob a complaint at their therapist. Many therapists are trained to interpret patient dissatisfactions or complaints as possible resistance to treatment itself. Patients' complaints are viewed as mere *transference*, a projection onto the therapist of the patient's historical familial dynamic. Given these assumptions, some therapists dismiss the face value of any complaints their patients might have about them or the therapy. Instead, they insist on guiding the patient through a scenic yet unnecessary exploration of the "unresolved historical conflicts" the patient's complaint is assumed to represent. One would think that of all people therapists should be able to recognize that sometimes a complaint is just a complaint.

This confusion about what should or should not be going on behind closed therapy doors is certainly not helped by the depiction of psychologists and psychiatrists in popular culture. We are usually treated to hour upon hour of emotionally unstable narcissists such as in *Fraser* or cannibalistic serial killers the likes of Hannibal Lecter. *The Sopranos* and *In Treatment* did give us some less objectionable depictions of what therapy sessions looked like. But rather than leaving the therapists to do their job simply and well, the therapist in *The Sopranos* was put through horrific violence, and the *In Treatment* Gabriel Byrne character is the kind of neurotic mess that makes for entertaining television but does not help the profession to be taken seriously.

If we have a complaint in our therapy, if something doesn't feel right, if we feel frustrated at our progress or lack thereof, we should always be brave and raise the issue with our therapist. Our mental health is too important to avoid discussing any concerns we might have. Most therapists should be able to handle our complaints, and productive new directions for the therapy can be explored in the discussion the complaint triggers.

Effective Complaining as Psychological Tool Kit

Our complaints can be practical, emotional, and psychological tools that we use to better our lives and they can benefit us tremendously. They can help us gain resolutions to meaningful problems. They can improve our moods, our self-esteem, and our general outlook on life. They can better and deepen our relationships.

However, as many sharp tools do, complaints can cut both ways when used incorrectly. When we complain excessively or, in some cases, too little, we can end up getting more cuts, nicks, and scratches than we do benefits. Some of the ensuing injuries could even run deep.

Now that we are alerted to the dangers of complaining, as well as to the numerous psychological, emotional, relationship, and societal benefits we can gain by complaining effectively, we can finally begin to use our effective complaining skills to get more out of our lives.

Chapter Five
The Ingredients for Serving a Delicious Squeak

I think a compliment ought to always precede a complaint, where one is possible, because it softens resentment and insures for the complaint a courteous and gentle reception.
—Mark Twain

The evening I wrote to my apartment's management company to complain about the construction noise, I had been up all night with a horrific cold, and thunderous drilling had kept me up throughout the next day. Only when my misery had reached its breaking point did I toss the covers aside, hack and sneeze my way over to the computer, and sit down to write my complaint letter.

The constant drilling had already made me incredibly irritable, and a fresh round of vibrations was starting up, making my keyboard vibrate and my patience snap. I wanted nothing more at that moment than to unleash my venom, to dump a steaming pile of anger and frustration onto the page, and to wrap it in the foulest language I could muster. After living and working in New York City for the past twenty years, when it came to foul language, I could muster with the best of them.

But the voice of reason inside my head prevailed. I knew that if I wanted my complaint to have any chance of succeeding, it could not be angry in tone. Desperate as I was to vent, I knew that anger never makes our complaints more effective, and it often makes our situation worse by inviting the very kinds of risks we seek to avoid.

Killing a Complaint Softly with Anger

While it is perfectly reasonable and acceptable for us to be angry at a situation, the same is not true of our complaints. An angry complaint cannot be more effective than a levelheaded version of the same complaint for one primary reason—anger is extremely distracting. When someone raises his or her voice angrily in a crowded room, we instinctively disrupt our own conversations and turn toward that person. Anger has that power: it grabs our attention by the collar and hogs it, even when it isn't directed at us. Anger not only draws our attention, but in the case of a complaint, anger draws our attention *away* from the content of our complaint, the actual matter we hope to resolve.

To avoid drawing attention away from the essence of our complaints, we have to keep our tone measured. Anger, sarcasm, name-calling, and condescension—however justified—guarantee the person to whom they are addressed will pay less attention to our actual grievance than to the obnoxiousness of our presentation. No matter how justified our anger seems or how culpable the recipient of our complaint actually is, angry complaints rarely garner satisfying resolutions.

Consider the tone of Professor Flynn's letter (from the previous chapter). He had placed dramatic emphasis on how angry the food poisoning had made him, and he referred to his emotional state repeatedly. (1) "I am *outraged* about a recent experience I had at your restaurant." (2) "It makes me *furious* just thinking that our special romantic evening …" (3) "Nevertheless, I am still *very angry* because it was I who fell ill." (4) "I felt *incensed* and therefore believed it was necessary to write you this letter." (5) "Now all I am experiencing is *extreme irritation.*" (6) "We will always *bitterly remember* this occasion." And finally, just in case it wasn't yet abundantly clear he was royally pissed, (7) "I am *furious* about this entire ordeal."

The professor's excessive emphasis on rage and anger did little to increase the impact of his letter. Despite the severity of the accusations and the potential damage to the restaurants' reputations, of the 240 establishments who received his fictional snit, only 60 bothered to respond. Three quarters of the establishments simply ignored Professor Flynn's thinly veiled threats entirely.

The problem with anger is even more profound when our outrage is actually authentic. What makes effective complaining a challenging skill set to master is that our anger sets us up for an "existential dilemma." Our motivations to complain are always strongest at the exact same time our irritation and frustration are peaking. Therefore, we feel most compelled to lash out in anger at the very moment clear thought and reason are most crucial to our success. We are thereby faced with a choice: do we indulge our irritability and get a nice cathartic bang for our buck, or do we labor to cool our hot heads and achieve a satisfying resolution? We cannot do both.

Although I have always been a fan of the latter option, that night my miserable and belligerent state of mind felt all-consuming. I remember wondering if it was even possible to change from such a strong and dominant mood, to shift by will alone from irritability and agitation to calm and composure. My own existential dilemma that night was, with the drilling raging outside, how could I possibly stop my raging within?

Tempted as I was to give in to my anger, my doctoral dissertation had been related to how we regulate our emotions. Therefore, even in the throes of upper respiratory misery, I knew I could use certain psychological techniques to reduce my agitation. However, any such methods require substantial effort, willpower, and strong motivation. If we want to marshal our full psychological resources, to get the most out of emotion-regulation techniques, we first need a clear understanding of what our feelings actually are.

Emotions, We Hardly Knew Ye

Imagine we cross the street and see a Mack truck bearing down on us at fifty miles an hour. In only milliseconds fear and instinct would make our heart leap into our mouth and our legs leap out of the way. Whatever thoughts, ideas, or beliefs we have at that moment are irrelevant. Only emotions and instinctive reactions are triggered fast enough to save our lives. If it were up to our thoughts and cognition to get us out of the way, we would have seen the truck and thought, "Jeepers! That truck's doing fifty in a school zone! Why I'd better—" At that point we'd already be smeared across the asphalt like cream cheese on a Sunday bagel.

Although our brains process both emotions and thoughts, the two are by no means equals. The pathways in our brains that transmit emotional reactions are far more ancient (evolutionarily speaking), wired far deeper in our brains, and operate more instantaneously than the relatively new pathways of abstract thought, cognition, and logic. Controlling our emotions by will alone is therefore a noble yet challenging pursuit. What makes it possible to do so is that those things we typically think of as our "feelings" are actually complex experiences composed of several different components.

Let's break it down with an example, say, of airline travel. After a long road trip, a looming snowstorm has us rush to the airport only to discover that our flight has been canceled. A quick glance at the board tells us only one other flight is leaving the airport, and we, along with dozens of other angry passengers, rush the airline's desk in an effort to get one of the limited available seats. What makes us even more desperate to get on the last flight out is that we have two longstanding family events to attend the next day.

Our emotional experience in that moment has several elements. First and most obvious is our actual "feeling," the subjective experience of the emotion. We most likely feel anger, frustration, irritation, and perhaps a drop of anticipatory guilt when we consider the possibility of missing our family events. Next, since emotional experiences are always accompanied by physiological responses, our heart rate and blood pressure are probably elevated; stress hormones have likely been released into our bloodstream, and the electrical chemical conductivity of our skin has likely changed as well.

Second, there are the behavioral expressions of our emotional state: our faces tighten, our voices get louder, and our elbows get sharper as we guard our place in line among the other disgruntled passengers. We scan the line from all sides, ready to object to anyone who tries to cut in front of us, or we may tap our feet or wring our hands in anticipation of our turn's coming up.

Lastly, we have our thoughts and beliefs about the emotional experience. We might believe missing the flight is terrible as it means we will miss our daughter's soccer game the next afternoon. Or we might realize how upset our parents, aunts, and uncles will be to have us miss the second family obligation, the debut of our unemployed second cousin's one-man rock opera about Bulgarian postal workers.

Our physiological reactions, our behavioral responses, and our underlying thoughts and beliefs about a situation are the three primary components of our emotional experiences. The question is, if we want to change how we feel about an upsetting or frustrating situation, which of these three components is easiest to manipulate, and which approach is more effective when it comes to expressing our complaints with level heads?

Zen and the Art of Emotional Regulation

Of the three components of our emotional experiences, our physiological responses are by far the hardest to control directly. Sure, we can try to lower our heart rates or blood pressure by measured breathing (in, two three; out, two three; and so on), and doing so might even affect them a tad. But truly controlling our autonomic nervous systems is simply not a possibility for most of us. Maybe the rare Shaolin monk or master yogi can drop his blood pressure on demand, but he's also far less likely to show up at Bed Bath & Beyond with a busted cappuccino maker.

That leaves managing our behaviors to gain control of our emotional responses or changing our thoughts and beliefs to do so. As for our behaviors, we are all experienced at trying to hide from the outside world what we feel on the inside, as doing so is part of life in civilized society. If our boss yells at us in the middle of a presentation we spent weeks preparing for, we try to cover both our embarrassment and our desire to whack the boss over the head with our notes. When the new object of our affections invites us for a romantic home-cooked dinner that tastes as if the butcher had a sale on ferret meat, we hide both our dismay and our gag reflex.

Controlling the behavioral expressions of our emotions by hiding them in such ways is called suppression. Let's assume that as stranded airport passengers, we know that spewing out our anger and frustration as soon as we're within spitting distance of the airline clerk will not likely endear us to them or result in our being bumped up the waiting list. Instead, we want to appear as calm and as reasonable as possible so we stand out from the other irate passengers and so we elicit whatever goodwill and favor the temporarily all-powerful reservation clerk has left.

But what can we do to suppress our rage and frustration at being stranded? First, we should probably avoid dwelling on vivid images of our daughter's scoring the winning goal in her soccer game, looking up into the bleachers with a tear in her eye and wondering why we are not there. Next, we might try speaking more slowly (unless we were slow talkers to begin with). Slower speech generally sounds less angry and agitated. Finally, we can try to force a pleasant smile when we reach the check-in clerk, even as we grind our canceled boarding pass to a pulp under the desk. With suppression, we still experience all the anger and frustration of the situation, but our efforts are focused on hiding those feelings from the person to whom we address our complaint.

Perhaps the best example of suppression is the game of poker, as playing it practically necessitates an expertise in hiding our emotions. Keeping a "poker face" means hiding our excitement when we hold a good hand and hiding our disappointment when we hold bad cards. Poker players' expressions have to be unreadable to other players. Watching a game of poker is watching raw suppression in action.

The second method we can use to regulate our emotions is to change our perspective of the situation such that it has less of an emotional impact on us. Psychologists call this process reappraisal or reframing. When we reframe a situation in our minds, we redefine it by examining it from a different point of view than we have previously.

How could we apply this method as the stranded airline passenger? We can remind ourselves that our daughter has soccer games every weekend, so we have plenty of further opportunities to see her play. Or we might focus on our unemployed second cousin's complete lack of artistic talent, his tone deafness, and his shoddy Bulgarian. We can even realize that the delay will allow us to catch up on work and thereby completely free up our Sunday. In each of these approaches, we essentially reframe our canceled flight as a blessing rather than a curse. Doing so changes our fundamental feelings about the event and modifies our emotional experience, allowing us to feel less angry and irritated.

We all use both suppression and reframing regularly in our daily lives. Some of us tend to use reframing more than suppression, and others favor suppression over reframing.

Reframe, Baby, Reframe!

Suppression and reframing have been studied by psychologists for many years, and as it turns out, they are not by any means equally effective. Reframing was shown to be far superior to suppression in its ability to decrease negative emotions. Although we are unable to affect our physiological responses directly, reframing does allow us to *somewhat* reduce our startle responses, lower our hormonal or endocrine responses, and even decrease our autonomic nervous system responses (even without training as a Shaolin monk).

Suppression is inferior to reframing in other ways as well. Trying to hide strong negative emotions actually causes us significant disruptions in memory and other cognitive functions. Repressing our emotions is a laborious task that taxes our ability to pay attention. Stifling our negative feelings also has social costs. In one experiment, the partners of people who used suppression reported feeling less comfortable and less at ease during interactions with them than those who interacted with people who were not instructed to use suppression.

If the advantages of reframing are so stark, why on earth would we use suppression as opposed to reframing to regulate our emotions? One of the problems is that each of our internal emotional thermostats is set at different baseline levels. Our ability to tolerate frustration varies from person to person. Some of us have triggers that are set low, making us quick to anger. Others have triggers that are set high, allowing them to stay cool and calm longer. Imagine driving along the freeway and spotting signs of a huge traffic jam. Some of us might react by exclaiming, "Oh, hell no! Damn it! Come on! Move already!" while others might say, "Traffic. I guess I can finally finish that book on tape!"

How quickly our temper cools down is just as important as how quickly it heats up. Once emotionally activated, some people's thermostats take far longer to calm down than others' do. Some of us who are quick to anger are also quick to cool, and some are not. The same is true of the calm types. In any event, someone who goes from zero to rabid in six seconds flat might have a harder time using reframing than someone whose anger is slower to boil.

Knowing all this came in extremely handy the evening I wrote my complaint letter. I tend to be a slow boiler myself, but at that point I had been doing a slow boil for almost twenty-four hours. My emotion-regulation solution was to reframe my prospective letter as an intellectual challenge, a puzzle of sorts. Indeed, my complaint was, in fact, rather challenging as the likelihood of success was extremely low (remember, my management company was not responsible for the noise and had turned down other requests).

Whether my complaining skills were sufficiently advanced to achieve a resolution where others had failed was an open question. Therefore, I hoped the concentration required to compose an effective letter would simultaneously divert attentional resources away from my anger, thus allowing my non-Tibetan nervous system to calm down.

Reframing our complaints as a challenge or a way to assess our skill sets is a technique we can all use to calm our emotions. Even the most annoying complaints are opportunities to test ourselves, to evaluate whether our knowledge and resources are sufficient to resolve the problem at hand in a satisfactory manner. Once we are focused on making our complaint more effective, our emotions will begin to fade from their previously distracting highs, allowing us to think more clearly and productively.

Emotion-regulation methods, much like effective complaining techniques, are skill sets that can be learned and improved, whether our emotional triggers are set high or low.

Common sense tells us that the best way to motivate another person to help us resolve our complaints is to make our grievances as palatable to them as we possibly can. When it comes to complaining, anger tastes bad to everyone. But removing the anger is only the first step in making our complaints tastier to their recipients. With the right techniques, it is possible to make most complaints downright delicious.

How to Prepare a Complaint Sandwich

Consider things from the complaint recipient's point of view for a moment. In my case, the building's management company was small, with a friendly staff, not a monolithic corporate entity. The person who answered their phones was an administrative assistant who probably had a variety of other responsibilities beyond taking calls from angry tenants. Now, imagine you were that administrative assistant. You have already fielded numerous complaints about the construction noise, all of which were denied outright. You are trying to get back to your work when the phone rings and yet another irate tenant opens with "I'm calling about the construction noise outside. It is [expletive of choice] unbearable! I pay too much rent for this! Do you have any idea how early the drilling starts? Do you?"

How much of the tenant's saga of noise and vibrations would you have indulged before you cut him off and got to the bottom line: "I'm so sorry, but there's nothing we can do." By the third or fourth call of the day, I would have interrupted the person midcomplaint or just continued with my work while the tenant finished venting. In either case, I would have tuned out rather quickly. Therefore, the first thing we write in our complaint letter (or the first thing we communicate verbally) has to be an *ear-opener.*

Ear-openers represent the top slice of bread in the complaint sandwich. The *meat* of the sandwich is the complaint itself, or the request for redress, and the bottom slice of bread in the complaint sandwich is the *digestive.* The digestive is a positive statement (much like the ear-opener) that comes at the close of the complaint.

Let's start with the top slice of bread. Ear-openers are important because we all become somewhat defensive when fielding complaints, much as we do whenever we feel attacked or criticized. If most of us even sniff a complaint coming at us from colleagues, friends, or loved ones, our defenses immediately kick in. We raise our emotional drawbridges, flood our moats, and release the crocodiles. Or, in less medieval terms, we naturally become less open to accepting fault or responsibility for any forthcoming matters.

Therefore, if we wish to be effective, we have to ease into our complaints in ways that do not trigger the recipient's defenses at our first words or utterances. Holding our tone and anger in check is crucial, but it is also insufficient. Starting with an ear-opener makes the recipient of our complaint far more receptive to whatever we say next, and ear-openers should be designed with that goal in mind.

Let's examine the complaint letter I wrote to my building's management company. Here is the opening paragraph:

> I have been a tenant for the past two and a half years (since the building opened) and have enjoyed living here very much. I am writing because as I'm sure you know, there is construction on the lot to the south of the building (which was a taxi parking lot for the first year I lived here). For the past few weeks, the noise level has escalated dramatically. Despite the double-glazed windows (which I am very thankful for) the drilling into concrete, banging, buzz saws cutting metal tubing, and other INCREDIBLE noise starts at 7 AM and goes on ALL DAY. As I write at home during the day (and go to my office in the afternoons and evenings), the noise has made it extremely difficult to get anything done at home as it is literally hard to concentrate for more than a few seconds or even hold a normal conversation on the phone.

The opening statement, "I have enjoyed living here very much," might appear simplistic, but it does something important. It opens up the reader's ears to what follows. Not only do I refrain from opening with the complaint itself, but also the only sentiment conveyed (so far) is a friendly expression of appreciation (i.e., "I've enjoyed living in your building").

Here is the meat section, the actual request for redress:

> I am fully aware that you have nothing to do with the construction and that you are under no obligation to provide any compensation or adjustments for the noise and inconvenience. However, as a tenant in good standing I would like to ask you to consider adjusting my rent downward to reflect the very different standard of living (again through no fault of yours!) that my apartment now provides. I would not be writing unless I found the situation to be extremely distressing as the construction has barely moved forward and many more months of this unbearable noise are yet to come.

Here the tone sounds more like a request for a favor rather than a complaint or a demand. Compare the tone of this letter to that in Professor Flynn's complaint. Whereas his tone was threatening and angry, I have clearly taken pains to appear nonhostile and agreeable.

The final slice of bread in the sandwich, the digestive, has two purposes. First, it serves as that spoonful of sugar that makes the medicine (our complaint) go down, making it more difficult for the recipient to dismiss our complaint outright. Second, it increases the listener's motivation to help. My letter ended as follows:

> I would appreciate anything you could do for me to help make my rent reflect the present realities of my living situation. I would be happy to sign any waivers you deemed necessary as I recognize you are under no obligation whatsoever to take any action and that you have no responsibility for the noise yourselves. But the situation has gotten so bad, I felt I had to ask …
>
> I do hope to hear from you soon and thank you in advance for any consideration you afford me.

Here the closing sentence ("thank you in advance for any consideration") is pretty much a standard closer with no "digestive powers" beyond mere politeness and civility. The real digestive is the sentence that precedes it: "But the situation has gotten so bad, I felt I had to ask …" It conveys that my expectations are not excessive and that I am ready to be appreciative. I make it as easy as possible for the management company to offer help, to *digest* my complaint. From their point of view, doing so will not entail a capitulation to any demand, nor will it represent an admission of responsibility or wrongdoing. Further, they are virtually guaranteed that any reduction in rent they offer is likely to be met with gratitude and appreciation.

The complaint sandwich is a simple formula (albeit one that requires some thought) that makes any complaint more likely to garner a positive response. While the complaint sandwich is necessary for our consumer complaints, it is just as effective and often more vital when complaining to family, friends, or colleagues.

Even once we become master chefs at complaint sandwich preparation, when the recipients of our complaints are our loved ones, we should anticipate an extra measure of natural defensiveness. Even my own friends and family, all of whom have been dining on my delicious anger-free complaint sandwiches for years, still stiffen whenever I ask them if we can "have a word." They get this momentary panicked look on their faces like "Sweet heavens, what did I do now?" No doubt, I react with similar anticipatory dread when they approach me with a complaint of their own. That's why the two slices of bread in the complaint sandwich are so important. They help us put the complaint recipient into a receptive and helpful frame of mind.

Certain circumstances might require us to beef up one or more of the complaint-sandwich components. If we anticipate the recipients to be especially unreceptive or if we know they are unlikely to be in a helpful frame of mind, we need to lavish more attention to the ear-opener or digestive sections of our complaint. When we have to provide an especially strong rationale for our complaint, the meat section most needs elaboration. Let's look at some examples.

The Bell Should Toll Just Once

In the last chapter, we saw how Mr. Bell opted for the "buckshot" approach to complaining: spray as many complaints as possible all around and hope some of them stick. Both his wife and his sons responded to his monsoon of dissatisfactions by simply ignoring all of them. While Mr. Bell's constant criticisms and negativity were oppressive for everyone, Tommy's only way of dealing with them was to shut down completely. But what if we helped Mr. Bell give his complaints an effective complaining makeover? How might Tommy respond to them then?

The first rule of complaining to our loved ones is to make sure to maintain eye contact. No matter whether we're complaining to a three-year-old, a thirty-year-old, or a ninety-year-old, we should always look them in the eye when we speak to them. And to be clear, eye contact *does not* mean staring at them with a red face and a maniacal glare. A calm, open, and caring expression is far more appropriate. If we feel too angry to pull off calmness, we need to first pause, reframe the situation in our head, regulate our emotions, and shed some of our visceral agitation before we proceed.

Here is a quick reminder of the opening lines of Mr. Bell's complaint soliloquy: "Tommy, don't sit on the floor. Brad, sit up. Tommy, must you sit with your back to me? Brad, stop fidgeting. And don't slouch. Tommy! It's not polite to sit on the floor. Why can't you [Mrs. Bell] say something to him? Why is it always my job?"

Now let's use the complaint sandwich to modify complaint number one. The first thing Mr. Bell should have done was to face Tommy, either by placing his hand on his shoulder so he turned around or by getting up and crouching in front of him. Then he should have remembered that when the recipient of our complaint appears emotionally distant or defensive (say, because he is sitting on the floor with his back to us), a more elaborate, convincing, and powerful ear-opener is required.

In Tommy's case, his ears were not *fully* sealed (as he did show up to the session), but they weren't exactly gaping open either. Given his recent suicide threat, a far warmer and more compassionate ear-opener was called for. Mr. Bell should have said something like "I know you've been through a difficult and traumatic week. We want you to feel better, that's why we're all here. But most of all we want to listen. So please don't sit on the floor. I want to be able to hear what you have to say. I really want to listen." Then Mr. Bell should have offered Tommy his seat on the couch and sat in the chair next to Brad.

It would not have been sufficient for Mr. Bell to just say those words; he would have had to mean them if he wanted to have an impact on Tommy. Reframing is a tool to change our underlying emotions in a situation, and we must make sure our frustrations and anger are both in check before expressing our dissatisfactions in delicate situations such as these.

As for the rest of Mr. Bell's complaints, he should have just dismissed them. Rule number two for complaining to our loved ones is—only one complaint at a time (i.e., per complaint session). It is far preferable for our loved ones to respond positively to a single well-phrased complaint than to have them feel ambushed by too many of them at once.

Beefing Up the Meat

Let's look at another example. Steve complained to his wife about mocking his fondness for all things *Star Trek*. Remember, he watched the show regularly and his wife mocked his viewing habits with equal dedication. Both the viewing and the mocking were quite an ingrained habit in their marriage. When we wish to complain about a situation that has already gone on for a long time or about behaviors that have become habitual, the aspect of the complaint sandwich we need to expand most is the meat section. We need to provide a rationale for our complaint that includes an explanation for why we are requesting the person to change a behavior when we have not been consistent in requesting such previously.

Steve wanted his wife to stop mocking him, but he also wanted her to understand why her supporting his viewing habits was important to him. Steve mentioned that he had already tried complaining to his wife by losing his temper and yelling at her to "Shut the hell up!" Even if Steve's outburst had prompted his wife to take a break from her criticizing, the change did not last. Nor should Steve have expected it to. Whatever resentments had been fueling his wife's need to mock him would not magically disappear just because he raised his voice. However, if Steve could explain the rationale for his request to his wife in a manner she could understand and with which she could empathize, she might cease acting out those specific resentments altogether.

After explaining this principle to Steve, I suggested he respond to his wife's next "Trekkie nerd boy" insult by doing something dramatically different—placing his show on pause and turning to look her in the eye. I assured Steve that doing so would get his wife's immediate attention, as he would be conveying that talking to her was far more important to him in that moment than watching *Star Trek.*

Once he had his wife's ear, Steve had planned to say something like "I know you don't like it when I watch my show. I don't do it because it annoys you. I do it because I really enjoy it. I love this show. Watching these episodes relaxes me. It makes me happy. And you could make me even happier if you allowed me to enjoy them in peace. If you have something you find enjoyable, whether it's a television show or anything else, I promise to be supportive as well. Really, if something is important to you and makes you happy, I'll be all for it. But please let me enjoy my show. I'll appreciate it and I'll reciprocate too, okay?"

That was the version Steve and I came up with in our session (he had taken copious notes). What actually transpired between them was probably somewhat if not altogether different. But regardless of how Steve phrased his complaint or exactly how his sentiments were conveyed, the conversation had gone well. Hopefully, at least some elements of the complaint sandwich remained intact during his delivery.

All Sales Are Mostly Final!

We've looked at an example in which it was necessary to expand the ear-opener, the first slice of bread in the complaint sandwich (Mr. Bell's complaint to Tommy) and one in which it was necessary for the meat layer to be beefier than usual (Steve's complaint to his wife). The bottom slice of bread is the digestive, a positive statement that should leave the complaint recipient with motivation to help us. When our complaint requires the recipient to go out of his or her way to resolve it, we have to thicken the digestive. The more effort our complaint requires from its recipient, the more elaborate or powerful our digestive should be.

A couple of years ago, I was able to get a concert-ticket company with a strict "No refunds under any circumstances!" policy to refund the full price of my tickets, including the service charge, and allow me to purchase tickets for the same concert on a different date. A customer-service supervisor had to use the code for an event's being canceled due to rain to get the refund to go through. This was entering a rainout code for a concert that had not yet even taken place. Clearly, he was doing something unusual for me. My digestive was the reason he was so helpful and went to such trouble. When purchasing the tickets, I looked at the wrong week in my calendar. I purchased the concert tickets for a family member's visit and got tickets for the week *after* they left. I called the company's customer service and asked to speak to a supervisor. As I labored through the meat section of my complaint, the supervisor clucked sympathetically but kept repeating how sorry he was their policies were so firm.

I knew it would come down to the digestive. I headed into the final stretch of my complaint exposition by openly admitting my mistake (choosing the wrong date). I then explained in simple and honest terms how special my family member's visit was and how much it would mean for me to attend the concert with him. Yes, it was my error, but, boy, would it mean a lot to me to have it corrected. Luckily, the customer-service representative handling my call was understanding and sympathetic. He insisted he would not have granted the same request to anyone else, as their policies were strict (albeit clearly not as strict as advertised), but he understood my predicament and would see what he could do to help.

What had changed his mind was my digestive. I wanted the supervisor to see my perspective, and the digestive was designed with that in mind. The message my digestive conveyed was that my complaint was not really about a mistake in dates but about being able to share a meaningful experience with a close family member visiting from afar. What motivated the supervisor to help me was my claim of special circumstances that emphasized family bonds and rare opportunities. Of course, telling the truth and being nice about it went a long way too.

Scooby-Doo and the Case of the Haunted Mailbox

A few years ago, I found myself in another predicament of special circumstances, and as well constructed as my complaint sandwiches usually were, coming up with one for this situation stumped me for quite a while.

I was working with a family in which the six-year-old daughter was obsessed with the film *Scooby-Doo.* It had nothing to do with their psychological issues, but the family had seen the film together, and their dialogue was rife with references from the movie. Being a *Scooby-Doo* novice, I decided to do my homework and prioritized the film in my Netflix account. I had not been a member for long and so the film was sent right away. It never arrived. I let Netflix know that *Scooby-Doo* had gone missing. They promptly sent another copy. That one too did not arrive. Now the situation was becoming strange if not slightly awkward. Still, the fault was not mine, so I let them know the second copy of *Scooby-Doo* was also missing in action. Netflix sent a third copy. Thankfully and much to my relief, it arrived safely. I watched the DVD a few days later and sent it back to Netflix right away. They never got it. They promptly sent me an e-mail notifying me my account was frozen. Now it was more than slightly awkward, it was downright embarrassing. Not to mention weird. The entire situation was beginning to sound like a typical episode of *Scooby-Doo.*

Still, I had done nothing wrong, so I decided to complain about the freezing of my young and mostly unexplored Netflix account. I realized I had something of a "reasonable doubt" problem. One doesn't have to be a mathematician to know the likelihood of the same film getting lost in the mail three times was exceedingly small. I realized the only alternative explanation Netflix could consider was that I was exploiting the company's fair mailing policies to hoard *Scooby-Doo* DVDs for nefarious purposes.

The rare event had actually happened, but how could I possibly get Netflix to believe me?

The complaint sandwich refers to the structure of the complaint, not to its content. Much as ear-openers and digestives can assure a more receptive audience for our complaints, it is also possible to make the complaint recipient (be it a store clerk, customer-service professional, or spouse) more likely to believe our claims and more likely to help us as a result. Several studies have examined which factors make people likely to believe some statements more than others. As we might expect, truth is not always objective, especially when dealing with complaints, perceptions, and missing Netflix movies.

Factors Affecting Our Perceptions of Truth

One of the most consistent findings in the "truth" literature is that statements that are more familiar to us are judged more truthful. When we hear a statement several times, we believe it more than statements we've heard only once. This phenomenon operates unconsciously and is especially strong when there is a sleeper effect—a delay between the first and second exposures to the statement. In one experiment titled Famous Overnight, subjects read a list of nonfamous names, including the fictitious name Sebastian Weisdorf. Then, twenty-four hours later, they were given a second list of names and asked to point out which were famous people. Compared to other fictitious and nonfamous names, Sebastian Weisdorf was thought to be a famous person far more often than names subjects had not previously been exposed to. The subjects recognized the name Sebastian Weisdorf but misinterpreted or misremembered where they had seen it before.

In writing to my management company, I was fortunate to be one of the last people in my building to complain (because I had previously assumed that doing so would be pointless). But my delay ensured that my claims of the noise being intolerable and my standard of living having taken a real hit had already been established by the many earlier calls and letters. Therefore, the person reading my letter could focus on my request, rather than on evaluating the merits of the basic facts.

Another research finding is that people tend to infer that an opinion they have heard several times is held by many. This remains true even when their familiarity is based solely on the repeated statements of *one* person. Complaining by sending several letters that are spaced out over time may be an effective way of changing someone's mind about the merits of our arguments.

Another factor that can affect our unconscious perception of truth is *perceptual fluency:* we tend to believe that which is more pleasing to the eye. So in written complaints, neatness, handwriting legibility, and the aesthetic appearance of the complaint on the page can affect whether our statements are taken as factual. In one study, subjects faced a computer screen and read statements about world geography, half of which were false and half of which were true. Statements written in colors that were easy to read because they contrasted well with the white background, such as dark blue, were judged to be truer than the same statements written in harder-to-read colors, such as yellow.

Findings about perceptual fluency and judgments of truth are disappointing news for those of us who favor emoticons or colorful animations at the bottom of our online correspondences. Sad as it might be, we should avoid concluding our riveting, compelling, and heartfelt demands for justice and restitution with smiley faces blowing raspberries or animated laughing panda bears.

A bizarre example of how perceptual fluency affects our perceptions of truth is rhyme. As it turns out, we love rhyme. We love rhyme so much that we tend to judge rhyming statements as truer than similar but modified versions of the statement that do not rhyme. For example, people judged the statement "What sobriety conceals, alcohol reveals" to be significantly more accurate than the statement "What sobriety conceals, alcohol unmasks" despite their exact same sentiment. Similarly, "Caution and measure will win you treasure" was judged to be truer than "Caution and measure will win you riches," and "Life is mostly strife" was considered more accurate then "Life is mostly struggle."

Johnnie Cochran used the bloody glove in the O. J. Simpson murder trial in just this way when stating to the jury, "If it doesn't fit, you must acquit." Had he presented the same evidence but said, "If he can't even get the thing on, he couldn't have worn it that night," O.J. might never have walked free.

This is not to suggest we handle our Netflix complaints by composing rap songs over the phone or reciting sonnets about the unreliability of the post office. But our tone and the cadence of our voice do impact how our complaints are received. When we complain, speaking plainly, clearly, and simply betters our chances of success.

Lastly, if we have obvious culpability in our complaint, we should admit so up front. Coming clean about our obvious mistakes or errors prevents us from appearing as though we're trying to hide them. We usually made a global judgment about whether someone is being honest with us. If we catch someone in a lie or an omission, we automatically suspect anything else he or she says. Confessing to obvious errors on our part (such as ordering concert tickets for the wrong dates) conveys the kind of honesty that makes our other claims more believable.

In my rift with Netflix, I had no culpability to admit to. But I could certainly admit that three copies of the same movie getting lost in the mail was indeed unusual. Doing so would convey to Netflix I was trying to be fair and realistic and should make it easier for them to believe the missing *Scooby-Doo* flicks were not a result of dishonesty on my part.

A *Scooby-Doo* Stakeout

Knowing that familiarity increased our perceptions of truth gave me an idea about how to resolve my Netflix dilemma. I knew I was not the only person whose DVDs got lost in the mail. Whatever steps people most commonly took in those situations would be the ones

Netflix would consider most reasonable. But what did people do in that situation?

The next day I staked out my mail carrier in the lobby of my building. Thirty minutes later he finally rolled in the mail cart. I pretended I had just come out of the elevator and nodded hello. "A couple of Netflix movies got lost in the mail," I explained casually. I then decided it would be more productive to come clean: "Maybe more like three."

The mail carrier nodded knowingly as if he'd heard this problem before and said, "You need to go to the local branch and fill out a complaint form for lost mail. Then you send a copy to Netflix with your letter." It was exactly the information I needed!

I thanked my mail carrier for the tip and went straight over to the post office. I sent a copy of the form to Netflix along with my complaint letter requesting my account be restored. I began by expressing my shared dismay at their *Scooby-Doo* losses. I explained that I had already taken strong action and filed a report with my local post office. I decided against adding rhymes since "I'm just as sad as you, for the loss of *Scooby-Doo*" was the best I had. Clearly, I was no Johnnie Cochran. I ended the letter by requesting my account be unfrozen and threw in a quick digestive that expressed my looking forward to enjoying a relationship with Netflix for years to come. My account was restored three days later.

The familiarity principle comes in handy in a variety of ways. For example, reading customer reviews of products online can tell us whether the problems we've encountered are unique to us or common. If we are not the only ones who struggled to collapse our new "one hand fold" baby carriage with only one hand, that would be the best argument to use when trying to return it. If, however, customer reviews online are glowing and feature pictures of smiling mothers folding their carriage with one hand while juggling twins and their purse in the other, we might conclude our complaint was rare, in which case we should beef up our digestive.

Eliciting Help from Strangers

Although our complaints are often demands for restitution, they are also requests for assistance. We complain about something when we have been unable to rectify the matter ourselves. All complaints, even the most justified or the most personal and intimate, are requests for cooperation or help from another person. Whether we're dealing with anonymous Netflix administrators, harried airline check-in clerks, or scowling customer-service representatives facing a long line of disgruntled customers, what are the best ways to go about eliciting help from strangers?

The study of altruism, helping behavior and kindness, is one of the more advanced fields of social psychology. After decades of research, we know quite a bit about the factors that affect helping behavior, and one of them is mood. Putting someone in a good mood does wonders for their motivation to help. In one early study, Cookies for Kindness, researchers gave out cookies to some students at a college library but not others. An "undercover" research assistant then approached students and asked for help with a research project. The study assumed cookies would help kindness—that people who received a cookie would be in a better mood and that their better mood would lead them to help more often than those who did not get a cookie. Indeed, those were the findings. People who got the cookies helped significantly more often than those who remained cookie-less.

The mood of the complaint recipient is important, but if our newly installed toilet overflows on a weekend and ruins the expensive new tiling in our bathroom, we do not need to dash to the kitchen and bake a batch of Toll House cookies. Sugar is not the only way to put a person (such as a plumber) in a good mood. We have our secret weapon—our smiles.

When we complain in person, the easiest and simplest way to tip a person's mood in our favor is to flash them an authentic smile. (The only way for our smile to be authentic is to master reframing.)

Authentic smiles are also called Duchenne smiles, after Guillaume Duchenne, a French physician who was the first to recognize that true emotional smiles involve our eye and cheek muscles as well as our mouth and lips. Saying *cheese* for the camera only works for the lower half of our face as it moves our lips and cheeks, but it does not make our eyes create crow's-feet. As far as authentic smiles are concerned, nothing says happiness more than deep crow's-feet. Without them our smiles look posed, forced, or tense.

How powerful is an authentic smile? One recent study demonstrated that kids who smiled more authentically in their childhood photographs, and college students who smiled more authentically in their yearbook photos (as measured by the intensity of crow's-feet around their eyes), were all less likely to divorce as adults than kids and college students whose smiles had less intense crow's-feet.

Duchenne smiles are contagious, even more so than yawning (or complaining), because people have automatic responses to Duchenne smiles—they give authentic Duchenne smiles back. Silly as it might sound, it actually works like magic. Getting people to smile authentically immediately puts them in a more receptive mood to hear our complaint. While we might not have cookies on us all the time, we always have our smiles.

Of course, we might require an emotion-regulation maneuver or two to be able to deliver both an authentic Duchenne smile and an effective complaint. Duchenne smiles are such a powerful social force that they are definitely worth practicing. We can practice both reframing and authentic smiling in many everyday situations, with store clerks, bus drivers, or delivery persons. For more advanced smile practice, post-office tellers, subway-booth attendants, or, if we're feeling especially adventurous, the photographer at the DMV. Remember, the only way we can be sure we gave an authentic smile is if we elicit one in return. No crow's-feet, no cigar.

Perhaps the most powerful technique to elicit help from the recipients of our complaint is simply to understand their perspective. Putting ourselves in the frame of mind of the recipient can help alert us to how our complaint might be received and whether any tweaks might be required. One way to do this is to imagine we are the complaint recipient and envision what it's like to spend our day reading letters of complaint—angry ones, incomprehensible ones, justified or rambling ones. Once we have the feel of the situation, we can read our complaint aloud and imagine how it might sound to its recipient. If listening to it does not make us feel compelled to respond positively, it probably won't compel the recipient to do so either. A quick round of fixes can make all the difference in eliciting assistance from the person to whom we plan to complain.

Reading our complaints aloud is generally a wise thing to do for other reasons as well. When we read aloud, we use a different part of our brains than we do when reading silently (our auditory comprehension as opposed to our visual comprehension). *Hearing* our complaints makes it much easier for us to catch accusatory wording, sarcasm, or a tone that sounded perfectly fine in our heads when we wrote it but actually comes across as too hostile. Reading aloud is also one of the most surefire ways of catching typos (which can interfere with the perceptual fluency of the letter).

Lastly, we must be specific about what we are asking for when we complain. Do we want a refund, a coupon, an apology, a hug and a kiss, some other benefit? We should always try to specify what might be a reasonable resolution for us.

Expressing our complaints politely, clearly, concisely, and without emotional involvement, smiling and saying "Hello" and "Thank you," and using the complaint sandwich should put the person to whom we are complaining in as favorable a mood and mind-set as possible. Not doing so could mean the difference between effective complaining and pointless frustration.

Complaint-Sandwich Condiments

We should insert the content of our complaint within the complaint sandwich. But how we present that content is of no less importance. Several additional factors affect how our complaints are received and handled, and consequently we must keep in mind a few more considerations to make our complaints more effective. Condiments such as the ideal letter length, the degree of its specificity, which kinds of details matter, and other helpful tips are presented in the notes to this chapter. However, most of the complaint-sandwich condiments are more relevant to consumer complaints than to dissatisfactions in our personal or work lives.

Personal complaints are delicate, as our relationships can be greatly impacted by them. When it comes to our loved ones, effective complaining means not only getting our complaint heard and handled, but also preserving bonds of friendship and love. Complaining effectively can enhance our relationships and strengthen them for the long term.

Chapter Six
The Art of Squeaking to Loved Ones

Honey, I complain about your performance all the time, and you don't care. Sometimes you don't even wake up.

—Peggy Bundy to Al Bundy,
Married ... with Children (1987)

Delays in construction meant that almost two years passed before tenants moved into the building that now stood only twenty feet from my bedroom window. I watched as a middle-aged couple moved onto the floor parallel to mine, guaranteeing an unavoidably intimate acquaintanceship. It was my first experience with a classic New York City phenomenon—strangers in adjacent buildings living their lives in full picture-window view of one another. I became an immediate and ardent believer in blinds and curtains. Alas, my new neighbors did not share my faith in window treatments. Nor did they believe in wearing clothing around the apartment as I rarely saw them in anything but underwear. Unfortunately, more often than not their newly installed track lighting illuminated every fruit in their loom.

However, what left an even greater impression on me was that my new neighbors seemed to have a wonderful relationship. Whenever I caught glimpses of them, they were cooking together, cuddling on the couch while watching television, or laughing with one another. I never once heard them argue or saw a moment of obvious tension.

Of course, I could not know such a thing for certain but after twenty years practicing couple therapy, when a couple walks into my office (or parades around in their bloomers with their blinds up), I can often tell within minutes if their marriage (or relationship) has a future. My conclusions have little to do with the severity of the problems the couple presents. Whether their issue is severe miscommunication, a torrid affair, or wet towels left brazenly on the bathroom floor, none of it has any relevance to their prognosis as a couple. It is rarely *what* couples argue or complain about that matters; rather, *how* they argue, *how* they complain, that tells me the quality of their couplehood and the potential longevity of their relationship.

Psychologists are usually loath to make predictions about human behavior because we typically cannot do so with any kind of accuracy. But in study after study, marriage researchers predicted which couples would remain together and which would split up, with accuracies of over 90 percent! While researchers use a specific set of tools and markers to make their predictions, experienced couple therapists combine scientific findings with clinical observations and gut intuitions to reach remarkably similar conclusions. What gives both researchers and couple therapists these insights into a couple's future is how they handle their complaints to one another; and one of the places in which couples express the most complaints to one another is in their first couple-therapy session—the consultation.

The consultation often presents a microcosm of how couples handle complaints. With both people airing their relationship dissatisfactions, the hour easily becomes a petri dish for marital complaints, chock-full of poisonous accusations, festering resentments, and mushrooming colonies of hurt feelings. Even for the least combative of couples, discussing meaningful complaints can become fertile ground for miscommunication and faulty assumptions. None of us is perfect when it comes to presenting our complaints to our spouse or, for that matter, when it comes to responding to their complaints to us. The majority of the mistakes we make when discussing relationship complaints with our partner are mild and leave no lasting impact. But some missteps result in huge wounds that, if repeated over time, can become deadly, matrimonially speaking.

John M. Gottman, the world's leading researcher on couples and marriage, describes four specific errors couples make when discussing complaints that are so toxic, they can spell doom for the relationship. He calls these couple-complaining errors the Four Horsemen of the Apocalypse. I believe a fifth couple-complaining error can be equally dangerous and will get to it later in the chapter. The outcome of our marital fates is determined not by the mere existence of these errors but by the extent to which they dominate our discussions of complaints.

All couples make some of these errors some of the time. But every so often, I encounter a couple whose communication style encompasses everything a couple can possibly do wrong when airing their grievances. The toxicity of their interactions erupts quickly, and with such hostility that the viciousness of their exchanges is often painful to watch.

Complaining Scenes from a Bad Marriage

I felt the tension radiating between Miral and Chad the second I stepped into the waiting room to meet them. The rigidity of their postures, the looks in their eyes, and the way they white-knuckled their iced Frappuccinos made a shiver go down my spine. Miral rose to greet me first, leaving her Frappuccino on the side table. Chad, still holding his, shook my hand next and took a step toward my office. Miral whipped around and hissed at him, "Aren't you going to bring my Frappuccino? I mean, really—selfish much?" Miral glanced at me and rolled her eyes to apologize for her husband's "obvious" lack of chivalry. She gave Chad another glare and stomped off to my office. Chad mumbled a quick "Sorry!" and hurried after her, an iced Frappuccino in each hand.

I reached my office just in time to see Miral grab her Frappuccino out of Chad's hand, sit in the center of the couch, and take a noisy sip. Chad moved two small side cushions between him and Miral and sat down between them and the edge of the couch. Miral promptly gave Chad a disapproving glance and tossed the two cushions aside. One of them landed on the floor. Chad vaulted forward to pick it up, then sat back down with the pillow on his lap. He turned away from Miral and sighed. The tension in the room was already stifling and we hadn't even started yet. I was pretty close to sighing myself.

I wanted to see if I could lighten the mood and give them a chance to shake off their nerves. "A little skirmish with the pillows?" I joked as I sat down across from them. Chad looked down embarrassed. Miral whipped around to him. "Why do you do that, Chad? Why do you always put up these barricades? You even do it with the pillows in bed!"

"So? You hog the blankets!"

Miral's eyes almost popped out of her head. "Are you calling me a pig?!"

"What? No! Why do you always take things the worst way possible?"

"Why? Because you called me a pig!"

I raised my hand to stop them. They could have spent the entire session arguing just as uselessly. I was already hearing the whinny of the first two Horsemen and we were barely five minutes in.

We all voice complaints to our partners, and at times we criticize them as well. But a crucial difference separates a complaint from a criticism. Complaints focus on specific behaviors in specific situations. Criticisms are generalized accusations about the other person's character; they ascribe blame that goes beyond the specific incident and assume negative motivations that go beyond it as well. Criticism is usually experienced by the recipient as a much more substantial emotional assault than a mere specific and encapsulated complaint. Miral and Chad had committed couple-complaining error number one—expressing complaints as criticisms—while still in the waiting room.

Miral's "Aren't you going to bring my Frappuccino?" was a complaint. However, "I mean, really—selfish much?" was a criticism, one wrapped in sarcasm for extra impact.

Doing it in front of me so unnecessarily gave the criticism added severity in my eyes, as did Miral's eye-rolling, huffing, and stomping. Miral's "Why do you always put up these barricades?" was also a criticism because of the generalization implied by words such as *always* and *never.* Such words can magically turn any valid complaint into a provocative and ineffective criticism.

Complaints are not considered toxic in and of themselves (although as we discussed in chapter 4, overdosing on them can be a real concern). Our complaints communicate requests to our partner, course corrections when circumstances require them. Yes, it usually stings when we receive a complaint from our partner, but when we manage complaints effectively as a couple, they do our relationships more good than harm. Criticisms, however, are never constructive. Every couple criticizes one another on occasion, but the question is how frequent the criticizing becomes. Pervasive criticism has been found to be extremely damaging both to marital satisfaction as well as relationship longevity.

The problem with Gottman's Four Horsemen is they tend to travel as a pack. When one appears, the others are soon to follow. Criticism, the First Horseman, often leads to the Second—defensiveness. Most of us get defensive when criticisms, global accusations, and character smears are hurled at us. Once we've entered a back-and-forth volley of criticism and defensiveness, our actual complaint becomes marginalized, and the result can only be a hurtful and unproductive argument.

Chad responded to Miral with defensiveness and criticisms of his own. His "Why do you always take things the worst way possible?" was a defensive criticism (note the *always*) in that he ignored Miral's complaint entirely and shifted the blame back onto her.

I'd already seen Miral on the offensive, so I decided to ask Chad what brought them to therapy to see if Chad would do the same. He did not. After giving me a brief history of their five-year marriage, he said, "I guess we're here because we fight a lot. Maybe I'm not always the most considerate husband. But I work really long hours so sometimes when I get home and I have to start making dinner, I'm not in the mood to ask Miral about her day or see how she's doing. And then she gets upset and laces into me from the living room and ... I try to be there for her and I think I am most of the time, but sometimes she sounds so angry and it's just too much. I guess I just tune out or something. I can't help it ..." Chad trailed off and hung his head.

I was about to ask Miral for her thoughts but she saved me the trouble. "Is that what you think the problem is?" she asked Chad with incredulity. "That you don't ask me about my day? What are you, stupid? You don't ask me about anything! You don't talk to me at all! You're always too busy, or you're on your BlackBerry or you're too tired. It's always about you, your needs, what Chad wants. It's never about me, ever! You are just so selfish!" Chad turned even farther away.

"I'm your wife!" Miral shouted at the back of his neck. "I'm supposed to be the most important thing in your life, the person you cherish! Do you remember that from our wedding vows, Chad? To love and to cherish! You promised me that! Do you call this love? Do you call this cherishing? You should be so ashamed!"

Chad said nothing. Miral turned to me, tears in her eyes. "He is so self-centered, it's just disgusting!"

Much as I sympathized with Miral's distress, her criticisms toward Chad were extremely harsh. Even more noteworthy, Chad had not objected to them even once.

"Chad, would you like to respond to your wife?" I asked.

Chad shook his head. "I have nothing to say."

Chad's silence in the face of Miral's all-out assault concerned me greatly. Withdrawal and disengagement represent Gottman's Third Horseman. When I see unresponsiveness in a consultation session, it can mean that the disengaged person is actively considering whether to leave the relationship. People often mull over divorce or separation for years before voicing it to their partner. In some cases, couples come to therapy when one of them, unbeknownst to the other, has already begun this mental exit. If that person feels emotionally prepared to leave, it can be extremely difficult to pull the person back from the brink. Overcomplaining to the point that our partners shut down is a seriously ineffective way of stating our dissatisfactions and can place our entire relationships at risk.

If our spouse turns away as we complain, seems disengaged or withdrawn, the most effective thing we can do is stop complaining. Until our partner has the space and time to regroup, nothing further we say will be effective. Frustrating as it is, we should say something like "You seem a little quiet or overwhelmed. I'm willing to take a break if we can continue talking later."

Much as Tommy became overwhelmed and shut down by the sheer volume of complaints he was fielding from his father, Chad was following a similar path. But unlike Tommy, Chad was free to leave whenever he chose. I needed him to communicate to Miral how desperate he felt.

I leaned forward in my seat. "Chad, can I ask you to turn to Miral?" Chad reluctantly turned to her. "Miral said you were selfish and disgusting. I'm sure that wasn't easy for you to hear." Chad shook his head. "Perhaps you can tell her exactly how you feel. She needs to understand why you shut down. Otherwise, she can only conclude it's because you don't care. And I don't think that's correct, is it?" Chad shook his head again. "So, tell her now. Look at her and tell her how you feel right now."

Chad took a deep breath. His lower lip began to tremble. "I feel like crap!" Chad finally exclaimed, his face crumpling into tears. "You make me feel like I'm failing you all the time, like I'm a horrible person. You hate my friends. You hate my family. You hate everything about me! You're angry with me all the time, all the time! You criticize everything about me! You make me feel like such a loser … I can't take it!" Chad covered his face and began to sob.

Miral responded to her husband's tears by stiffening in her seat. Her face quickly registered anger and resentment. She responded to every shudder of Chad's shoulders as though he were shooting her with bullets of wrongful blame. Her face showed no sign of concern or compassion. Meanwhile, Chad could not stop sobbing. The poor man appeared truly distraught. I began to worry for him. Remember, I had just met them. I nodded at Miral, urging her to do something about her husband's distress. She did. She recoiled.

"Look at him crying!" she said to me with disgust. She then turned to Chad, who was still sobbing. "Look at you," she spat. "You're a grown man! You're a professional! How can you be such a weak, pathetic human being? I am so ashamed of you right now, Chad! I am just so embarrassed by you!"

Miral's shocking cruelty in the face of Chad's breakdown was extremely disturbing. It was even more distressing to think about how much worse things probably were when they were home. Couples are typically on good behavior when they come to therapy, at least comparatively speaking. When interactions look bad in the therapy office, it is usually safe to assume they get far worse in the privacy of the home. I quickly raised my hand to shut off Miral's tirade before it did more damage. She took the hint and stopped speaking. She gave Chad another glare, sat back, folded her arms, and took another sip from her Frappuccino.

Gottman's Fourth Horseman—to me, the most destructive of them all—is having contempt for our partner, lacking basic human compassion. If the deep emotional distress of one member of the couple leaves the other member cold, chances are they will be unable to bridge the gap of partnership and collaboration necessary for the relationship's long-term viability. The only reason I was not certain Chad would leave Miral was that he hadn't already done so. He had been suffering in the relationship for a long time, yet here he was in therapy instead of at his lawyer's office.

Empathy and compassion were so lacking between Miral and Chad, I felt it was the first thing I had to introduce into the session. I leaned forward in my chair and said softly, "Chad, I want to say some things to you. It's okay to cry while I'm speaking. In fact, you've been feeling bad for a very long time. That's why you're hurting so much. But no one can keep that much pain inside without its erupting at some point. So I'm glad you're letting some of it out now. I can tell there's a lot there." Chad nodded, grabbed a tissue, and blew his nose. But Chad was not the only one hurting.

Miral was certainly extremely critical and hurtful to Chad. But she felt just as rejected, unwanted, and unvalued by Chad as he did by her. Indeed, Miral's self-esteem was probably doing no better than Chad's. We all have moments of deep frustration in which anger causes us to lose touch with our compassion for a loved one. However, if we want to preserve our relationships, we have to engage our emotion-regulation strategies to cool our heads and refill our hearts with empathy. We should never allow cold anger to fester without employing an emotion-regulation strategy such as empathy to bring our anger down to manageable levels.

The Fifth Horseman of Marital Apocalypse

I feared Chad was close to leaving Miral, but she clearly did not realize it. He had been signaling his exit by silences and withdrawing, but she was as deaf to his cues as she was blind to his distress. Her own emotional and psychological pain distracted her from seeing Chad's inner torment. Being blind to our spouse's anguish and deaf to critically important complaints is the fifth complaining error couples make, and I believe it deserves an apocalyptic horse of its own.

Ralph and Sonya, another couple I once treated, came to therapy to deal with disputes over finances. Ralph had left his corporate job to begin a new business. He worked from home to keep expenses down but the venture was doing poorly nonetheless. That financial burden placed a huge stress on their marriage, causing frequent arguments about money. Ralph felt resentful that Sonya was critical of him at a time when his self-esteem was low. Sonya, who had not been in favor of Ralph's leaving his job, was also concerned about their finances. But she was even more upset that Ralph had gained thirty pounds in the last year and had completely neglected their sex life.

After a couple of sessions, I understood that Sonya was in far greater distress than Ralph seemed to realize. He seemed to want to discuss only their financial disagreements. Whenever Sonya brought up their lack of intimacy, Ralph heard it as another complaint about their current financial stressors and his decision to leave his job. Sonya tried repeatedly to get back to the topic, but Ralph just could not hear her. By the middle of the second session, she seemed to stop trying.

I was concerned their marriage was drifting into dangerous waters. It was important Ralph not ignore Sonya's complaint when next she voiced it. I steered the discussion away from finances and brought up the intimacy issue myself. It allowed Sonya another chance at her complaint.

"I get home and you're still in pajamas in front of the computer screen," she said. "At least you shower before you go to sleep, but … do you realize you bring a pint of ice cream to bed with you almost every night?"

Ralph immediately stiffened. "Sonya, you know what I'm going through with my business right now. Why can't you be more supportive? I'm trying my best to get this company off the ground and you're counting my calories? Ever since I left the firm, all you do is criticize me!"

"But that's not what I'm saying!"

"You keep harping on anything I do that gives me a little comfort. So I eat some ice cream in bed, why is that so terrible?"

"Because, Ralph," I interrupted, "ice cream is not what Sonya's been asking you to eat in bed."

Stunned silence filled the room. Sonya turned red. Then she snorted with laughter. Ralph got much redder but he chuckled as well. Yes, I made the point *extremely* crudely. However, once an issue has been ignored for too long, subtlety, tact, and even my laying things out often do not work. Ralph heard what Sonya was saying, he was not denying their sex life was bad; he was denying the *emotional importance* of their sex life's being bad.

Breaking emotional denial can be challenging. One has to convey the message in as dramatic and memorable a manner as possible.

Being crass and vulgar with a couple who were both far from crass and vulgar themselves was the best way to make my message one Ralph could not ignore. Of course, once I had his full attention, I conveyed in politer terms that Sonya's desire for intimacy and sex was as important as his desire for comfort foods. I suggested if she had more of the former, she would allow him more of the latter. I also mentioned that having a better sex life would provide them both with a nice boost to their marital satisfaction as well as their individual self-esteems.

Although some stereotypes suggest men complain about marital sex lives more than women do, in my experience there is no difference. Women are just as likely to complain about sex as men are, and men are just as likely to ignore such complaints as their wives are. Complaints about sex are equally common in gay and lesbian couples. When our partner complains about sexual dissatisfaction, awkwardness or embarrassment has to be expected (in addition to the defensiveness that comes with receiving a complaint). Managing sexual complaints is always emotionally uncomfortable, and that prompts many of us to shunt them aside.

However, few of us can voice repeated complaints such as Sonya's and not feel rejected or even unattractive to our partner when they are constantly ignored. When our partner expresses a complaint about our sex lives, we should man up (or woman up), put our discomfort aside, and listen with an open mind. More often than not, we have sexual dissatisfactions of our own that need to be voiced, and doing so can make the discussion much more productive for each member of the couple.

Effective Complaining as a Couplehood Enhancer

While Miral and Chad encapsulate everything couples can do wrong when they discuss complaints, some couples do everything right. Their discussion of complaints demonstrates the behaviors and communication styles that are associated with *increased* long-term marital satisfaction. These *relationship enhancers* are evident in how members of the couple voice complaints to one another as well as in how they respond to complaints from their spouse. Relationship enhancers are skill sets any couple can acquire if they work hard enough at them. I've met numerous couples who were blessed in their natural and superior complaint-handling skills, but perhaps none more so than Eden and Harvey.

I first met Eden and Harvey only months after opening my private practice. I had already acquired five years of specialized training in couple therapy, but I was still new to working without supervision and flying solo. Harvey and Eden were in their midthirties at the time. Both of them were dressed in colorful tie-dyed T-shirts, and Eden's showed that she was six months pregnant with their first child. Harvey was the first to greet me in the waiting room. He introduced Eden, then himself, then patted Eden's belly and said, "And this is Jonathan." He smiled, bent down, and whispered to his wife's pregnant belly, "Don't worry, Mommy and Daddy love each other, we're just here for a tune-up." Eden kissed Harvey on the cheek, took his hand, and they walked down the hall to my office. I loved them already.

I asked what kind of help they were seeking as a couple, and in response they did something too few couples do in a consultation session—they turned to face each other. Eden began speaking first. She addressed her comments directly to Harvey. She told him she wanted to discuss a sensitive but pressing issue that seemed to lead to protracted arguments whenever they broached it at home (related to their finances). Harvey looked at Eden the entire time she spoke. When she described the topic, Harvey met her eye and nodded in agreement. That simple act alone spoke volumes about their couplehood.

We teach our children to look people in the eye when spoken to, but when it comes to our romantic relationships, we often fail to do so ourselves. Fully half the couples I see in my practice have little to no eye contact when discussing complaints with one another. We might think of eye contact as a minor issue or a mere nuance, but when discussing our complaints with our partner, this minor nuance can have major implications.

Jeanne Flora of the University of La Verne and Chris Segrin of the University of Arizona measured how long members of a couple gazed at one another as they discussed complaints. They found the longer a husband gazed at his wife when she complained, the higher the marital satisfaction of both members of the couple tended to be. Men's gaze was so crucial because it conveyed an open-mindedness, a willingness to consider what the other person had to say. On the other hand, turning away too frequently (or, like Chad, all the time) conveys a closed-mindedness and a resistance to listening to the other person, which has a significantly negative impact on the entire interaction.

Interestingly, how long a woman gazed at her husband when he complained did not make a difference to the couple's marital satisfaction. On average, women are far better at maintaining eye contact during emotional discussions than men, and they're more practiced at doing so as well. Men's relative discomfort with "relationship" topics means they are less sensitive to their wives' turning away during emotional discussions, and they do not interpret such cues as close-mindedness.

Flora and Segrin also found that when wives took more turns speaking than their husband, the marital satisfaction of both members of the couple was lower than when the couple took turns speaking evenly. Because women have a basic advantage in their comfort and experience with relationship discussions, some men feel flooded or outargued when their wife or girlfriend dominates the discussion lopsidedly. If a man who had maintained good eye contact then begins to look away in the discussion, it may be a good time to let him do some of the talking.

Maintaining eye contact and balanced talk times represents relationship enhancer number one. The good news for couples is that improving these habits is not difficult. This one simple tweak can potentially have an immediate and positive impact on their discussions of complaints, and potentially on their entire relationship. Simply stated, men should look their wife or girlfriend in the eye when listening to a complaint even if it feels difficult or uncomfortable. Women should make sure to share the floor evenly, no matter what the verbal output of their husbands. Women whose male partner insists on speaking in telegraphic sentences and is overly pithy should equal their husband's minimal output. Despite popular wisdom, at times in a woman's life she *should* enter a *pithing match.*

One of the advantages of maintaining eye contact is that it allows us to see if our partner begins to tear up. Eden's eyes began to well up a few minutes into our session, and Harvey quickly passed my "tissue-box test." Most therapists have a tissue box on their coffee or side table, but I have two, one on either side of the couch. Someone usually gets tearful in a consultation session (it is just as likely to be the husband as the wife, and at times it can be both). How members of a couple respond to one another's tears can provide me with vital information. Some spouses immediately lean in toward their partner, put an arm around their shoulder, stroke their knee or neck, or pass them a box of tissues (which is why I make sure each of them has a box handy). All of the above are sufficient to pass the tissue-box test. These responses demonstrate compassion, engagement, basic caring, and the ability to put one's own feelings aside when the partner needs support.

Much as a lack of compassion represents a warning sign for couple longevity, authentic concern and compassion for our partner's emotional distress represents the opposite—the kind of true caring that rises above any dissatisfactions or resentment of the moment. Demonstrating such nurturing instincts, especially during discussions of complaints, represents relationship enhancer number two.

Relationship enhancer number three is to balance out complaint talk with fun and efforts to lighten things up with humor. I made a joke about Miral and Chad's "skirmish with the pillows" to see if they could switch gears even during a tense moment and access a lighter, more playful side of their relationship. Although they could not, many couples can, even in the middle of an argument. I had an opportunity to see if Eden and Harvey had such flexibility when they paused between topics. I did so almost out of necessity, as facing their extraordinarily loud tie-dyed T-shirts for over thirty minutes was beginning to make my head spin with color shock. I wasn't sure what would hit first, the headache or the seizure.

"I couldn't help noticing your T-shirts," I said, as my eyes blinked uncontrollably. Harvey and Eden both brightened immediately and began discussing their love for the Grateful Dead. They had met at one of the group's concerts and still had a large group of "Dead Head" friends they met with regularly. "Actually, we even danced around to the Dead a little last night," Eden confessed.

"We wanted little Jonathan to get used to Mommy and Daddy rocking out," Harvey added. "Plus, we thought it would be a good tension reliever."

"What do you think the tension last night was about?" I asked thoughtfully.

"Coming here, of course," Eden replied, stating the obvious. I nodded sagely, trying to hide that my question had been stupid. As I said, I was just starting out. Even so, I quickly recognized their dancing as a sign of their ability to have fun together. Harvey and Eden found ways to mix their serious complaint talk with lighter moments so that their discussions rarely became too negative.

Fun might seem like a frivolous topic for couple therapy, but having fun, creating light moments, is extremely important for couples. I find myself addressing the issue far more often than I might have expected. When a relationship starts running into trouble, one of the first things couples tend to neglect is having fun together. We conceive of "working on the relationship" as sitting through hours of grueling talks and negotiations about complaints and issues. We quickly forget how important it is to be silly, laugh, play, and frolic with one another. Well, perhaps frolicking per se isn't for everyone, but certainly laughing, playing, and even silliness should be.

Being able to have fun together and make each other laugh is a significant relationship enhancer. Couples who exhibit moments of lightness even as they share their complaints with one another, especially in a therapy session, are usually able to navigate even stormier waters when they run into them. People are always nervous when starting couple therapy, and anxiety is fertile ground for humor, especially for a couple for whom joking around is an established part of their togetherness repertoire.

For example, a few years ago, an attractive young couple in their late twenties came for a consultation. I knew little about them and so I tossed them my usual opening question, "Tell me what brings you to couple therapy."

The husband took a deep breath, slapped his hand down on his wife's knee, and announced with utmost seriousness, "Well, doc, she's very gassy!"

His poor wife turned a deep shade of red and quickly elbowed her husband in the ribs. But she was hysterically laughing as she did it. "Just kidding!" the husband quickly reassured me as he and his wife laughed. "He always cracks jokes when he gets nervous," the wife added, then gave her husband another playful elbow in the ribs for good measure. We enjoyed the moment and quickly turned to discussing serious matters.

A number of studies have investigated the use of humor in couples and its relation to long-term couple satisfaction, but the results are not yet conclusive. There are many types of humor (for example, self-effacing versus aggressive), and other aspects, such as whether the joke is actually funny, well timed, or appropriate, play a crucial role as well. The key to successfully using humor to diffuse tense moments is distinguishing when to refrain from doing so. Regardless, couples who laugh together more easily than others are often able to use their humor to create an extra layer of insulation from the stresses of long-term couplehood.

While humor and fun are important, a couple doesn't have to crack jokes to be able to enjoy light and entertaining times together. By the time couples arrive in the therapy office, they've already spent some time and effort working on their issues, usually with insufficient success. Therefore, their dialogue and manner is often strained and tense no matter what the topic of discussion. When I ask such overly serious couples what they do for fun or relaxation, they often blink at me hesitatingly, confused as to what fun could possibly have to do with their problems.

The purpose of having fun together, besides being a huge part of what makes life enjoyable, is specifically to balance out our complaint talk by reminding ourselves of our fundamental friendship with our partner. The stronger a couple's friendship is, the stronger their couplehood is as well. Much as with Eden and Harvey's dancing together on the eve of starting therapy, any couple who share a foundation of strong friendship can use such bonds to balance the stresses of managing complaints when they find themselves in relationship realignment or negotiation. A foundation of strong friendship is one of the more significant prognostic signs for relationship longevity and is relationship enhancer number four.

If we've let friendship and fun take a backseat to life's demands and challenges, we can always take action to remedy the imbalance. Focusing on recapturing our friendship and making time to do so is one of the most important things we can do both for ourselves and for our relationship. If we enjoyed spending time with one another during the early days of our courtship, we can work to reconnect to that aspect of our couplehood. Even with the demands of parenthood and careers, we can still make time to recapture old ways of laughing together.

One of the ways in which we can do so is to engage in a shared and mutual passion such as Harvey and Eden's love of the Grateful Dead. Sharing a mutual passion with our partners serves as an ongoing reminder that we are on the same team, and it cements our sense of partnership and couplehood. The excitement and anticipation of attending our favorite band's concert, crying with joy or sadness when our sports team wins or loses the big game, or booing and yelling at the TV together when our favorite contestant is booted off a show we both love, all unite us in emotional experiences. Sharing strong sentiments together in such ways, be they of disappointment or elation, always provides a bonding experience, and it is a powerful dynamic in balancing our complaint talk and relationship troubles. Therefore, having a mutual passion represents relationship enhancer number five.

I once asked a couple who had been married for forty years what their happiest memory was, and they both responded, "When the '86 Mets won the World Series." After watching thousands of games together over the years, seeing their favorite baseball team achieve the highest honor in the sport had united them more than their wedding day had. Whether we share a devotion to a specific sport or team, a belief in a political candidate, an obsession with daytime soaps, or a weakness for rare-bird watching, having a mutual passion and powerful shared experiences always deepens our bonds of friendship and couplehood and helps inoculate us against the dangers of separation or divorce.

Some couples' mutual passion is each other, in that their sex life remains highly fulfilling and satisfying for both of them, even in times of heightened conflict. The absence of a fulfilling sexual relationship does not necessarily affect a marriage adversely, as plenty of satisfied couples have generally unsatisfying couplings. However, the presence of a passionate sexual relationship can often be a mitigating factor when dealing with stress and conflict.

Detoxifying a Toxic Couple

Miral and Chad enjoyed none of these mitigating factors. As one might have expected, their sex life was in shambles. Both romance and intimacy were practically absent in their relationship at that point (as were my hopes for their treatment). Some couples can become allergic to one another over time, and Miral and Chad were prime examples. Unless they were both willing to devote themselves to change, I could do little to help them. I started out my feedback to them by letting them know I thought their marriage was in deep trouble. I went into some detail and emphasized that at least 95 percent of the work required to fix things would have to be done by them at home.

But I wanted to end on a softer note and I needed to see if I could break through some of their walls and defenses. "Chad, you feel Miral is too critical and harsh, and she is," I began. "And you, Miral," I continued before she could object to my previous statement, "feel Chad is dismissive, cold, and distant, which he is. But which of you is more right than the other has long ceased to matter. From where I'm sitting, you both look equally miserable. Sure, on any given day, one of you might be suffering more than the other, but it's pretty even in the end. You both feel unheard and underappreciated, and you both feel unloved. You're both hurting. Yet the war rages on."

I knew I had their attention. Now I needed them to get on board with the treatment plan, and the only way to do that was to offer them hope. "You have to change almost everything about your communication to one another. You don't have to reinvent it; you just have to go back to the care and caution you displayed when you first started dating. But you do have to decide whether you feel up to doing the work, whether you want it enough." I motioned for them to turn to one another. "Talk together. Try and come to a decision together about how you want to proceed."

I had to direct Chad to maintain eye contact with Miral before he even got a word out. Then, as soon as Miral started speaking, he turned away. I insisted Chad turn back to his wife as she spoke. He was so uncomfortable he ended up overcompensating. The resulting expression on Chad's face was so grim, so over-the-top serious, Miral's lip began to twitch. Then she broke into a giggle.

"I'm not used to him looking at me when I talk!" she insisted, embarrassed.

I pointed at Chad. "Fine, but say that to Chad, not to me."

Miral turned back to Chad. She opened her mouth to speak, snorted, and burst out laughing. Chad could only stay serious for so long. He smiled despite himself. Soon they were both in hysterics. I decided to end the session on this positive note as I wasn't holding my breath for another to come down the pike anytime soon.

They filed for divorce three months later.

It was the best thing that could have happened to either of them. Separating allowed Miral and Chad to start the long healing that both of them would need for their self-esteem to recover fully. Couple complaint errors leave deep emotional and psychological scars. They aren't called the Horsemen of the Apocalypse for nothing.

The Teen Whisperer

Ashley was fifteen when Elliot, her father, found a pack of tiny copper screens in the back pocket of her jeans after a sleepover at the home of her best friend, Donna. Being a child of the seventies, he knew exactly what they were. He planned to confront her over breakfast, but Ashley had an agenda of her own. "Pop, Donna's having a party next weekend, can I go?"

Elliot ignored Ashley's question. He sat down next to her at the breakfast table and asked calmly but firmly, "When did you start smoking weed?"

Ashley eyes opened wide in shock. "What do you mean? I never smoked weed!"

Elliot produced the screens from his pocket and held them aloft as though he were showing a jury Exhibit A.

Ashley was unfazed. "What's that?"

"They were in your jeans, you tell me!" Elliot demanded.

"You went through my jeans?" Ashley's face crumpled into tears. "You can't go through my clothes like that! And I've never seen those things before. Someone must have put them there by mistake!"

"Oh, come on!" Elliot sputtered.

"We all have the same jeans!" Ashley protested.

"You're grounded until you start telling me the truth. And hand over your cell phone. Until you tell me what's going on, there'll be no phone, no TV, no iPod, no computer. So you'd better start talking!"

"Fine!" Ashley screamed. "I hate you! Is that enough talking for you? I hate you!" She stormed out of the kitchen, went to her room, and slammed the door.

As Elliot concluded in our next session, "I guess it didn't go so well."

Indeed, it did not. Elliot's efforts continued with his cornering his daughter in her bedroom later that morning, along with her other father, Elliot's life partner, Mitch. Both men spoke calmly and reasonably, but Ashley kept to grunts and monosyllabic words, both of which were expressed with exclamation points. Their "conversation" lasted twenty minutes. Not surprisingly, little came of it.

The Parent-Teen Demand/Withdraw Merry-go-round

Teenagers come with two built-in, factory-installed defense mechanisms to ward off complaining parents. They either explode in a rage or glaze over with emotional glaucoma. Both responses are hard to miss, and they both signal the same thing for parents: our conversation has derailed and it is no longer on an effective track. The most productive thing we can do in that moment is to stop complaining.

The challenge for parents with teens is to make our complaints effective enough for our teenager to hear them in their entirety before their glazing or raging response is triggered.

Most parents respond to raging teens by attempting to have the exact same conversation when their teen is calmer. Of course, the teen begins raging again as soon as the discussion starts. We respond to glazing teens by expressing our complaint more frequently and more persistently but, alas, no differently. Both of these strategies only make adolescents withdraw further. The more we approach them with our complaints and concerns, the less responsive they become as a result. That makes us try even harder, which in turn makes them even less communicative. Most parents are familiar with this vicious cycle but nonetheless fall into its trap regularly.

Repeatedly complaining to, pestering, blaming, or nagging our teenagers while they make efforts to avoid the discussions and ignore our nagging is called demand/withdraw communication, and it is the most common complaining error we make as parents. Demand/withdraw styles of communication are not limited to parent-teen interactions as they can be seen in many kinds of relationships. But in all of them, their presence renders the interactions not only pointless, but destructive and damaging as well. It harms both the individuals involved and, more important, their relationship.

A broad body of research has demonstrated that parent-adolescent conflict is associated with relatively poor adolescent self-esteem. An even broader body of research shows that adolescents with low self-esteem have more risk-oriented behaviors and higher incidence of drug and alcohol use. But now studies are finding *direct* associations between demand/withdraw communication and teen substance abuse.

In 2004, John Caughlin of the University of Illinois at Urbana-Champaign and Rachel Malis of Northwestern University explored the demand/withdraw dynamic among parents and teens and its relationship to both self-esteem and drug and alcohol use. They asked parent-teen dyads to discuss topics of importance both to the teen and to the parents. They found that parents and teens whose discussions were characterized by frequent demand/withdraw dynamics *both* had lower general self-esteem than parents and teens for whom demand/withdraw featured less prominently. Thus parents and teens paid a similar price for ineffective interactions around complaints as expressed by poorer emotional well-being.

In addition, teens who participated in frequent demand/ withdraw interactions with their parents were found to be significantly more likely to use drugs and alcohol than teens whose interactions with parents involved less demand/ withdraw communication (see chapter notes for parent resources). The implication for parents such as Elliot and Mitch is even more complicated. Once the pattern of demand/withdraw communication is established, it can be difficult to change. Each party to the dynamic assumes its position automatically, often before the discussion even starts. Teens are ready to withdraw at the first sign that an innocent chat has an "agenda," and parents are ready to begin an ill-advised pursuit at the first sign of their teen's withdrawal.

Getting Off the Demand/Withdraw Merry-go-round

Despite the obvious ineffectiveness of the demand/withdraw complaining style, the vast majority of us fall victim to its strong current at some point on one side of the interaction or the other. What makes the demand/withdraw dynamic so insidious is that most of us can tell when we're in it. We know our conversation has become futile, but we forge ahead with it regardless. Many of us simply don't know what else to do when it happens. As Elliot explained, "If she's not going to respond, at least maybe she'll think of what I said later." Such parental false hopes can persist despite all evidence to the contrary. Once we've been swept up into a demand/withdraw war of attrition with our teenagers, how do we end it and get back to a productive dialogue? Another finding from the 2004 study hinted at possible resolutions. The researchers found that when teenagers wanted to discuss topics that were important to them, parents often considered those topics less of a priority and withdrew from these conversations, much as their teens withdrew when the topic was important to the parent. In other words, *demand/withdraw between parents and teens often works both ways.* One of the first changes we can make as parents is to avoid dismissing or minimizing topics that are important to our teens. If we want our teens to consider our priorities, we have to be equally aware of theirs.

When Elliot ignored Ashley's request about her friend Donna's party, he conveyed to her that refusing to engage in a discussion was acceptable behavior. Instead, he should have welcomed Ashley's request to discuss the party as it would have provided the perfect segue into a discussion of drugs and alcohol. Discussing topics that are less urgent to us but of great importance to our teens often provides us with entrées into conversations that are otherwise tricky to initiate. One of the primary things we can do to avoid demand/withdraw dynamics is to make a habit of engaging our teens in a mutual and constructive dialogue about smaller or less disputed topics. Doing so would allow us to establish a history of mutual problem solving upon which to build when we need to communicate about issues that are more serious both to us and to them.

Second, when we do need to discuss heavy issues such as drugs, sex, social behavior, or academic problems, we should approach these discussions as neutrally as possible. Teenagers have great noses. They can sniff out an agenda a mile away. Our goal should be to do no more than half of the talking during any discussion with them. We should listen and learn their thoughts and feelings on the matter *before* we introduce any of our own beliefs, demands, standards, or agendas. In short, we have to become "teen whisperers." We have to learn how to approach our teens only a half step at a time, then wait for them to take half a step themselves before we take another.

Elliot and Mitch, as all parents of adolescents, have to minimize their complaining and stop wasting their efforts. A simple rule of thumb about the overall tone of our verbalizations to our children is: We should keep our positive or neutral communications to them at around 80 percent, leaving only 20 percent for directives or complaints. Since we tend to give our children a large variety of directives (e.g., come to the dinner table, time to go to bed, finish up that television show, careful with that breakable vase, etc.), it doesn't leave much room for complaints and neither should it.

Male Friendships: Complaining in Silence

If complaining to our children requires us to be judicious in choosing which complaints to voice and which to let go, the same is even truer when complaints arise in our friendships. The differences between how men and women handle complaints in their friendships are huge; when it comes to complaining or having relationship conversations, male friendships and female friendships are different animals entirely.

Carlos, a fifty-year-old engineer, was hugely disappointed when his childhood friend Raul didn't make it to his fiftieth birthday party. Maria, Carlos's wife, was equally upset, as she had gone to considerable effort to plan a lavish surprise party for her husband. Raul had assured Maria he would happily make the three-hour drive to their Westchester home and that he would definitely be there for his friend. But Raul, who was notoriously late for everything, mistimed his drive and missed the party entirely. Maria was certain Carlos would give Raul a piece of his mind the moment Raul got home. But several days later, realizing Carlos had not yet spoken to his friend about how disappointed he still felt, Maria decided to bring up the topic in their couple therapy session.

"Just call Raul and tell him how you feel," Maria suggested to her husband. "Talk to him. You're good friends. You just have to talk it out."

"I'll talk to him at the end of the month," Carlos replied.

He and Raul had their seasonal fly-fishing weekend coming up in a few weeks. Although the men had not spoken since the party, Carlos had no doubt they were still on for their annual tradition. They had not missed a fishing trip in over ten years.

"Why wait that long?" Maria insisted. "He's your best friend. Surely you can talk to your best friend if something's bothering you."

"I will talk with him—when we go fishing."

The two men met at a rented cabin at the end of the month. They first busied themselves setting up for the next day, then promptly went to bed at sundown. Not a word was exchanged between them. They got up at the crack of dawn, grabbed their gear, and made their way down to the stream, where they stood side by side for the next four hours. As the time came for them to gather their rods and head back to the cabin, Carlos began to wonder whether he should wait for Raul to broach the topic or just bring up the issue himself. Finally, just before they were about to start packing up,

Carlos brought up his complaint and addressed the current rupture in their long friendship.

"About last month," Carlos said softly so he didn't scare away the fish.

"Man, that was ..." Raul trailed off, shaking his head.

"Yeah," Carlos said, for emphasis.

Raul gave Carlos a momentary sideways glance. Not too long a look because, as Carlos later explained in their session, "that would just be weird," but a quick glance.

"It's just ..." Raul shrugged and trailed off again. He turned and gave Carlos another quick glance.

Carlos caught his friend's eye and nodded.

Raul exhaled. "So, we're good?"

"Yeah," Carlos said, relieved, "we're good."

"It went okay," Carlos concluded in our session after describing the full interaction. "It was good to talk about it."

Maria blinked at her husband, highly perplexed. "Are you kidding, Carlos? That was the extent of the big discussion?" Carlos nodded sincerely. Maria turned to me, exasperated.

"They barely said two words to each other!"

"Ah, yes," I acknowledged, "but there was quite a bit of subtext and nonverbal communication going on as well. The absolute word count might appear to have been a tad on the low side, but each utterance packed a whole lot of nutritional information about their friendship."

"It was a sincere apology," Carlos agreed.

Maria turned to her husband. "You were so disappointed that night, remember? Did you really feel he apologized?"

"Of course. He felt really bad about it," Carlos said, bewildered that his wife couldn't see what to him was so patently obvious. "But we figured it out. Things are good between us, really."

"Okay." Maria sat back, rolled her eyes, and sighed, "You men really make me crazy."

Just as there are significant differences between men's friendships and women's friendships, male friends resolve conflicts and deal with complaints differently from female friends. Men are usually much less verbal in their processing of friendship and relational issues than women are (indeed, most men might cringe at the characterization of a friendship conflict as a "relational issue").

When men describe their "buddies" as supportive or providing caring and listening, they are usually referring to brief moments of intimate disclosure during *activities*, much as fly-fishing provides for Carlos and Raul. For men, opportunities for male bonding, sharing, and conflict resolution occur mostly in shoulder-to-shoulder-oriented activities such as golfing, backyard barbecue grilling, and campfire extinguishing.

Because male friendships are more activity-oriented than discussion-oriented, when one male friend complains to another, they should do so in a way that best matches their typical verbal interaction. Carlos and Raul were great friends but not great talkers. They were able to discuss their complaints in shorthand because that matched their usual style. Male friends who have more verbal or verbose interactions should present their complaints accordingly, with greater exposition and choice of phrasing.

The complaint sandwich is an extremely important element to include in such discussions. Men's typical (and at times stereotypical) reluctance to engage in "relationship talk" as well as "complaint talk" can best be overcome by deploying the complaint sandwich and keeping the emotional volume of the complaint to a minimum. Further, men are highly sensitive to loss of face in confrontations, and the complaint sandwich significantly limits the accusatory and disapproving tone of our complaints by couching them in between positive and reassuring statements (ear-openers and digestives).

The most abbreviated male complaint sandwich I heard was when a twenty-year-old college student described confronting one roommate about not taking his side in an argument with the other. The young man packed all the elements of the complaint sandwich into one short sentence: "You're my bro, dude, have my back, you and me are tight." Perhaps not the most moving appeal ever made, but effective.

Female Friendships: Complaining Deeper and Growing Closer

Male and female stand-up comedians rarely agree about anything. They each see the world from either side of the gender divide, and they make their living by writing funny observations about their very different perspectives on life.

But the one thing almost all male and female comics agree upon is the difference between male and female friendships.

Carol Siskind shared her thoughts about female friendships with the men in her audience when she pointed out, "You're better friends than we are. Think about it. Men seem to have friendships that last for years. You know why? You guys don't talk to each other!" Mike Yard expressed similar ideas about friendships to his female audience members: "Women know deep stuff about their friends. They talk intimate stuff. Guys, we don't really have that. Our friendships are shallow. I got people I've been friends with for fifteen years—I don't even know their real names."

Indeed, women's friendships are often characterized by a far more pervasive and sophisticated verbal communication. Women's dialogue with their friends utilizes more emotional language than men's does, and their affective communications are both broader and deeper than is typical of male friendships. Obviously, this puts women ahead of the (male) pack when it comes to their innate and practiced ability to discuss complaints with female friends.

A 2009 study out of the University of Michigan demonstrated that for women, a short twenty-minute task aimed at eliciting emotional closeness with another woman who was a stranger was so powerful, it significantly boosted the levels of the participants' progesterone (the hormone) compared to women who participated in an emotionally neutral task. The increase in progesterone helped boost the women's feelings of well-being and reduced their levels of anxiety and stress.

For women, compared to men, greater and richer verbal expressiveness creates a greater sensitivity to the nuances of verbal and nonverbal communication. Women employ more sophisticated and sharper instruments in their conversations and friendship dialogues than men do, and therefore they have to wield these powerful instruments with a greater degree of care and caution.

The complaint sandwich does much to dull the cutting edge of complaints that can be conveyed or received as too sharp. While men get through their "friendship complaint talk" in one or two rounds, women often require numerous volleys back and forth to resolve a single complaint. Therefore, women tend to be more cautious in their expression of relationship dissatisfactions, and they tend to be better at monitoring the vital signs of their friendships as they go through such talks. Nonetheless, women might want to attend to the amount of time they spend in "complaint talk" within a given friendship so they achieve a balance. Extensive complaining, even if productive, could associate a friendship with conflict and negativity as opposed to sharing and support.

Receiving Complaints from Others: How to Eat a Complaint Sandwich

Now that we know how to complain to our loved ones, we should also take a moment to consider how best to respond to complaints from them as well. Our natural inclination is to respond to a complaint as though we're being attacked. This kind of response set has obvious evolutionary advantages as in our less civilized pasts, complaints probably served as precursors to actual physical attacks more often than not. For example, "Hey, that's *my* mammoth pelt you're wearing!" was unlikely to be followed by a long chat about hurt feelings and respect for the property of others.

Although our natural defensiveness persists, when our loved ones serve us a complaint sandwich, we should do three things to consume it correctly, whether it was served with bread or not. Let's say you just left a restaurant after having dinner with your partner and his or her ex-college-roommate and spouse. Your partner turns to you angrily and says, "You spent the entire night on your BlackBerry checking up on the babysitter! It was rude to our friends and incredibly annoying to me!" What would be the most correct way to respond?

If our BlackBerry use had indeed been excessive and unnecessary, an immediate and sincere apology would be appropriate. But what if the opposite was the case? We might feel tempted to point out the babysitter was new and had never sat for the kids before, so, yes, we checked in several times. Also interruption-worthy might be the fact that both kids had tests the next day for which they were supposed to be studying, even though according to the new and slightly inept sitter, they were not. Therefore, some of the texts we sent were actually to the kids to get them cracking on their books. We would have much preferred to participate more fully in the dinner and the evening as a whole, but we were being both generous and considerate by handling things ourselves and giving our partner a chance to catch up with the old roommate.

All these counterarguments are incredibly compelling and, in our minds, render our partner's complaint null and void, *but we should always let our partner finish speaking without interruption nonetheless.* True, shelving such potent responses for a few moments is not easy. But holding on to our winning hand for just a little longer is far more productive than indulging our natural tendency to become defensive when we feel attacked.

Remember, our partners complain because they are angry, frustrated, or disappointed. Cutting them off midstream would only make them more so. Allowing them to complete their complaint (provided they remain respectful, even if angry) and vent some steam can only make it easier for them to calm down and accept how wrong they were when it is our turn to present our deeply persuasive side of things. We also know that by complaining, our partners are seeking to have their emotions validated. Since we're already amassing some feelings of our own in the situation (after having our good intentions become fodder for a complaint), we will probably like to have our feelings validated as well. Being sympathetic to our partners' distress (even if we are about to demolish their case for complaining with unimpeachable counterarguments) only makes it more likely they will reciprocate by being sympathetic to ours.

Therefore, the second thing we should do when eating a complaint sandwich served by our partners (after listening fully to their complaint) is to take a moment and reflect back our understanding of their complaint to them. In this case, and with justice so blatantly on our side, even a terse "Look, you're pissed because I was texting back and forth with the babysitter too much, I get that" would suffice.

Paraphrasing our partners' complaints is a crucial step because not only does it provide them with the first ingredient of emotional validation—an understanding of their point of view—it also prevents us from arguing about the wrong thing. Relationship complaints can be misinterpreted in numerous ways, and at least some miscommunication is extremely common when couples discuss complaints. When one person complains, the other often hears the words correctly but interprets their meaning differently from what was intended. For example, in this case, we might hear our partner's complaint to mean we busied ourselves with our BlackBerry on purpose because we didn't care for his college roommate; which could in turn easily lead to a fascinating but irrelevant spat about who is the more supportive of the other's friendships.

The third thing we should do when our partners complain is to acknowledge their feelings, even if we don't think they are warranted, and even if we are convinced that we had no part in eliciting them. We lose nothing by acknowledging our friends' or loved ones' feelings are hurt even if we never intended to hurt them, and even if they misinterpreted our original intent and were hurt by a misunderstanding. Acknowledging their feelings will both provide them emotional validation and create a dynamic of fairness and respectfulness that can only facilitate further discussion.

Acknowledging our partners' feelings becomes more difficult when we are not clearly justified in our actions. For example, we might have been fiddling with our BlackBerry because, as our partner suspected, we have always disliked his ex-college-roommate and we acted out passive-aggressively. In such cases, we can still acknowledge our partners' feelings even as we then demand they acknowledge ours. "Yes, I get that I was rude and that you were annoyed. But as usual, I had to sit through two hours of you and your friend reliving college experiences about people I don't know in a way that totally excluded me from the conversation. Can you understand how I felt?"

After we do these three things (listen, paraphrase, validate) we can feel free to voice our compelling arguments or countercomplaints as long as we do so clearly and respectfully. To the extent that our arguments are indeed winning ones, we will still have plenty of time for smugness and a victory lap.

By taking these three important steps, we by no means concede any ground in the matter itself. Being understanding and compassionate does not mean we give up our right to disagree, countercomplain, or claim hurt feelings of our own. All it does is clarify our partners' communications and validate their emotional experiences. Much as companies that handle consumer complaints satisfactorily increase their customers' loyalty, when we handle our friends' and our partners' complaints well, our friendships and partnerships can only be strengthened.

Chapter Seven Getting Squeaked At for a Living: *The Customer Service Professional*

Oh, a satisfied customer. We should have him stuffed.
—Basil Fawlty, *Fawlty Towers* (1975)

A couple of years ago, I arrived at a crosstown-bus stop just as a well-dressed man in his forties stepped out of line and placed a quick call to his medical insurance carrier. Apparently, he had been denied reimbursement for simple blood work that should have been covered under his insurance plan. I, as well as everyone else at the bus stop, learned these details because they were conveyed loudly and with much impatience and condescension to the customer service representative on the other end of the line.

"No, *you* told me it would be covered if my doctor sent you the form!" the man shouted into his phone. "No, *you* told it me it *would* be covered!" The man paced back and forth, oblivious of the line of people only a few feet away. "This is the fourth time I've spoken to you about this, and each time you tell me ... No! I am listening! You're not listening! You keep telling me ... No! I won't lower my voice because each time you tell me something different!" The man listened for a few blessed moments of silence. Then: "You idiots don't know what you're doing! ... No! How about you morons learn to do your [expletive] job! ... No, I can't send the form in because my doctor already sent it in twice!" The man's neck muscles strained as he screamed into the phone, "You don't know what you're talking about! You're just repeating the same thing! I told you he sent it in already ... Uh, you know what, just go [expletive] yourselves!"

The man snapped his cell phone shut in disgust, stomped over, and joined the back of the line, breathing slightly heavily. Everyone on line developed an immediate fascination with the pavement, pretended to check text messages, or picked imaginary lint off their outerwear. Of course, we had all been paying rapt attention and heard every word of the man's rabid tirade. I'm sure it would not be too great a leap to infer the matter had not been resolved to his satisfaction.

For effectiveness, the interaction was practically a master class of everything we should *not* do when complaining. First and most obvious was the man's terrible temper, his rudeness, and his hostility. Angry complaints are ineffective because anger distracts the complaint recipient from the complaint's actual message. But this *bus stop lunatic* was not merely angry; he was openly abusive to the person on the other end of the phone. As much as I understood his sentiments, he was calling the customer service department to ask for their assistance. Delivering every sentence with disdain is hardly the best way to coax someone into a helping frame of mind. Screaming "idiot" and "moron" while dropping F-bombs is equally unlikely to galvanize someone into a frenzy of altruism.

But what truly prevented the bus stop lunatic from being effective was something else entirely—a complete misperception of how call centers function. Many of us have faced similar hurdles when calling customer service, technical support, or sales hotlines. All such calls are answered in *call centers*—tightly run and highly technological businesses whose services are often outsourced from third-party companies. To get a scale of the numbers involved, despite the outsourcing of many call centers to India and other countries, in 2008 almost *two million* customer service representatives were working in the United States alone.

Almost everything a call-center employee does is dictated to them by the rules and highly specific procedures of the companies they represent. Unless we have a basic understanding of how call centers operate and a grasp of the scope and limitations of the representatives who work in them, it will be difficult for us to pursue our consumer complaints successfully. Knowing how to navigate a system that can be frustrating, contradictory, and even surreal can make the difference between achieving a quick resolution to our problems and achieving a quick anxiety attack.

Miscommunications are frequent when speaking to call-center representatives, with occasional moments of true befuddlement when we begin to question if anything we said got across. We might even suspect the representative is being dense and difficult on purpose. Despite how common such experiences are, in the majority of instances none of our fears are justified. John Goodman's research has repeatedly demonstrated that 80 percent of our problems are due to a company's faulty systems and procedures, not mistakes by their service employees.

The bus stop lunatic is a perfect example of this faulty perception on our part. That he had to call four times about a matter that should have been simple and easy to resolve pointed to a clear problem within the systems of his insurance carrier. But the bus stop lunatic mistakenly leaped to a far less likely conclusion, that the call-center employee had access to more information than the employee could possibly have. That one erroneous assumption actually caused most of his frustration and fueled his growing temper tantrum. (We will revisit the bus stop lunatic's incorrect assumptions later in this chapter.)

While not everyone gets worked up into a maniacal frenzy when dealing with call centers, aggravation is an integral part of the experience for many of us. Anyone who has ever called a consumer hotline knows how frustrating such encounters can be. The current system of ever more complicated automated menus and tightly scripted call-center representatives is so annoying it could easily whip the calmest and most mild-mannered consumer into a blithering rage.

The Call-Center Customer Service Obstacle Course

Samuel, a senior executive at a major financial institution, once spent an entire therapy session describing the elaborate preparation he went through just to make a simple call to dispute his bank's interest fees. His checking account was covered by an overdraft line of credit that kicked in automatically if he became overdrawn. He had dipped into the line of credit during a summer vacation with his family but paid the balance in full as soon as the statement arrived. The next month he got a second bill, as apparently his overdraft balance had continued to accrue interest until his payment arrived. The new statement was for $85. Samuel paid it immediately and again in full. The following month he received a third statement for $2 and change for the interest that had accrued on the previous balance of $85. "Every time I opened one statement, there was another smaller one inside!" Samuel complained.

Determined to challenge his bank's financial homage to Russian babushka dolls, Samuel prepared for his complaint call much as a warrior prepares for battle. He waited for the weekend when his wife and kids were out on an errand. Then he quickly put on his best "power suit" and walked around the house warming up his voice as if he were about to audition for the county-fair yodeling competition. Then he did neck stretches, followed by a round of loud knuckle-cracking. The only thing missing from his pre-call rituals was war paint. Only once he felt "ready and powerful" did this highly paid and senior financial executive tackle a phone call to a low-paid and entry-level service representative.

Despite the fact that corporations spend billions of dollars training and supervising their customer service representatives, most of us approach making complaint calls with the kind of anticipatory dread we usually reserve for IRS tax audits, emergency root canals, and colonoscopies. Like Samuel, many of us feel the need to prepare for such calls both mentally and psychologically. We try to get ourselves into the right frame of mind, we gather our documents, we take deep breaths, and we gird our loins in preparation for the inevitable obstacle course.

The first call-center test we face is the "automated menu—key-punching test of finger dexterity." These days we have to go through so many menus before we reach a live person, I often wonder how those of us with meatier fingers such as butchers, professional wrestlers, or Seinfeld's dinner date who had "man hands" can possibly get through them without making a mistake. My own personal downfall in such situations is that I'm so busy composing my complaint in my head, by the third menu I lose focus, select the wrong options, and suddenly find myself hearing, "Para llegar a apoyo técnico, pulse dos."

The next obstacle we face is the "serial-number scavenger hunt." The launch code for the nation's nukes probably has fewer digits than the average toaster oven's serial number. Most products have identifiers that include fifteen to twenty numbers and letters, and they're always located in the most inconvenient places possible—carved onto the back of the plasma television we just mounted on the wall or printed on a flimsy sticker on the bottom of a three-ton industrial washing machine we just bolted to the floor.

Next, we play "name that tune while on hold," which is annoying because for some unfathomable reason, every company in the world believes the only song capable of soothing our frazzled nerves is Dolly Parton and Kenny Rogers's "Islands in the Stream." Even that chestnut is interrupted every minute for a recorded voice to thank us for our patience and reassure us, without a shred of irony, that our time is *extremely* valuable to the company. My personal record for being put on hold is forty-eight minutes, roughly fourteen and half repetitions of "Islands in the Stream." I am well aware many people have been put on hold for hours, not minutes, but for me the forty-eight-minute wait was excruciating. I guess I break easy.

Of course, getting to a live representative does not mean we've arrived in the promised land, as we then face a few rousing rounds of the "name game." My first and last names have only one syllable, yet they're both butchered regularly. I can only imagine what people with more complicated names go through. A few years ago I completed a call to Dell technical support without one of the three people I talked with getting either my first or last name correct even once. How is it possible to screw up a name as simple and generic as Guy? Here's what happened: My printer had jammed as I was printing out notes for a lecture on couple therapy that I had to give that afternoon. Hoping for the best, I called Dell's toll-free number. After innumerable automated menus and seven plays of "Islands in the Stream," I was put through to a real live representative with a strong Indian accent.

"Thank you for calling Dell. My name is Tiffany. How may I help you today?"

"I'm having problems with my printer."

"I'm sorry to hear you are having problems with your Dell printer. May I have your name please, sir?"

"It's Guy Winch."

"Thank you. May I call you Buy?"

"I prefer Guy."

"Yes, Mr. Gay. How can I help you today?"

"You can start by getting my name right … Tiffany. It's Guy. Guy Winch."

"Yes, of course. Sorry, sir. Is Die Wench correct?"

"Only if you're channeling Jack the Ripper."

"Who …? I … Sorry, how may I help you with your printer today, Mr. Wench?"

I sighed inwardly but was in too much of a hurry to belabor an irrelevant detail. "The paper feed spins but doesn't grasp the page," I explained.

"Okay, I see here that your warranty is still good, Mr. Wench, so I will now transfer you to a Dell technical support representative."

"Please make sure I don't get disconnected before … Hello …?" I waited for Dolly Parton to tell me how "We ride it together, uh-huh!"

But Dolly and I were no longer riding it together, uh-huh. Instead, a heavily New York-accented recording barked, "Please hang up! There appears to be a receiver off the hook! Please hang up and try your call again!" How most phones survive such moments without being hurled into walls, thrown onto floors, or stomped into pieces is a miracle of emotional regulation on all our parts. I quickly checked the time. It was tight, but I decided to call Dell again.

After another twenty-minute wait, a lovely Indian woman named Brittney assured me, "You don't get disconnected this time, Mr. Wink!" and mercifully transferred me successfully to a technical support representative named Sebastian. Sebastian's English was incomprehensible. His most coherent sentence was "I think is bust your printer, Witch."

I should mention that since my chats with "Sebastian,"

"Tiffany," and "Brittney," Dell has received so many complaints about outsourcing to India that they've relocated a huge portion of their technical support operations right back to the United States.

What the Bus Stop Lunatic Needed to Know About Call Centers but Didn't

The first call-center representative we reach is usually the lowest-paid, least-trained, and least-experienced employee in the entire operation. These representatives also have the least authority. Some are able to handle our complaints themselves, while others (such as Tiffany) only do triage and transfer us to other departments. Even those representatives who are authorized to take action on our behalf vary greatly in the limits of their authority and in how much they can do for us. But when we call, we have no idea what the call-center employee's limitations are, nor is this information ever disclosed to us.

For example, the bus stop lunatic kept emphasizing the representative's overall responsibility: "*You* told me it would be covered," "This is the fourth time I've spoken to *you*," and "Each time *you* tell me," as though the person he was speaking with had handled each of his previous calls. Given that he was dealing with a huge national health-care provider, that was extremely unlikely.

Most large companies require many call centers to service their clients, all of which run multiple shifts throughout the long workday. The chances of our speaking to the same representative twice are extremely slim. Certainly, we cannot assume the person taking our call knows anything beyond what might be noted in our file. Yet, the bus stop lunatic clearly expected his service representative to be familiar with the conversations he had had with a different person who might have been located in an entirely different state or country.

The bus stop lunatic was also unaware of the extent to which call-center employees must follow *prewritten scripts.* Programs on their screens tell them exactly what to do as well as what to say, in many cases literally word for word. But our complaints do not always fit into the company's specified script paths and when they don't, the conversation can get off track rather quickly. Indeed, the bus stop lunatic's representative suggested he send in a form even though he had mentioned only two sentences earlier that his doctor had already submitted the form twice.

This kind of overly rigid scripting can make a call-center employee appear distracted, incompetent, or simply dense. When we find ourselves scratching our heads in confusion at a representative's non sequitur, it is usually a sign of a script miscommunication. We should interrupt the person politely and rephrase the point of our call. Using phrases such as "just to make sure we're on the same page" and "let me just clarify something" is a good way to alert the representative to a possible script problem or miscommunication.

But had the bus stop lunatic been better informed, could he have handled the complaint call more effectively? We now know a little about how call centers operate. Could we manage a similar call more productively ourselves? True, we only have one side of the conversation to work with, but it isn't difficult to reconstruct the entire exchange.

Lunatics No More: An Effective Complaining Redo

Let's examine the bus stop lunatic's first belligerent set of responses: "No, *you* told me it would be covered if my doctor sent you the form!" and "No, *you* told it me it *would* be covered!"

Obviously, the call-center employee's screen indicated the blood work was not covered, but that was probably because of the missing form. Therefore, discovering what happened to the crucial form should be the first point we clarify with our representative: "My doctor sent in the form a second time. Did you guys receive it?" If the company had not received the form, we need to figure out why. "Your system is showing you never received it? It was sent in last week. Is it possible it was not entered into the system yet?" If it should have been in the system by now, we need to verify our doctor sent it to the right place. In which case we should ask for the address and fax numbers for confirmation purposes.

Belligerent response number two was "This is the fourth time I've spoken to you about this, and each time you tell me … No! I am listening! You're not listening! You keep telling me … No! I won't lower my voice because each time you tell me something different!"

Let's assume the lunatic was correct, that his doctor had sent the form to the right place (as the address or fax number we received match). If so, the error was on the insurance company's part, and we would have to explain that to the representative. "Thanks for that address, but that is the address it was sent to, and it has been sent more than once. This is actually the fourth time I'm calling about this, and each time we resend the form to the address you specify and yet it doesn't register in your system. Do you have a suggestion as to what might be going wrong here? I really cannot keep troubling my doctor with paperwork."

The representative might then have a solution for us, but more likely will not. If so, it might be time to speak with someone with greater authority and experience. "Look, I really appreciate your trying to help me, but there seems to be a problem with the form as either you guys are not getting it or it's not getting entered into the system correctly. Since you don't have any suggestions about how to remedy that situation, may I please speak with a supervisor?"

If we get resistance to our request, we should be polite but firm: "I understand you're suggesting I send it in again, but since that hasn't worked more than once already, I would rather speak to someone who can offer me an alternative. Again, I appreciate your efforts, but I would like to speak with a supervisor." If we insist on speaking with a supervisor or manager, a call center would not usually refuse that request, especially if we've already established the representative is unable to assist us.

The supervisor should be able to find out why our form keeps taking a one-way journey into the twilight zone and clear up any confusion about where such forms should be sent and what might be preventing them from being entered into the system. Once we have a supervisor or manager on the case, the likelihood of our getting an effective resolution is significantly higher. We can also ask for their names and direct phone lines, so we can call them directly if we keep having trouble.

The Correct Way to Handle Customer Complaints

On a few occasions I've had the pleasure of being on the receiving end of top-notch, state-of-the-art complaint handling, and I found the experience to be both incredibly soothing and surprisingly satisfying. By the end of those calls, my mood had gone from irritable and nasty to calm and satisfied, as I was practically awash with the warm tingle of emotional validation. How these companies achieved this is no great mystery. The science of customer service is by no means new and has been thoroughly researched.

There are established and empirically verified guidelines for handling customer complaints that work like magic the vast majority of the time. Why are we so unfamiliar with them? Some companies do not bother to seek out the most effective complaint-handling procedures, but most are simply unwilling to pay for the time and training necessary to instill these procedures in their employees. Consequently, few companies consistently manage customer complaints with excellence.

Those that do enjoy a strong and loyal customer base, while those that don't often find themselves bleeding established customers faster than they recruit new ones. One of John Goodman's most important messages to companies has been "Do it right the first time!"

Janelle Barlow and Claus Møller, authors of *A Complaint Is a Gift*, lay out eight steps companies should follow when handling complaints. Since this information is readily available to all company executives or customer service managers, I believe we should hold companies to these specific standards. I keep a list of the steps beside me whenever I call a customer service hotline and check them off as we go through the call. I find it interesting to see how many steps the representative gets right. I recommend making a quick list for easy reference. Lamination is optional.

Customer service representatives should respond to our complaints by doing the following, preferably in this order:

1. *Thank us for letting them know about our complaint.* After all, we're taking time out of our day to give them free feedback.
2. *Explain to us why our feedback is appreciated.* For example, because it helps them prevent other customers from having similar issues.
3. *Apologize for the mistake or the problem,* whether they caused it or not (i.e., they should not get defensive). However, their apology should come only after we have explained our problem (otherwise, they don't know what they're apologizing for), and it should match the severity of our complaint.
4. *Take responsibility for the problem* and promise to handle it immediately.
5. *Ask us for necessary information* and detail.

6. *Correct the mistake promptly* or within the time frame they give us.
7. *Check our level of satisfaction* with the complaint handling by following up with a phone call or e-mail.
8. *Prevent further mistakes* by fixing their procedures or systems.

The first time I used the list when making a complaint call, it was fascinating to observe how with each step a representative "did right" I actually felt a little calmer and a little more reasonable. The representative's calm, sympathetic, and reassuring manner, and knowledge and skill level, were surprising and incredibly effective. John Goodman believes companies should always aim to surprise us by exceeding our expectations because, when they do, they create what Goodman calls "customer delight." "Delighted" customers are far more loyal and spread extremely positive word of mouth that can be highly influential in recruiting new customers. However, although customer delight has long been considered the brass ring of customer service, few companies make a sincere effort to reach for it.

When a service representative misses too many steps (if not all of them), it is usually because the company has not adopted these steps, not because the representative chose to omit them. Therefore, it would be unfair to blame the call-center employee for handling our call in the manner their systems instructed them to. For this reason, I've trained myself to conduct complaint calls with civility and patience (even when I'm feeling neither) for the sheer purpose of having my complaint be effective and getting a satisfying result.

However, I should admit that in the darkness of my pre-effective-complaining days, I too was part of the pulsing masses that take out their consumer frustrations on hapless call-center representatives (I never cursed or belittled, but I was a shouter more than once). For too many of us, customer service representatives and especially call-center employees have become the approved societal punching bags of the twenty-first century.

Unmasking the Call-Center Representative

Gil C. is a twenty-five-year-old man who works in a call-center that services a large cell-phone company. Although his job is typical of call-center employees, his story is not. Gil was born as the most fragile of premature babies in the twenty-seventh week of his mother's pregnancy. His biological parents abandoned him at the hospital, where he battled for his life for many months. He emerged from that early struggle almost completely blind, with no vision in his left eye and only 5 percent in his right. He is also completely deaf in one ear and has only one kidney and numerous other complications. Gil spent his early years in hospitals and in foster care, where he experienced difficult times and even abusive situations. When he was eighteen, he volunteered for a year of national service and fell in love with telecommunications. Today he lives in an independent-living residence for adults with special needs where he shares an apartment with nine other men.

"The day I got the job at the call center was the happiest day of my life," Gil recalled. "I went out and spent a bunch of money buying snacks for all my friends at the residence. I got home, put the food out on the table, and blasted the music as loud as I could to celebrate. It seemed like a dream come true."

Gil started out as a sales representative. His job was to call existing subscribers and offer them products such as warranties. Some customers become annoyed when receiving unsolicited calls, and a few even let out an expletive or two before hanging up. From what I understand, those are few. When I talked with Gil, I wasn't sure if he had ever experienced truly hostile or abusive exchanges, so I asked about his experiences.

"Oh, I've been through everything already," Gil assured me. "I've been called every name in the book and then some." I was curious to hear an example of an incident in the "and then some" category.

Gil had many from which to choose. "I called this one customer and explained about our warranty service. He seemed interested in hearing more, so I started explaining how expensive it was to replace lost or damaged equipment and how much a warranty could save him. He was cool until I got to pricing. He seemed shocked at the cost. I told him I understood his concern but I explained how the benefits could be more than worth it. That seemed to make him even angrier. He suddenly started screaming at me at the top of his lungs, 'I'll make sure you get screwed! I'll make sure you get fired! You're an idiot! You son of a bitch! Why don't you go screw yourself and give yourself a disease!' "

Gil was taken aback by the intensity of the man's rage. But Gil's job was to mollify the customer and salvage the call. So he took a deep breath and gave it his best effort. "I tried to get him to stop yelling at me. I calmly asked him not to speak to me in that manner, but he kept yelling. I asked him again to lower his voice. Then I asked him to stop cursing at me. I even asked him to dignify my humanity as a person. But he kept cursing and threatening me until he hung up."

I wondered what dealing with hostile and abusive customers did to Gil's mood and self-esteem. "When I started working here, I used to get my feelings hurt all the time," he admitted. "I wanted so much to do well here, I gave everything ... I gave my soul to this job ... to have people just scream at you, curse at you ... it hurt. People cry here all the time."

Working a job in which we are cursed, dismissed, or belittled by the public regularly might seem unfathomable to anyone with the possible exception of soccer referees and street mimes. What makes Gil's job even more complicated is that despite his own history of abandonment and abuse, he is expected to take his customers' hostility on the chin.

Not only must he continue speaking with such customers, he is expected to remain calm, patient, and understanding while doing so.

Staying calm and pleasant while abusive callers or bus stop lunatics are hurling insults and threats at us is no easy task. I've dealt with a lunatic or two in my day as well, but as a trained mental health professional. Therefore, the incidents took place in a locked psychiatric ward where most hostile "lunatics" were strapped to gurneys or restrained by security staff. While I too had to remain calm when, for example, a delusional paranoid schizophrenic tried to attack me for "poisoning the yogurt with monkey spit," I was not expected to thank them for relaying their concerns, sound pleasant as I listened to their raving, or coo sympathetically.

Call centers are virtual stockades that shackle their employees to their posts and leave them exposed to an angry public toting bucketfuls of consumer angst and cartloads of verbal rotten tomatoes. Unfortunately, bus stop lunatics are hardly the only ones throwing them. Over the years, I've heard many otherwise kind and decent people describe using horrifically insulting and abusive language when dealing with call-center representatives.

What makes our general public animosity toward service representatives such a rare phenomenon both psychologically and sociologically is how often the details of these verbal assaults are relayed not with embarrassment or chagrin but with actual pride, satisfaction, and even glee. It is hard to imagine another context in which ordinarily kind and compassionate people *boast* about being emotionally abusive to a complete stranger who is merely trying to do his or her job.

Studies demonstrate that the typical call-center employee handles an average of ten hostile calls per day. John Goodman has worked with call centers for many years. I asked him how frequently call-center employees were cursed, insulted, or threatened by their customers. "Oh, that happens all the time!" Goodman exclaimed. "We tell the representatives that most people have only seven good curses in them. So we suggest they write out the curses as they hear them, and by the time they reach the seventh, most customers should have spent their anger."

I am unaware of any other professional that has to list the curses hurled at them regularly just so they won't find them so upsetting. Clearly, society has declared open season on call-center employees. But how did things devolve to this point?

One of the main reasons we tend to dehumanize customer service employees so readily is they are the literal representatives of the companies responsible for our grief and aggravation. Since we don't have direct access to the company managers, executives, or decision makers, we consider their *official representatives* to be equally deserving of our wrath. In addition, our speaking to an anonymous, faceless stranger whose reactions we cannot see allows us to switch off psychological filters such as empathy or civility. This gives free rein to the kind of battle mentality and combative mind-set Samuel assumed when preparing for his call. If we saw a service representative's eyes well up with tears, most of us would never allow ourselves to get so ruthless.

Hostile and angry customers are only one aspect of what makes Gil's job so demanding. The actual work conditions in call centers present an equal if not greater challenge to many of the employees. A couple of years ago, I visited my first call center, which is where I met Gil and his fellow call-center workers and got my first taste of what it is like to work in these cramped hives of telecommunications activity. After learning what call-center employees go through, it was much easier for me to use empathy to reframe my anger and regulate my emotions when complaining to a call-center representative.

A Day in the Life of a Professional Punching Bag

Gil sets three alarm clocks to make sure he wakes up every morning at five thirty A.M. It then takes him two to three hours to commute to work *in each direction* (remember, he is legally blind). His computer is located in a large hall surrounded by dozens of other workstations. Supervisors on elevated platforms monitor Gil and the other employees constantly, both electronically and by sight. A large monitor and a ZoomText program allow him to see his screen a couple of words at a time. Gil's computer tracks the number of calls he handles, the length of each call, and the number of sales he makes an hour. His calls are recorded, and every month random conversations are selected by his supervisors and managers for "training and quality-assurance purposes." One can get away with little at a call center. Gil cannot even go to the bathroom without notifying his supervisors because the computer has to be alerted to stop measuring statistics about his calls (number per hour, call length, products sold, etc.) until he returns to his station.

Gil is required to follow strict behavioral guidelines such as being pleasant, patient, polite, and understanding when speaking to customers. Indeed, call-center and customer service employees are often hired because they have "positive energy" or are upbeat, and they are often expected to demonstrate these characteristics in their work. "Service with a smile" and other forms of behavioral directives are called display rules, and companies are usually quite strict in their application. Display rules can include conveying patience, understanding, empathy, and calm no matter how abusive a customer becomes. Some companies insist their representatives display even nebulous characteristics such as friendliness, helpfulness, or enthusiasm. Given how frequently call-center representatives are expected to demonstrate one set of emotions while feeling another, one might conclude call centers would do best by recruiting their employees straight out of acting schools (most graduates could probably use the work).

Considering the technical demands of call-center work, display rules can add a huge layer of stress to an already challenging job. Call-center employees are expected to handle back-to-back calls while simultaneously navigating long chains of complex menus on their computer screens to process sales, file warranties, issue refunds, and the like. The mental effort required to regulate their emotions and behavioral reactions while also performing their jobs correctly and without mistakes is called emotional labor.

All jobs include some aspects of emotional labor. None of us can afford to yell at our bosses when they make us stay late or curse colleagues if they annoy us in a meeting. But it should come as no surprise that call centers are considered more emotionally laborious than the vast majority of other professions.

So how do besieged call-center representatives manage the demands of display rules when we call and yell at them? Call-center employees are expected to adhere to display rules by doing something we are familiar with—regulating their emotions. They typically use one of two methods to do so. The first, "surface acting," is a form of suppression and requires modifying tones or facial expressions and hiding emotions such as anger, frustration, or boredom that conflict with the company's display rules. The second technique, "deep acting," is a form of reframing. It involves the call-center employees changing their underlying feeling by focusing on something pleasant to distract them (e.g., only fifteen minutes are left in the shift) or by changing their fundamental attitude about the encounter (such as by empathizing with a customer's distress).

We know that suppressing our true emotions can interfere with our performance on cognitive tasks. But call-center employees are expected to take orders, issue warranties, process refunds, and do other administrative duties while simultaneously interacting with customers (hostile ones or otherwise). If representatives get flustered, become too emotional, or lose concentration and make too many mistakes, they can lose their job. We also know that reframing strains our intellectual resources less than suppression does. But reframing is hard to do when a customer is shouting, "Why don't you go screw yourself and give yourself a disease!" In general, the greater the discrepancy between the display rules and the representative's emotional state, the more effortful emotional regulation becomes and the more stress the employee experiences.

Other studies have found that representatives with strict display rules feel more distressed, report higher levels of exhaustion, and accrue more sick days than those with more autonomous display rules. Strict display rules have also been linked to chronic elevated stress levels and burnout. Call-center employees are thus thrust into battle with their customers with the huge disadvantage of display rules and little or no protective armor. It should be no surprise to learn they sustain both emotional and health-related injuries as a result.

For those readers wondering how most people survive the stresses of working at call centers, the simple answer is, most people do not. The average length of employment in call centers is around eighteen months. Since it can take anywhere from one to several months to train new employees, precious little time is then left for companies to capitalize on their investments before the employee buckles under the pressures of emotional labor and leaves.

In some ways, we the public are responsible for call-center employees' inexperience or incompetence because our treatment of them is one of the main reasons they don't last in their jobs. If we were as polite to call-center employees as we are when making any other noncomplaint-oriented business call, their attrition rates would be far lower. Whether we are at fault for this or not, better treatment of customer representatives would benefit us because it would facilitate achieving a more satisfying resolution.

Of course, the plight of call-center employees isn't entirely our fault. The management of such establishments is as much to blame as are the companies they represent. Why? Because at least one call center has found a way to provide the kind of corporate culture that significantly alleviates the stresses and pressures of emotional labor and hostile customers. How this company revolutionized their training and management approaches is even more remarkable given the additional challenges they faced. But despite having to interface with difficult and hostile customers regularly, the employees of this call center could not be happier or more satisfied with their jobs.

The Heavenly Call Center

At the time he sat down for an interview, Gil had already been at his call center for eighteen months and had absolutely no intention of leaving. Neither did any of the other employees with whom I spoke. In fact, when employees were asked if anyone thought of leaving, one woman looked up quizzically and said, "Why would anyone want to leave heaven?" In the customer service field, the words *call center* and *heaven* are rarely used in the same sentence. But the place that hired Gil was no ordinary call center.

Gil's call center, Call-Yachol (CY), is a start-up company in Israel and the first business of its kind in the world to *employ solely people with disabilities.* Gil is one of CY's many legally blind workers, but they also employ people with cerebral palsy, stroke victims, injured veterans, amputees, and paraplegics as well as people with mental disabilities, such as victims of post-traumatic stress disorder or survivors of trauma and abuse. But CY employees are given absolutely no leniency when it comes to their job performance. They have to be able to compete directly with other call-centers peopled by nondisabled personnel that service the exact same clientele and customer base.

CY's managerial philosophy blends principles of both management and *parenting* to create a unique work environment that holds employees to high standards of performance without sacrificing caring and support. By design, *CY's corporate structure is as reminiscent of a family as it is of a business.* All senior staff at CY undergo unique sensitivity training to give them insight into the specific challenges each disability presents. For example, managers might be told to circle every 5 on a page filled with tiny numbers. After a few minutes, when the strain causes their eyes to sting, they can appreciate why someone such as Gil might need to take a break for a few minutes if his eyes begin to sting.

Although most of the training and management techniques CY has developed are considered proprietary, I do have permission to disclose their guiding principle of "management as parenting." This prime directive has led them to create training protocols that are incredibly effective and even emotionally transformative experiences for those who go through them. CY's emphasis on supporting and nurturing their employees while expecting the highest professional standards has directly translated into empowering frontline representatives such as Gil.

The care and personal investment CY's workers experience from their managers and supervisors give them a layer of extra resilience when they are faced with the emotionally laborious challenges of interfacing with a hostile public. The result is radically reduced attrition rates and vastly increased job satisfaction.

"This place is like a family to me," Gil said earnestly. "These days when customers call me a son of a bitch, I shrug it off." Gil chuckled. "After all, I've never actually had a mother ...

But now, what I finally do have ... is a home."

Gil C. is never far from my thoughts whenever I place a call to a service, sales, or technical-support hotline. Thinking of how hard he works to do his job well is the most powerful method I've found to help me reframe my anger or frustration of the moment and regulate myself into a calmer state of mind. To that end, we can all be mindful that call-center representatives are hardworking people with extremely difficult jobs. They are our allies. They are the people who can resolve our problems, not the people who caused them.

However annoyed we might feel, reminding ourselves of those facts can only make our complaints more effective. Being treated with decency, consideration, and respect by their managers and executives brings out the best in Gil and his fellow employees at CY. Respecting the humanity and decency of customer service representatives in call centers or in stores will not only help us resolve our complaints but will prevent us from working ourselves into a frenzy of bus-stop lunacy that gets us nothing but a one-way ticket to consumer learned-helplessness.

Chapter Eight
Squeaking as Social Activism

One person can make a difference and every person should try.
—John F. Kennedy

In the fall of 2007, Beckie Williams, a twenty-five-year-old copywriter for children's books from Brighton, England, was shopping for brassieres in Marks & Spencer, the British retail giant. She noticed that bras sized DD and larger cost two pounds (a little over $3) more than smaller-sized bras. Being in the "and larger" category, Ms. Williams was rather displeased by the pricing discrepancy. So when she got home, she dashed off a quick letter to Marks & Spencer to question the surcharge. The company responded to her complaint, explaining the higher prices were necessary to defray the costs of the extra material larger brassieres required.

Ms. Williams found their explanation rather irritating. "They don't charge more for larger knickers, do they?" she argued. "Larger blouses require extra material too but they're priced the same." Ms. Williams decided to write back to the company. She pointed out the flaws in their logic and again protested their unfair pricing. This time, she received no response at all. Now she was even more annoyed. "Marks & Spencer is a British institution. They always say they care about their customers. It was very wrong of them to just fob me off."

Fobbed off and out of options, Beckie Williams continued discussing the complaint over the next few months with a number of friends "who were also quite busty." She found much emotional validation in doing so as they were equally outraged by the discriminatory pricing policy. However, the initial rush of emotional validation did not last long as, over the months, her dialogue with friends began to feel more frustrating than validating. "I don't like complaining about things without trying to change them," Ms. Williams explained. "It's a waste of time to do that."

Then she heard about a Facebook group that had formed to petition Cadbury, the giant chocolate company, to bring back a discontinued chocolate bar. "It struck me as a fun and easy way to get a few more people together," Ms. Williams realized. "So I discussed it with a friend and we decided to start our own Facebook group to petition Marks & Spencer. We called our group Busts 4 Justice."

Busts 4 Justice seemed to strike a chord with busty women as within days their numbers swelled to over one hundred members. Ms. Williams provided her complaint letter to the group for members to e-mail Marks & Spencer as well, all to no avail as the giant retailer refused to jiggle their pricing even by a penny. Then a journalist came across the Facebook group and contacted Beckie Williams. Soon after, the story of her complaint and the Facebook group ran in a London newspaper. What happened next took Beckie Williams completely by surprise.

"The story went viral!" Ms. Williams said, amazement still evident in her voice when we spoke almost a year later. In the week following their national exposure, Busts 4 Justice amassed over eight thousand new participants and ballooned to extralarge proportions. Marks & Spencer responded by releasing a statement in which they essentially repeated their arguments about extra material costs. As far as the prices of their brassieres were concerned, Marks & Spencer were determined to stand firm.

Ms. Williams was highly disappointed. "They basically told us they're one of the few companies who even stock things for women with our bust sizes so we should be grateful and pay what they tell us to pay." The Facebook group was equally dismayed by the response. The discussion forums on Busts 4 Justice soon heaved with activity. Women began posting stories about other negative experiences they had in Marks & Spencer stores. Many women in the group had faced a lifelong struggle to find clothing that fit their body type. Most largely endowed women develop early. Consequently, they frequently struggle with issues of body image and feelings of self-consciousness during their adolescence. Being unable to find appropriate clothes as children and then being penalized for their body type as adults only added to their feeling angry and marginalized.

"Some women in the group had a really hard time growing up," Ms. Williams explained. "They might have been only twelve or thirteen years old, but people associate a certain bawdiness with having a big chest. It could be very uncomfortable for young girls to go through that." Indeed, many women in the group still dealt with the psychological scars of a challenging adolescence. The Facebook group was actually tapping into years of painful resentments and frustrations. Stories women shared on discussion boards became more personal and more emotional. "It was becoming something very positive," Ms. Williams acknowledged. "Eight thousand women who shared this frustration began talking, sharing their experiences and supporting one another. We were becoming a community."

Marks & Spencer invited Ms. Williams to a meeting in which they promised to explore different pricing options with manufacturing facilities in China. But then, in the fall of 2008, the global economy crashed, and Great Britain found itself in a severe recession. "The company backed down," Ms. Williams reported to her group. "They claimed they really couldn't do anything in the current economic climate."

Marks & Spencer's willingness to risk alienating eight thousand of their most vocal customers was obviously staggering in its shortsightedness. Beckie Williams again pressed Marks & Spencer to reconsider their position. But despite a looming public relations debacle, Marks & Spencer, the corporate Goliath, continued to ignore the young woman with a larger-size slingshot.

Beckie Williams's next move was nothing short of brilliant. In early May 2009, she went out and purchased a single share of Marks & Spencer stock for three pounds and forty pence (roughly $5). She then called the journalist who had first reported on her story and let her know of the group's plans. "I told her I was going to attend the Marks & Spencer's annual shareholders meeting in July and that I planned to confront the company chair, Sir Stuart Rose, in person on behalf of our group."

The specter of Beckie Williams and her busty friends publicly confronting the company's stockholders was too good a story for any journalist to pass up. By the next morning, Beckie Williams was in London taping a widely watched breakfast television show in which she discussed her much anticipated confrontation. By the time she arrived back in Brighton, her phone was ringing off the hook. Within fewer than forty-eight hours, Marks & Spencer had backed down.

The company not only agreed to price all bras equally, they issued an apology to Beckie Williams and her entire group. Finally taking advantage of the incredible marketing opportunity that had been staring them in the face all along, they promptly declared a huge brassiere sale to kick off their new era of bust size equality. Of course, being a British company, they were unable to resist inserting the obligatory pun into their official statement. "Basically," the spokesperson for the company admitted, "we've boobed!" Indeed, they had. Their first boob was penalizing women with larger cup sizes in the first place. But their far bigger boob was underestimating the determination of an effective complainer such as Beckie Williams as well as the powerful social pressure complaining activism can generate.

Beckie Williams started out writing a letter about a biased pricing policy and ended up creating change on a national level that benefited tens of thousands of women across the United Kingdom. Her simple complaint evolved into a grassroots campaign of social activism. The most remarkable aspect of her story is that Ms. Williams won her battle against the largest retailer in Great Britain without lawyers, pamphlets, candlelit marches, or financial sponsorship. She achieved these results using the same tools all of us have at our disposal—sheer determination and the Internet, both of which are free.

Many of our most commonly shared complaints and irritations remain unresolved because no one has yet stepped up, complained, and done something about them. A single person's speaking up is often enough to persuade others to join in and for entire communities to benefit. When I witnessed the rude employee in the drugstore that I described in chapter 2, a similar thing happened. At first people muttered and did nothing. But the moment one single person spoke up about "doing something," others joined in, and soon action was taken to alert the manager.

When our complaint is shared by other people in our neighborhood or community, it is the perfect opportunity to take our new effective complaining skills for a test-drive. We should always tell others when we complain because most of us get annoyed and frustrated by the same problems and our disclosure might galvanize others to complain as well.

Beckie Williams learned this lesson well. Her Facebook group developed into a supportive forum for women to discuss difficult experiences resulting from having a specific body type and a challenging adolescence. She thought it would be a shame for such a unique and valuable resource to disband simply because they'd won their battle against Marks & Spencer. "The experience awakened something in me," she told me when I asked her what she planned to do next. "I'm working on a Web site where girls can go and share their mixed emotions about being busty. It would be amazing if we could comfort these girls and normalize their experience." With thousands of her Facebook-group friends behind her, Beckie Williams is determined to continue her social activism and hopes to benefit girls and women all over the world.

But we do not need thousands of Facebook friends to make a difference in our own communities. Even a lone voice can be surprisingly effective in bringing about societal change by pursuing a complaint. When justice is on our side, speaking up passionately and making sure our story gets out to the relevant people can even empower us to take on the government and the Pentagon and take our fight all the way to the White House.

Dead Heroes Cannot Complain

On November 15, 2005, Matthew Holley and three other soldiers of the 101st Airborne Division from Fort Campbell, Kentucky, were killed in a bomb blast in Iraq. A few days later, Holley's devastated parents went to Lindbergh Field in San Diego to receive their son's remains. It is hard to imagine a more heartbreaking moment for a family, but their distress was about to become compounded. When the Holleys arrived, they learned their son's body was being shipped home in the cargo hold of a U.S. Airways flight from a military base in Delaware. Matthew's body would not be met by a military honor guard but by civilian baggage handlers. These civilian personnel would load the casket onto a luggage trolley and cart it to the airline's freight area, where they would await the family.

John Holley, himself a veteran, was outraged that his son's remains were to be handled by nonmilitary personnel using trolleys and forklifts. He could not believe the military would allow Matthew's coffin to leave the plane with no flag on it, no honor guard saluting it, none of the respect and dignity befitting the brave men and women who gave their lives for their country. John Holley was even more horrified to learn that such procedures were regularly used when handling the transfer of remains to families.

Mr. Holley knew he had to act immediately to prevent his son's coffin from being handled disrespectfully. Families of fallen soldiers are assigned a casualty-assistance officer from the appropriate service branch. John Holley called the family's casualty officer and insisted Matthew's casket be removed from the plane only by an honor guard from Fort Campbell and only once it had been draped with the flag. But U.S. Airways is a civilian airline with an established and tight flight schedule to which they have to adhere. Time was going to be of the essence.

The casualty officer began making frantic phone calls, one of which was to California senator Barbara Boxer. After some haggling with the airport-security regulators, the officer got an honor guard from Holley's unit, the 101st Airborne Division, based at Fort Campbell, Kentucky, over to Lindbergh Field in time to receive Matthew Holley's remains. John Holley's son was afforded the proper military honors on his journey to his final resting place.

But Mr. Holley was still reeling from the realization that other soldiers' remains were subject to the horrifically insensitive Pentagon procedures. He initiated a complaint to his congressional representative, Duncan Hunter, a Vietnam War veteran who was then the chair of the House Armed Services Committee, and secured continued assistance from Senator Barbara Boxer's office. Hunter insisted on the inclusion of a casket-transport provision in the House version of the 2007 National Defense Authorization Act. But the legislation could potentially cost the military millions of dollars for the transportation of remains, and with the costs of the war escalating, the provision might not be passed.

John Holley refused to back down. He decided to use the publicity and platform his initial complaint had generated to benefit every other parent who had to face the unspeakable agony of losing a child to war. He threatened to single out every single member of Congress who opposed the Holley Provision and publicly call them on their lack of support and respect for our country's fallen heroes. No elected official dared risk such negative publicity, and the defense authorization bill passed in both chambers soon thereafter. President Bush signed it into law on October 17, 2007.

Few of our complaints are as serious or as heart-wrenching as John Holley's. But the true lessons of Mr. Holley's complaint are unrelated to its emotional impact. Mr. Holley succeeded because he had the necessary psychological mind-set to do so—he was determined to prevent his son's remains from being disrespected. His certainty and determination came across in every interview he gave.

Beckie Williams was just as certain of her own victory. I asked her at which point she first realized she could win her fight against Marks & Spencer. She found it difficult to answer because the thought of not winning had never crossed her mind. "When we decided to start the Facebook group, I knew it was only a matter of time. I just didn't see how they could avoid backing down at that point."

But Marks & Spencer did not initially back down. They stood their ground on three separate occasions and held out for over a year after the group was formed. But Beckie Williams (like John Holley) had an unwavering determination and fundamental belief in her ability to create change and the righteousness of her cause.

Having faith in our own effectiveness is a crucial ingredient in our motivation to pursue meaningful complaints. One study examined the role of self-efficacy (how effective we believe ourselves to be in any given situation) on our tendency to withhold relational complaints. The largest predictor of whether people voiced complaints to another person was their belief in their ability to do so effectively. Using the techniques in this book to practice (and master) our effective-complaining skill set will give us greater faith in our abilities and therefore make us more likely to pursue complaints in the future.

Having faith in our effectiveness can allow us to influence our environment in matters both large and small. Pursuing our complaints with confidence can lead to change for the better all around us, whether our cause has national ramifications such as Beckie Williams's or John Holley's did or whether our purpose is merely to improve our communities in small but meaningful ways.

Complaining and, Yes, Complimenting Our Way to Better Communities

Life presents us with frequent opportunities to influence our communities and change them for the better because we can do so simply by giving feedback. Each time we visit a store, have a meal in a restaurant, take a bus or taxicab, or interact with a service provider, we have the option of letting them know what we thought about their service or product. Of course, most of our daily experiences are not worthy of comment as they fall somewhere in the "adequate" range. But when we encounter extremes in either direction, we have the perfect opportunity to take a quick dip in the waters of community activism.

We've all encountered rude employees in stores, filthy taxicabs, or inedible food in our local restaurants. Our families, friends, and neighbors encounter the same rude store employees, take the same dirty taxicabs, and dine in the same bad restaurants. If more of us complained effectively, store-owners would have more ammunition with which to terminate rude employees, cabdrivers would have more incentive to clean and air out their cabs midshift, and restaurants would improve their menus and stop serving bad food.

In New York City, rude service employees are far from being an endangered species. Yet, a single complaint to the people in charge would allow them to take another step toward replacing the offending employee with a pleasant one. When local businesses are staffed by pleasant people, it makes a huge difference to the general tone and friendliness of a neighborhood. Using complaints to effect such small changes in our communities is not a Herculean project, but rather a matter of daily mindfulness. We need only open our eyes to the daily opportunities we have for providing feedback to our neighbor-hood businesses and service providers.

Compliments have the same power to improve our communities as complaints do. However, as a society, we are even worse at complimenting than we are at complaining. We might enjoy good service experiences and might even tell friends about them, but we rarely let the people who provided the positive experience know that their efforts were appreciated. The same holds true when it comes to complimenting our friends, colleagues, and even our loved ones.

Compliments Seem to Be the Hardest Words

Why are we so bad at giving compliments? Because counterintuitive as it might seem, we find it socially and emotionally uncomfortable to compliment people in person. Complaints have the historical background of being transactional, and therefore most of us perceive them as being somewhat impersonal. But compliments are considered both more personal and more intimate than complaints. This greater implied intimacy takes most of us out of our comfort zones.

However, compliments are not inherently intimate or personal. They are merely a form of positive reinforcement (much as complaints are a form of negative reinforcement). With compliments we can increase the likelihood of getting more of what we like in the future. It is just as important for service professionals and businesses to hear from us about what they do well as it is to learn about what they should improve. When we encounter exceptional service at restaurants, knowledgeable sales staff in stores, or extremely understanding and helpful customer representatives, we should express our appreciation to them and detail what impressed us.

This simple directive is more complicated than it seems. Even when we are determined to compliment someone, we often struggle to find the words with which to do so. "Thanks, you were, um ... great!" is the best most of us do. As a sentiment, it's nice, but as feedback it's useless because it conveys no detail about what aspect of the person's efforts we appreciated most. It doesn't reinforce anything specific. On the other hand, "You were very patient and knowledgeable" expresses exactly what it was we appreciated. When we encounter a bank or post-office teller who processes twice as many people as the person next to them, "You're really fast and efficient. Thanks!" also conveys appreciation for specific efforts. We could provide similar feedback to a call-center employee who handled our complaint well by complimenting specific things they did that we appreciated: "Thanks. You were extremely pleasant, patient, and understanding."

All these compliments convey not just gratitude but the elements we would like the person to continue emphasizing in the future. Giving positive feedback to service employees around our communities, be they store clerks, waiters, post-office tellers, or cab-drivers, creates a pay-it-forward system that improves customer service for everyone. Such improvements give us further opportunities for positive reinforcement, which improves service even more, and so on. In time, this kind of positive societal dynamic can become self-perpetuating and have a significant positive impact on our communities.

Ironically, we tend to be even more miserly with our compliments when it comes to our loved ones. When my patients describe something their partners, friends, or family members did for them in superlative terms, I always ask if they expressed appreciation clearly and thoughtfully to that person. Far more often than not, we neglect to do so adequately. Too often, we complain to our spouses about something, then forget to pay attention and compliment them when they make efforts to change, even though it is clearly in our best interest to compliment any efforts in the desired direction as overtly as we possibly can. Complimenting small favors or efforts when our loved ones make them is the best way to increase the likelihood that those behaviors will reoccur.

Further and even more powerful reasons exist for us to increase our general mindfulness and identify complimenting opportunities in our daily lives. Complimenting others and expressing appreciation (especially with a Duchenne smile) has been shown to boost the mood of the person providing the feedback as much as it does the recipient's.

For those of us who might be skeptical about the "powers of gratitude," it is easy to set up an experiment and experience them for ourselves. All we need to do is wait for a service provider to do a job really well. Then we should give the provider a real Duchenne smile (remember not to skip the crow's-feet) and a specific and sincere statement of appreciation. If we did so correctly (crow's-feet and sincere gratitude), the provider's face will light up and we will get a Duchenne smile back.

Pursuing even minor complaints can improve our communities in small ways, and they can be just as important as addressing larger complaints. Most neighborhoods have numerous minor deficiencies and problems that we notice but do little to remedy. We typically leave the complaint making or action taking to others. But now that we are effective complainers, we can wave the flag of civic duty ourselves. Doing so is both satisfying and empowering. Small community complaints can also be good choices to practice complaining therapy.

When a tree falls in the forest, it does make a sound even if no one is there to hear it. But as I discovered when I interviewed Cari, when one falls in Manhattan, people not only don't hear it, they fail to see it as well. Luckily, all it takes is one effective complainer to hear it, see it, and make sure something is done about it.

A Tree Grows in Manhattan

In April 2007, New York mayor Michael Bloomberg announced the million tree initiative—a publicly and privately funded project to plant one million trees in New York's five boroughs within the next decade. The project inspired many tree-starved New Yorkers, including Bette Midler, who planted tree number 250,000 in October of 2009. Cari, a longtime New Yorker, embarked on her own tree initiative in October of 2008. Although she was hoping to plant only one tree, she soon discovered that getting a single tree planted in New York City could be just as challenging as planting a million of them.

Cari lived in the West Village in downtown Manhattan and knew it well. When a new tree was planted, she noticed it even if most did not. When an old tree died, she noticed that as well. One crisp fall afternoon, Cari noticed a tree had died outside a Wendy's restaurant in her neighborhood. The soil around the tree hinted at the cause of death.

"It was this disgusting sewerlike goo." Cari recoiled at the memory. "There was this stench … it reeked!" Cari noticed oily stains on the pavement surrounding the square yard of contaminated soil. Although not a sleuth by profession, it took only one glance over to the Wendy's restaurant to give Cari a strong hunch as to the culprit in the tree's premature demise.

Cari went into the Wendy's restaurant and asked to speak with the manager. She showed him the refuse-enriched soil and pointed at the dead tree interred within. The manager claimed the fault lay with the tree itself, as it stubbornly stood right smack where they put the garbage out at night. Cari suggested that since the tree was unable to move, the restaurant should place the garbage bags farther from the tree's base. The manager dismissed her suggestion and mumbled that city ordinances made that impossible.

Cari realized she was wasting her time with the obviously reluctant manager. So she decided to put her considerable complaining skills to use. She went home and, after a quick Google search for the relevant contact information, wrote a complaint letter to Roland C. Smith, Wendy's president and CEO, and carbon-copied Adrian Benepe, the commissioner of New York's Department of Parks & Recreation. Within a week, she received a response from Wendy's director of area operations, who forwarded her complaint to Andy Chan, the district manager. Mr. Chan contacted Cari soon thereafter and assured her he would handle the situation personally and would make sure another tree was planted in the same spot.

Cari was grateful Wendy's was being so responsive, but she also knew that no sapling could survive the soil of death currently filling the small plot. Mr. Chan listened to Cari's lingering concerns and agreed to replace the semi-radioactive soil with fresh, healthy dirt. However, such efforts would have to be coordinated with the city government, which was not an easy maneuver. In addition, the end of the year was approaching and no planting could be done until the spring. Mr. Chan promised to stay on the case and to keep Cari informed of any progress.

Cari was delighted when in the spring of 2009 and true to his word Mr. Chan called to let her know the new tree was finally in the ground. But the moment Cari lay eyes on the sapling ensconced in fresh, clean soil, she knew the tree was doomed. "The restaurant still placed their garbage there and still washed out the dirty chemical-filled water onto the sidewalk after cleaning the floors every night," she explained to Mr. Chan on the phone. "All those toxins go right into the new soil. It is only a matter of time before it kills the new tree as well." Cari suggested they cement stone bricks around the plot to prevent the poisonous fluids from spilling into the soil.

Mr. Chan again promised to take care of the matter. The next time Cari passed by the tree, it was protected by stone bricks that had indeed been cemented to the sidewalk. In addition, Mr. Chan had even taken the extra step of placing a wrought-iron fence around the plot to prevent any garbage bags from being placed directly around the trunk. The tree was safe at last! Today the tree remains healthy and strong, protected by Cari's single-tree initiative and its patron saint, Wendy's amazing Mr. Chan.

What makes Cari's complaint even more remarkable for its effectiveness is that at no point during the process did she imply or even insinuate that she was a Wendy's customer—as she is not. But Cari has always viewed New York as a collection of small neighborhoods, a place where people look out for each other and speak up about things that matter. Cari believes that even in a huge city such as New York "complaining is just another way citizens can improve their communities," a feeling apparently shared by Wendy's and Mr. Chan.

Cari wrote her last letter to Wendy's in July 2009, addressed again to Roland C. Smith, Wendy's president and CEO. Demonstrating her knack for delivering both negative and positive feedback, she followed up her complaint letter with one of gratitude and compliments. She thanked the company for replacing the tree and "doing a truly great and elegant job of it." She also singled out Mr. Andy Chan, whose caring and responsibility would make any company proud. As for the tree and the soil around it, the two couldn't be happier.

Of course, New York and any other major city have far bigger problems than dead trees. But the principle of how we might go about fixing these problems is the same. We have to speak up effectively. Wendy's local branch manager was not interested in helping Cari, but he probably did not have the authority to replace the tree even had he wanted to.

It is always crucial that we target the correct people for our complaints. *We need to first identify who has the power to make the changes we seek and then complain to that person directly.* Doing so makes our complaints more likely to get resolved quickly and thoroughly than if we make our way up corporate channels one executive at a time.

The Joy of Overrepresentation

We have one huge advantage living in a society of ineffective complainers. Those of us who wish to influence our communities have a better chance of succeeding than we may realize because of a phenomenon called *overrepresentation,* which guarantees those few of us who do speak up to have a far stronger impact than we would have had otherwise. When few people express their opinions, those who do so always have a larger say than their numbers suggest they should—they become overrepresented. Overrepresentation occurs every day in our society because the majority of us take advantage of only a fraction of the potential opportunities we have to make our opinions known.

A common example of overrepresentation occurs in elections. I vote in every general election or two-year primary, but I tend to skip voting when only city or state politics is involved. Why would I skip voting at local elections when they are obviously the contests that have the most direct impact on my life? Good question. But I am hardly alone in doing so. While voter turnout in the 2008 general elections was 62 percent, in off-year elections, voter turnout in some states drops to less than 25 percent. If only a quarter of us vote, those who do will have four times the influence on the outcome than if the turnout had been a full 100 percent. As a result, smaller groups who vote in atypically large numbers are overrepresented in the results, and they wield much larger political influence than their numbers alone suggest they should.

Another example of overrepresentation occurs in customer surveys. It is difficult to walk out of a store without finding a survey on the receipt (usually on the bottom—except when companies get desperate for feedback and smack it right at the top). These surveys provide us with simple and quick ways to give feedback or express specific complaints, as most surveys give us the option of describing any "incidents" in our own words. Yet the vast majority of us don't take these opportunities to let our opinions be known, even though companies, institutions, and government services, everyone from the Gap to Best Buy, from Starbucks to the U.S. Postal Service, are practically *begging* for our feedback.

Many survey requests have even begun offering raffles for cash prizes and multithousand-dollar spending sprees as a reward for the two to ten minutes it might take us to complete them. But evidently, the prospect of winning thousands of dollars in cardboard boxes, Bubble Wrap, and Homer Simpson stamps just doesn't do it for us.

I asked John A. Goodman about this outcry of institutional insecurity that has gone ignored by a helplessness-induced public. He suggested that few of us notice these ubiquitous survey offers or even know they exist. "Online surveys are the new comment cards," he said, "and they get ignored just as thoroughly. Only one to two percent of people complete them, if that." I asked a Starbucks manager how many customer surveys people complete a month. "We'd be ecstatic with fifteen but we pray for ten" was his response. Ten responses out of thousands of customer transactions every month!

Such a tiny response rate is bad news for the companies and government services, but good news for consumers. Those of us who do respond are guaranteed to have a much bigger impact when it comes to survey results. Our lone opinion might well be the straw that breaks the company's back and forces it to attend to the things that annoyed us in the first place.

I once completed a survey about my local Best Buy electronics store and included a specific complaint about the sales representatives' lack of attentiveness. The next morning an apology e-mail from James Lawrence, the branch manager, was waiting in my in-box. He apologized for the incident, gave his direct phone number, and offered to have a salesperson personally take me around the store. I declined the offer as I had already made my purchase, but I was impressed with it nonetheless. "Businesses definitely look at these survey numbers," Goodman confirmed (although he noted that few companies are as responsive as Best Buy to descriptions of specific complaints in online surveys).

Businesses are also beginning to pay attention to online customer review sites such as Trip Advisor (.com), Yelp (.com), as well as comments on social networking sites such as Twitter and Facebook. Both Yelp and Trip Advisor now allow businesses to respond to customer reviews, and many of them are doing so, at times even aggressively. Some small-business owners search out and read every review about them posted online, making it as easy as possible for us to make our opinions heard by those empowered to change things.

But can one single voice really make a difference by completing a customer survey or online review? Beckie Williams had thousands of supporters, yet it still took her a couple of years to pursue her complaint successfully. Is there really a point to us speaking up when for all we know we might be completely alone in doing so?

How Many Complaints Does It Take to Change a Lightbulb?

When I was in graduate school at New York University, I lived in a slightly run-down area of the East Village in Manhattan. My apartment was a dump but it was cheap. Unfortunately, the building manager was even cheaper. Whenever anything broke, it was always a battle to get it fixed. One day in the entrance to the building the circular neon light affixed to the thirteen-foot-high ceiling shorted out. The building superintendent said he would replace it as soon as he got authorization from management. To move things along, I called the management myself. Nothing happened. A neighbor I saw in the stairwell the next day said she too would call, but still nothing happened. A week later, she alerted a third neighbor, who called that very day, and a new bulb was installed within hours.

With complaints, three is often the magical number. One complaint might indicate an exception, two a coincidence, but three represent an undeniable pattern, enough for most people to begin to pay attention. This information can be extremely useful when our complaints are about common problems that many of us find frustrating. For example, few people enjoy arriving at a previously scheduled doctor's appointment on time only to spend two hours in the waiting room. Similarly, few women relish spending three times as much time waiting on line for bathrooms in public places as men (the Roman Empire favored unisex public bathrooms but it's been downhill for women's bladders ever since). Lastly, many kids in elementary and middle school struggle daily to complete exorbitant amounts of homework that leave them little time to do much of anything else.

In each of these common situations a single person is unlikely to have a sufficient impact to cause a change. But when decision makers hear complaints from three different people, it is often more than enough to spur them into action. The next time we find ourselves pacing with boredom in a doctor's waiting room, hopping up and down in an effort to control our bladder during intermission, or rocking back and forth with frustration as we help our eleven-year-old tackle the ninety-seventh math problem of the evening, we should consider doing something about it. Here's how.

Drowning in Homework

I first met Timothy, a quiet, overweight eleven-year-old boy, when his mother brought him to therapy to discuss his slipping grades. A few minutes with Timothy were enough to confirm that his mood, self-esteem, and general happiness had slipped right along with them. Timothy attended one of the top private schools in Manhattan, an environment in which slipping grades were no idle matter.

I asked about Timothy's typical day. He awoke every morning at six thirty so he could get to school by eight and arrived home around four thirty each afternoon. He then had a quick snack, followed by either a piano lesson or his math tutor, depending on the day. He had dinner at seven P.M., after which he sat down to do homework for *two to three hours a night.* Quickly doing the math in my head, I calculated that Timothy spent an average of thirteen hours a day hunched over a writing desk. His situation is not atypical. Spending that many hours studying is the only way Timothy can keep up and stay afloat academically.

But what if, for comparison's sake, we imagined Timothy spending thirteen hours a day hunched over a *sewing machine* instead of a desk. We would immediately be aghast at the inhumanity because children are horribly mistreated in such "sweatshops." Timothy is far from being mistreated, but the mountain of homework he faces daily results in a similar consequence—he too is being robbed of his childhood. His academics leave him virtually no time to do anything he truly enjoys, such as video games, movies, or board games with his friends. During the week he never plays outside and never has indoor play dates or opportunities to socialize with friends. On weekends, Timothy's days are often devoted to studying for tests, working on special school projects, or arguing with his mother about studying for tests and working on special school projects.

By the fourth and fifth grade and certainly in middle school, many of our children have hours of homework, test preparation, project writing, or research to do every night, all in addition to the eight hours or more they have to spend in school. Yet study after study has shown that *homework has little to do with achievement in elementary school and is only marginally related to achievement in middle school.* Play, however, is a crucial component of healthy child development. It affects children's creativity, their social skills, and even their brain development. The absence of play, physical exercise, and free-form social interaction takes a serious toll on many children. It can also have significant health implications as is evidenced by our current epidemic of childhood obesity, sleep deprivation, low self-esteem, and depression.

A far stronger predictor than homework of academic achievement for kids three to twelve is having regular family meals. Family meals allow parents to check in, to demonstrate caring and involvement, to provide supervision, and to offer support. The more family meals can be worked into the schedule, the better, especially for preteens. The frequency of family meals has also been shown to help with disordered-eating behaviors in adolescents.

Experts in the field recommend children have no more than ten minutes of homework per day per grade level. As a fifth-grader, Timothy should have no more than fifty minutes a day of homework (instead of three times that amount). Having an extra two hours an evening to play, relax, or see a friend would constitute a huge bump in any child's quality of life.

So what can we do if our child is getting too much homework? We should complain to the teachers and the school. Sara Bennett, author of *The Case Against Homework: How Homework Is Hurting Our Children and What We Can Do About It,* believes most parents are unaware that excessive homework contributes so little to their child's academic achievement. They are also unaware they can complain about this to teachers or school principals, especially when younger kids are involved (K–4).

It is often easier to get policies changed in private schools than in public schools. However, even in public schools, educating the teachers and principals about homework research is a good place to begin and an even better way to create allies within the system.

See the chapter notes, which list Sara Bennett's informative Web site and blog for numerous resources including sample complaints parents have written.

Waiting-Room Blues

Americans are spending much more time at the doctor these days, not because we are less healthy as a nation but because wait times in most doctors' offices have reached outrageous proportions. We arrive in the waiting room on time for our *scheduled* appointments (walk-in clinics are obviously a different story), then wait anywhere from several minutes to several hours before we are even called into an examining room. Once in the examining room we wait again, often an additional fifteen to thirty minutes before the doctor rushes in. Then the doctor leaves so the nurse can do our blood work (nurses are typically far more punctual than doctors), after which we have to wait for the doctor again. And wait. And wait. Even the most basic of medical visits can take several hours for what often amounts to less than five minutes of face time with our doctor. The problem is the system.

Doctors usually schedule several patients at the same time, then shuttle between the different rooms. Booking several patients in the same time slot allows doctors to process more patients a day and maximize their billing. However, once the slightest complication with any one patient occurs, the other patients are left waiting even longer for the doctor to return. Most of us find this practice inconvenient and annoying, not to mention *incredibly disrespectful of our time.*

I wondered whether any studies had examined the effect of excessive wait times on patient loyalty and consequently on the bottom line of medical practices. Indeed some had, and the research was done by none other than John A. Goodman. He was asked to consult with a leading healthcare provider, and his team identified four main issues that had a negative impact on their bottom line.

Sure enough, one of these primary problems was extended wait times both for and during medical appointments.

"Often it's the leading doctors that are responsible," Goodman explained. "They are always fully booked. But then they have to shoehorn in these extra emergencies, and that makes them overbooked. One appointment nurse told me she had started telling patients that they had a ten A.M. appointment but they should bring their lunch." I asked Goodman how bad things could get. I was slightly horrified by the answer: "The average wait time in some of the clinics we looked at was five hours." *Five hours!*

Few of us complain about wait times in our doctor's offices and fewer complain to the right people. We might mention our dissatisfaction to a nurse or receptionist, and the rare brave souls might hint at their displeasure to their doctor during their examinations, but the majority of us simply seethe in silence. This is no ordinary complaining situation. It isn't easy to confront an authority figure with confidence and assertiveness while wearing only our underwear and a gown possessing the structural integrity of toilet paper. In addition, all the regular justifications we have for not complaining still apply: we're not sure to whom our complaints should be addressed, we're afraid complaining will do no good, and we fear retaliation by the complaint recipient (who is in this case authorized to stick needles in us, not to mention fingers).

Consequently, precious few of us write a complaint to the patient-relations officer at the hospital, the office manager at the clinic, or the head physician of the group about wait times. But hospitals and medical practices are businesses. They exist to serve their customers—us. Keeping their customers should matter to them, especially given the long-term nature of most patient-physician relationships. Therefore, a letter to the head physician, clinic manager, or president of the hospital in which we threaten to take our aching back, suspicious-looking moles, and irritable bowels elsewhere might get their attention.

I asked Goodman how many letters he thought it would take to get a clinic to start doing something about excessive wait times. "If physicians get three complaints, they start looking into it," Goodman confirmed. Again three is the magical number that makes people take our complaints more seriously. Therefore, when next you find yourself waiting too long for a medical appointment, all you have to do is recruit two other annoyed patients from the waiting room who keep checking their watch and muttering. Offer to e-mail them a copy of your complaint letter, and ask them to send their own version to the people in charge. It is preferable to space out the three complaint letters by a few days or a week for maximum impact.

Potty Parity: When Equal Means Twice as Many

In 2005, New York City mayor Michael Bloomberg signed the Potty Parity Bill, a long overdue piece of legislation that calls for newly constructed or renovated public sites such as cinemas, concert halls, and the new Mets and Yankees stadiums to have two women's bathroom stalls for every men's stall. Finally, an age-old injustice has been resolved. No longer will women have to wait three times as long on bathroom lines as men do. Mayor Bloomberg was not the first person to take on this issue. That honor belongs to Professor John F. Banzhaf III of George Washington University's School of Law. Professor Banzhaf filed the first federal "potty parity complaint" in 2002. He went on to make tireless efforts to establish potty legislation all around the country, eventually earning himself the dubious title Father of Potty Parity.

Such legislation was hardly slapped together willy-nilly. Scholarly research had already substantiated the horrors of bathroom inequality. Sandra Rawls of Virginia Polytechnic Institute wrote her doctoral dissertation on the subject—"Patterns of Behavior in the Use of Male-Female Restrooms." Professor Savannah Day of Virginia Tech studied exactly what men and women do differently in the bathroom. Mind you, most of us could probably guess the answer to this question, but the bottom line is that whatever women do differently from men takes twice as long.

Those of us who live in communities that are as of yet untouched by potty parity might wonder how to bring such enlightened toilet policies to our own areas. In general, tapping into complaints that have already been argued effectively elsewhere can save us a lot of time and effort. Since this matter requires passing legislation, our complaint letters would have to be addressed to our elected officials. We might do best by identifying local congressional representatives or assembly members who are up for reelection and sending our potty-parity complaints to them. We might also include copies of the legal complaints filed by the Father of Potty Parity himself (Professor Banzhaf kindly offers links to those on his Web site, which I list in the notes to this chapter).

Since few of us complain about such things to our elected officials, three complaint letters to any candidate might well be sufficient to spur him or her into action, especially during election cycles. We might also mention in our complaint letters that acting on an issue that will benefit a full 50 percent of the elected official's constituents could only be a winner. Their efforts are likely to get attention in the local press and consequently appeal to many female voters with weary bladders in their district.

Effective-Complaining Utopias

If more and more of us spoke up about issues we would like to change in our communities, if more of us complained effectively instead of venting to the wind, if more of us demanded our most common complaints be addressed and resolved, imagine the collective impact we could have. Our local businesses and service providers would all rise to a new standard of customer service that truly prioritized our needs and desires as consumers. We could walk down the street and pop into stores or restaurants knowing we would encounter pleasant, kind, and helpful staff who would in turn inspire us to be more pleasant, kind, and helpful ourselves.

In part we complain excessively today because of the great need for improvement in customer service, product development and reliability, and especially consumer-complaint handling. We should never have to have our days ruined by spending hours in a doctor's waiting room, getting disconnected by a call-center worker after our call has been transfered for the third time, or being insulted by rude store employees. By complaining effectively and by getting others to do so with us, we can change our communities, we can start our own small campaigns of social activism, we can make a difference.

We can also create equally meaningful change in our personal lives. All it requires is for us to speak up about the things that bother us, and to do so in ways that promote and improve our relationships in the long term. We can learn to receive complaints better, to be patient and responsive when our friends and family members voice their own dissatisfactions. Better responses on our part can easily turn such situations into opportunities for further dialogue about the things that could make our relationships happier, more satisfying, and more fulfilling.

But most of all we can use effective complaining to improve our own self-esteem and strengthen our own mental health. We can use complaints as psychological tools that have the power to banish feelings of resignation and helplessness that can threaten to overwhelm us when things go wrong. Doing so will allow us to feel more confident, competent, and proactive in other areas of our lives as well. By pursuing even minor complaints effectively and successfully, we might become inspired to take on new and greater challenges that we would never have considered otherwise.

Beckie Williams would never have started a Web site to empower young women had she not experienced winning her battle against Marks & Spencer. John Holley would never have changed how fallen soldiers are transported on their final journeys had he not been successful in making sure his own son's remains were given the proper and dignified treatment.

We can and should start with the most doable, the smallest and most trivial of matters, because one successful and effective complaint resolution empowers another. Every day is an opportunity to go through our Rolodexes of dissatisfactions, to choose one and begin pursuing it using the effective-complaining techniques and guidelines in this book. Our self-esteem, our mental health, our relationships, and our communities would all benefit as a result.

Together we could bring about a true revolution, a grassroots campaign to change our lives, our homes, and our neighborhoods for the better. The next time we find ourselves venting a complaint to a friend instead of to the person who can do something about it, we should remember that the door to our own psychological revolution could start with that very complaint. Life presents us with new and challenging problems every day. We have no shortage of dissatisfactions and complaints from which to choose. It is time instead to stock up on solutions and resolutions. After all, they are only one effective squeak away.

Epilogue
Squeaking on Social Media

The explosion of social media Web sites, such as Facebook, Twitter, YouTube, and others, has provided consumers with new venues through which they can voice their complaints to businesses. Consumers need no longer fear that registering complaints will require too much time and effort in determining who to address written complaints to or spending precious time navigating automated telephone menus or being left on hold for extended periods of time.

For example, Twitter users can simply tweet their problems in 140 characters or less using dedicated Twitter handles (@ CompanyHandle) and hashtags (#CompanyName) and many companies respond within minutes. A growing number of companies now monitor social media sites as an important source of customer feedback and a way to stay on top of what's being said about their company or their product. The power of social media to catch the attention of corporations was evident when a Groupon ad campaign that aired during the 2011 Super Bowl drew a flood of complaints on social media. According to "Milk Campaign Ended Amid Social Media Firestorm" by Stuart Elliott in the *New York Times*, Groupon withdrew the campaign after being "taken aback at how quickly the complaints came in—many only a day or two after the campaign began—and how intense, even angry, the critics were."

Beyond the convenience, complaining on social media helps those people who find the specter of face-to-face (or voice-to-voice) confrontations so intimidating or aggravating that they would rather remain silent. By making complaining less nerve-wracking, as well as less time-consuming, social media is having a positive impact on our collective complaining psychology and empowering the public. This is especially welcome news for younger consumers who in the past have been less likely to complain or less skilled in complaining effectively.

As is often the case when presented with new tools, not everyone uses social media to complain correctly at first. Many consumers simply slam companies rather than observe the same techniques that work when complaining by traditional means. Tweeting to a company "I need help!" or "Cable out 5 times this week!" is more useful than "You suck!" You may not be able to deliver a complete complaint sandwich on social media but you can serve up an open-faced version by stating your problem in palatable wording (no epithets), followed by a positive statement or request for specific remediation. For example, @HelplessBill could tweet this to his cable company: "@NYCableCo Two tech visits already but to no avail. Glitch still locks me out of system every day. Can't enjoy new TV! Please help!"

Social media, when used properly, is one more arrow in the quiver of effective complainers.

NOTES

Introduction

2 a waste of our limited emotional resources: M. Mauraven and R. F. Baumeister, "Self-regulation and depletion of limited resources: Does self-control resemble a muscle?" *Psychological Bulletin* 125, no. 2 (March 2000): 247–59.

2 Bacteria ... greater than that of all other living things: S. J. Gould, *Full House: The spread of excellence from Plato to Darwin* (New York: Random House, 1997), 194.

3 Sydney Hotard: www.foxnews.com/story/0,2933,480726,00.html.

Chapter 1: The In effective Squeaker Doesn't Get the Grease

11 our complaints have become almost entirely unproductive: M. D. Alicke et al., "Complaining behavior in social interaction," *Personality and Social Psychology Bulletin* 18, no. 3 (1992): 286–95.

12 complaint choirs: See comlaintchoirs.org or youtube.com. The Helsinki choir is often at the head of the "hit" list. Enter *complaint choir* and a specific city or country of interest to see complaint-choir performances from that area.

13 Henry Wheeler Shaw (Josh Billings): David B. Kesterson, *Josh Billings (Henry Wheeler Shaw)* (New York: Twayne Publishers, 1973).

14 "The Kicker" by Josh Billings: Christine Ammer, *The American Heritage Dictionary of Idioms* (Boston: Houghton Mifflin Company, 1997), 607.

15 Gregg Easterbrook, *The Progress Paradox: How life gets better while people feel worse* (New York: Random House, 2003).

16 discontinued candy bar: www.guardian.co.uk/media/2008/nov/05/ advertising.

17 complain primarily to vent our emotions: Alicke et al., "Complaining behavior"; and R. M. Kowalski, "Complaints and complaining: Functions, antecedents, and consequences," *Psychological Bulletin* 119 (1996): 179–96.

21 Kowalski defines complaining behavior: Kowalski, "Complaints and Complaining," 180.

22 complaints serve four primary *social* functions: R. M. Kowalski, *Complaining, Teasing and Other Annoying Behaviors* (New Haven: Yale University Press, 2003).

25 One of the chief advocates of the complaint slim-down: Will Bowen, *A Complaint Free World: How to stop complaining and start enjoying the life you always wanted* (Garden City, NY: Doubleday, 2007).

25 six million purple bracelets: www.acomplaintfreeworld.org.

26 depression might be the least of their problems: Kowalski, *Complaining,* 29.

28 Goodman's group published their first report: The original study is out of print. A summary of the 1974–79 and 1984–86 studies called "Increasing Customer Satisfaction" was published by the U.S. Consumer Information Center in Pueblo, Colorado, in 1986.

29 "Why would companies *ever* want to talk": Quoted by John A. Goodman in our interview.

31 a mind-boggling 95 percent of disgruntled customers never complain: John A. Goodman, "Basic facts on customer complaint behavior and the impact of service on the bottom line," *Competitive Advantage,* June 1999, 1–5.

31 80 percent of customer problems are caused by: John A. Goodman, "Manage complaints to enhance loyalty," *Quality Progress,* 2006, 28–34.

32 Goodman identified four primary reasons we fail to take action: Ibid.

Chapter 2: The Trouble with Bill—the Hidden Costs of Ineffective Squeaking

43 maximum commission as a whopping $1,000: http://consumerxchange.com/OPENprice.htm.

44 new customers could cost a business *five times* as much: John A. Goodman, "Basic facts on customer complaint behavior and the impact of service on the bottom line," *Competitive Advantage*, June 1999, 1–5.

45 we actually become more loyal as customers: John A. Goodman, "Manage complaints to enhance loyalty," *Quality Progress*, February 2006, 28–34.

47 "Top Corporate Hate Websites": Charles Worlich, "Top Corporate Hate Websites," www.forbes.com/2005/03/07/cx_cw_0308hate.html.

48 Girls Gone Wild: www.girls-gone-wild.pissedconsumer.com (accessed January 4, 2010).

49 Better Business Bureau: The BBB uses over 120 local franchises in the United States and Canada. Their goal is to foster fairness and trust between businesses and their customers. They provide information such as the consumer-complaint histories of companies and offer dispute-resolution services. The BBB Web site (bbb.org) is a great resource for names and addresses of a company's top executives.

Other sources for consumer complaints and disputes: Consumer Action (consumer-action.org) has guides and resources for consumers in several languages. Call for Action (callforaction.org) is an international nonprofit network of consumer hotlines. They have volunteers around the world to assist consumers in disputes with businesses as well as governmental agencies. Their services are free and confidential. They claim to resolve 90 percent of all their cases. You can reach them through the above Web site or in the United States by calling 301-657-8260.

52 self-defeating prophecies have repeatedly been studied: Beginning with Robert K. Merton, "The self-fulfilling prophecy," *Antioch Review* 8 (1948): 193–210.

52 the Pygmalion effect: R. Rosenthal and L. Jacobson, "Teacher expectations for the disadvantaged," *Scientific American* 218 (1968): 19–23.

52 negative impacts of the Pygmalion effect: A. E. Smith, L. Jussim, and J. Eccles, "Do self-fulfilling prophecies accumulate, dissipate, or remain stable over time?" *Journal of Personality and Social Psychology* 77, no. 3 (September 1999): 548–65.

55 while studying learning behavior in dogs: J. B. Overmier and M. E. P. Seligman, "Effects of inescapable shock upon subsequent escape and avoidance responding," *Journal of Comparative and Physiological Psychology* 63 (1967): 28–33.

57 trained hopelessness: J. A. Goodman, and C. Grimm, "Beware of trained hopelessness," *ICCM Weekly*, May 2007; and J. A. Goodman, *Strategic Customer Service: Managing the customer experience to increase positive word of mouth, build loyalty and maximize profits* (New York: AMACOM, American Management Association, 2009).

60 learned helplessness—their ability to generalize across situations: D. S. Hiroto and M. E. P. Seligman, "Generality of learned helplessness in man," *Journal of Personality and Social Psychology* 31 (1975): 311–27; and L. D. Young and J. M. Allin, "Persistence of learned helplessness in humans," *Journal of General Psychology* 113 (1986): 81–88.

60 and came up with a vitally important insight: M. E. P. Seligman, *Authentic Happiness: Using the new positive psychology to realize your potential for lasting fulfillment* (New York: Free Press, 2002), 23.

62 how we make those attributions, whom and what we blame: L. Y. Abrahamson, M. E. P. Seligman, and J. D. Teasdale, "Learned helplessness in humans: Critique and reformulation," *Journal of Abnormal Psychology* 87 (1978): 49–74; and P. C. Henry, "Life stress, explanatory style, hopelessness, and occupational stress," *International Journal of Stress Management* 12 (2005): 241–56.

64 The difference between optimists and pessimists: M. E. P. Seligman, *Learned Optimism* (New York: Knopf, 1990).

65 it reduced their later rate of adolescent depression by half: M. E. P. Seligman, *The Optimistic Child* (New York: Houghton-Mifflin, 1996); and Seligman, *Authentic Happiness.*

65 A high school varsity team: M. Miserandino, "Attributional retraining as a method of improving athletic performance," *Journal of Sport Behavior* 21, no. 3 (1998): 286–97.

66 Let's revisit those poor dogs: E. M. Altmaier and D. A. Happ, "Coping skills training's immunization effects against learned helplessness," *Journal of Social and Clinical Psychology* 3, no. 2 (1985): 181–89.

67 We can teach ourselves that the harness of trained hopelessness: E. Ramirez, A. Maldonado, and R. Martos, "Attributions modulate immunization against learned helplessness in humans," *Journal of Personality and Social Psychology* 62 (1992): 139–46.

70 Comprehensive Soldier Fitness Program: A. Novotney, "Strong in mind and body," *Monitor on Psychology* 40, no. 11 (2009): 40–43.

Chapter 3: Complaining Therapy—Squeaking Our Way

79 Millions were spent on self-esteem programs: J. Crocker and L. E. Park, "The costly pursuit of self-esteem," *Psychological Bulletin* 130 (2004): 392–414.

79 They were all fool's gold: R. F. Baumeister et al., "Does high self-esteem cause better performance, interpersonal success, happiness, or healthier lifestyles?" *Psychological Science in the Public Interest* 4 (2003): 1–44; and W. B. Swann Jr., C. Chang-Schneider, and K. L McClarty, "Do people's self-views matter? Self-concept and self-esteem in everyday life," *American Psychologist* 62, no. 2 (2007): 84–94.

79 Undeterred, the State of California commissioned an entire task force: California Task Force to Promote Self-Esteem and Personal and Social Responsibility, *Toward a State of Self-Esteem*

(Sacramento: California State Department of Education, 1989). The person behind the task-force initiative was California assemblyman John Vasconcellos, who was a champion of and true believer in the impact of having high self-esteem: John Vasconcellos, *The Social Importance of Self-Esteem,* www.lightparty.com/visionary/ importanceselfesteem.html.

80 People have attitudes about themselves that are both *global*: M. Rosenberg, et al., "Global self-esteem and specific self-esteem: Different concepts, different outcomes," *American Sociological Review* 60, no. 1 (1995): 141–56; and A. Kohn, "The truth about self-esteem," *Phi Delta Kappan* 76, no. 4 (1994): 272–83.

81 The more meaningful a domain of specific self-esteem is to us: L. Hardy, and T. Moriarty, "Shaping self-concept: The elusive Importance Effect," *Journal of Personality* 74, no. 2 (2006): 377–402.

82 many aspects of our self-esteem do not remain static: J. Crocker and C. T. Wolfe, "Contingencies of self-worth," *Psychological Review* 108 (2001): 593–623.

83 the only thing that can undo feelings of victimization: No studies have been conducted on victimization as resulting from complaints. However, taking action and having faith in our ability to manage our environment (such as by pursuing a complaint and getting a resolution) have been demonstrated to facilitate mental health and self-esteem for victims of traumatic events (such as terrorist attacks, rape, and others). For a review see C. C. Benight and A. Bandura, "Social cognitive theory of posttraumatic recovery: The role of perceived self-efficacy," *Behavior Research and Therapy* 42, no. 10 (2004): 1129–48.

85 Research on lottery winners shows: P. Brickman, D. Coates, and R. Janoff-Bulman, "Lottery winners and accident victims: Is happiness relative?" *Journal of Personality and Social Psychology* 36 (1978): 917–27.

85 the importance of identifying our "signature strengths": M. E. P. Seligman, *Authentic Happiness: Using the new positive psychology to* *realize your potential for lasting fulfillment* (New York: Free Press, 2002).

90 a type D personality: J. Denollet, "DS14: Standard assessment of negative affectivity, social inhibition and Type D personality," *Psychosomatic Medicine* 67 (2005): 89–97; and J. Denollet, J. Vaes, and D. L. Brusaert, "Inadequate responses to treatment in coronary heart disease: Adverse effects of Type D personality and younger age on 5-year progress and quality of life," *Circulation* 102 (2000): 630–35.

90 They called these people type A personalities: M. Friedman and R. H. Rosenman, *Type A Behavior and Your Heart* (New York: Knopf, 1974).

90 (I was briefly involved in such research at the time): T. E. Lobel, L. Bar-Nof, and G. L. Winch, "Type A behavior pattern and assertive behavior," *European Journal of Personality* 2, no. 4 (1988): 295–301.

91 Dr. Johan Denollet of the Netherlands found something interesting: J. Denollet et al., "Personality as independent predictor of long-term mortality in patients with coronary heart disease," *Lancet* 347 (1996): 417–21.

93 once asked her students to list pet peeves: R. M. Kowalski, *Complaining, Teasing and Other Annoying Behaviors* (New Haven: Yale University Press, 2003), 36–37.

98 a result of its depictions in film and television: *One Flew Over the Cuckoo's Nest* (1975); and *Frances* with Jessica Lange (1982).

Chapter 4: When to Squeak—How to Avoid Complaining Dangers

107 Unfortunately, we usually find out about the latter group the hard way: www.wltx.com/news/story.aspx?storyid=59423&provider=top.

108 stabbed to death by a woman for complaining about her barking dog: www.smh.com.au/national/woman-killed-man-who-complained-about-her-dog-court-20090310-8twq.html.

108 shot in the arm at a South Carolina Waffle House by her waitress: privateofficernews.wordpress.com/2009/05/13/

waffle-house-waitress-shoots-complaining-customer-www-privateofficer-com/.

108 sporting events are often the venue of choice: Thomas Junta, a hockey dad, complained to the referee (who was also the father of another player) about a call during the game. Junta beat the referee to death. abcnews.go.com/GMA/story?id=126414&page=1.

108 Adrienne Shelly was murdered: gothamist.com/2006/11/07/shellys_murder.php.

108 I am writing this letter to you: The full text of the letter can be found in J. Lefkowitz, *Ethics and Values in Industrial-Organizational Psychology* (New Jersey: Psychology Press, 2003), 362.

110 The hapless Professor Flynn was humiliated: A couple of examples: www.nytimes.com/2004/02/08/nyregion/following-up.html?fta=y; and a British newspaper, www.timeshighereducation.co.uk/story .asp?storyCode=166964§ioncode=26few.

110 Professor Flynn was promptly sued: The court ruling can be found at www.nycourts.gov/comdiv/Law%20Report%20Files/January %202003/Chez.htm.

111 Psychologist Amanda Rose: A. J. Rose, W. Carlson, and E. M. Waller, "Prospective Associations of Co-Rumination with Friendship and Emotional Adjustment: Considering the Socioemotional Trade-Offs of Co-Rumination," *Developmental Psychology* 43, no. 4 (2007): 1019–31.

113 our identities are shaped by the stories we construct: M. White and D. Epston, *Narrative Means to Therapeutic Ends* (New York: Norton, 1990).

117 depression and co-rumination formed a vicious cycle: Rose, Carlson, and Waller, "Prospective Associations of Co-Rumination."

121 or there could be more suicide threats: D. Shaffer, M. S. Gould, and P. Fisher, "Psychiatric diagnosis in child and adolescent suicide," *Archive of General Psychiatry* 53 (1996): 339–48.

126 recruited over one hundred illegitimate complainers: K. L. Reynolds and L. C. Harris, "When service failure is not service failure: An exploration of the forms and motives of 'illegitimate' customer complaining," *Journal of Services Marketing* 19, no. 5 (2005): 321–35.

129 Web site's efforts to educate and inform the public: Examples of private and government medical-information sites: www.webmd.com; mayoclinic.com; www.nlm.nih.gov/medlineplus; wrongdiagnosis.com.

130 Few of us speak up in such situations: J. A. Goodman and D. Ward, "Satisfied patients lower risk and improve the bottom line," *Patient Safety & Quality Healthcare,* March/April, 2008.

134 In a 1999 study, Professor John Hunsley: J. Hunsley et al., "Comparing therapist/client perspectives on reasons for psychotherapy termination," *Psychotherapy: Theory, Research, Practice, Training* 36 (1999): 380–88.

136 in almost every psychotherapy-outcome study: A review and analysis of many outcome studies can be found in D. J. Martin, J. P. Garske, and M. K. Davis, "Relation of the therapeutic alliance with outcome and other variables: A meta-analytic review," *Journal of Consulting and Clinical Psychology* 68, no. 3 (June 2000): 438–50.

Chapter 5: The Ingredients for Serving a Delicious Squeak

142 emphasis on rage and anger did little to increase the impact of his letter: S. Carder and L. Gunter, "Can you hear me? Corporate America's communication with dissatisfied customers," *Journal of American & Comparative Cultures* 24, no. 3/4 (Fall 2001): 109–12.

143 my doctoral dissertation had been related: G. L. Winch, "Intrinsic motivation and self-regulation: Applications to psychotherapy," *Dissertation Abstracts International* 53, 3-B (1992): 1620.

146 hiding them in such ways is called suppression: J. J. Gross and R. W. Levenson, "Emotional suppression: Physiology, self-report, and expressive behavior," *Journal of Personality and Social Psychology* 64 (1993): 970–86.

147 Psychologists call this process reappraisal: O. P. John and J. J. Gross, "Healthy and unhealthy emotion regulation: Personality processes, individual differences and life span development," *Journal of Personality* 72, no. 6 (2004): 1301–33.

148 they are not by any means equally effective: J. J. Gross and O. P. John, "Individual differences in two emotion regulation processes: Implications for affect, relationships, and well-being," *Journal of Personality and Social Psychology* 85 (2003): 348–62.

148 In one experiment titled Famous Overnight: L. M. Jacoby et al., "Becoming famous overnight: Limits on the ability to avoid unconscious influences of the past," *Journal of Personality and Social Psychology* 56, no. 3 (March 1989): 326–38.

163 people tend to infer that an opinion they have heard several times: K. R. B. Weaver et al., "Inferring the popularity of an opinion from its familiarity: A repetitive voice can sound like a chorus," *Journal of Personality and Social Psychology* 92, no. 5 (May 2007): 821–33.

163 factor that can affect our unconscious perception of truth: R. Reber and N. Schwartz, "Effects of perceptual fluency on judgments of truth," *Consciousness and Cognition* 8 (1999): 338–42.

164 We love rhyme: M. S. McGlone and J. Tofighbakhsh, "Birds of a feather flock conjointly (?): Rhyme as reason in aphorisms," *Psychological Science* 11, no. 5 (September 2000): 424–28.

167 In one early study, Cookies for Kindness: A. M. Isen and P. F. Levin, "The effect of feeling good on helping: Cookies and kindness," *Journal of Personality and Social Psychology* 21 (1972): 384–88.

168 How powerful is an authentic smile?: M. J. Hertenstein et al., "Smile intensity in photographs predicts divorce later in life," *Motivation and Emotion* 33, no. 2 (June 2009): 99–105.

170 Complaint sandwich condiments: Additional considerations when constructing complaint letters:

- *Professionalism*: Try to sound as professional as possible. Complaint letters are in essence business letters; they should look and sound like one.

- *Detail*: Include all relevant detail such as date and time of purchase, model and serial numbers of products, names of persons involved and their job titles (i.e., sales associate, shift manager or floor manager).
- *Brevity*: Try to keep your complaint to one page or less.
- *Clarity*: Keep your sentences short and simple. It should be easy for the reader to understand what happened and what went wrong.
- *Resolution Specificity*: State specifically what you are asking for or what would constitute a satisfying resolution for you, and be reasonable and fair in doing so (e.g., a refund, an apology, a free delivery of the missing part, a free month of the service, rent abatements, and so on). It is much easier to respond positively to a complaint that includes a clear indication of what the person considers a fair resolution.
- *Personal Information*: Don't forget to include your own information, including how it is best to reach you. Provide your name, address, and telephone number as well as an e-mail address if you have one, and specify which of those is preferable for them to contact you.
- *Target the Complaint Recipient Correctly*: Identify who within a company has the authority to resolve your complaint and address your complaint to that person. Information on many companies is available at the Better Business Bureau (bbb.org). You can also try the company's Web site by searching for the CONTACT US tab at the top or bottom of their home page or a CUSTOMER SERVICE tab. Those should give you the names and e-mail addresses of the persons or department handling complaints or queries. If your complaint is to a smaller business such as a restaurant, call them and ask for the name of the manager or owner. You can also check to see if a company has a toll-free number by calling 800-555-1212. Typically, the highest person in a company is the CEO (chief executive officer), but other C-level officers

are also empowered to address problems, such as the chief financial officer (CFO).

- *Perceptual Fluency:* Use spell-checks and grammar-checks, then check for typos by reading the letter aloud. Typos and spelling errors can interfere with perceptual fluency.
- *Record Keeping*: Always print out and save a copy of your complaint letter as well as a copy of all receipts, warranties, or documentation.
- *Turnaround Times*: Expect to get a response in less than thirty days. If you do not, try someone higher up in the company, preferably a C-level executive.

Chapter 6: The Art of Squeaking to Loved Ones

172 marriage researchers predicted which couples would remain together: J. M. Gottman, *What Predicts Divorce?* (Hillsdale, NJ: Erlbaum, 1994).

173 Four Horsemen of the Apocalypse: J. M. Gottman et al., "Predicting Marital Happiness and Stability from Newlywed Interactions." *Journal of Marriage and the Family* 60, no. 1 (1998): 5–22.

175 But a crucial difference separates a complaint from a criticism: J. M. Gottman and N. Silver, *The Seven Principles for Making Marriage Work* (New York: Three Rivers Press, 1999), 27–29.

176 Criticism, the First Horseman, often leads to the Second: Ibid.

178 Withdrawal and disengagement represent Gottman's Third Horseman: Gottman et al., "Predicting Marital Happiness."

183 gay and lesbian couples: J. M. Gottman et al., "Correlates of Gay and Lesbian Couples' Relationship Satisfaction and Relationship Dissolution," *Journal of Homosexuality* 45, no. 1 (2003): 23–43.

185 measured how long members of a couple gazed: J. Flora and C. Segrin, "Affect and behavioral involvement in spousal complaints and compliments," *Journal of Family Psychology* 14, no. 4 (2000): 641–57.

187 to balance out complaint talk with fun: Gottman and Silver, *Seven Principles.*

190 The stronger a couple's friendship is, the stronger their couplehood: Ibid.

192 Some couples can become allergic to one another: M. R. Cunningham and L. K. Ault, "Social allergies in romantic relationships," *Personal Relationships* 12, no. 2 (2005): 273–95.

196 they can be seen in many kinds of relationships: J. P. Caughlin and T. L. Huston, "A contextual analysis of the association between demand/withdraw and marital satisfaction," *Personal Relationships* 9 (2002): 95–119.

196 *direct* associations between demand/withdraw communication and teen substance abuse: J. P. Caughlin and R. S. Malis, "Demand/ withdraw communication between parents and adolescents: Connections with self-esteem and substance abuse," *Journal of Social and Personal Relationships* 21, no. 1 (2004): 125–48.

199 Second, when we do need to discuss heavy issues such as drugs: Resources for parents dealing with teenagers and drug or alcohol use can be found at Parents: The Anti-Drug's Web site, www.theantidrug.com.

204 Carol Siskind and Mike Yard jokes about gender and friendships: www.jokes.com/stand-up-search//all/?keywords=friendships (accessed January 4, 2010).

204 A 2009 study out of the University of Michigan: S. L. Brown et al., "Social closeness increases salivary progesterone in humans," *Hormones and Behavior* 56, no. 1 (June 2009): 108–11.

Chapter 7: Getting Squeaked At for a Living: The Customer Service Professional

212 in 2008 almost *two million* customer service representatives: U.S. Department of Labor, Bureau of Labor Statistics' 2008 report, ftp://ftp.bls.gov/pub/special.requests/lf/aat11.txt.

212 80 percent of our problems are due to a company's faulty systems: J. A. Goodman and M. Wilke, "The Call Center Is the Place for the VOC," *Call Center Magazine,* May 2007, www.callcentermagazine.com/shared/printableArticle.jhtml;jsessionid=KJDRLXW1U40Q4QSNDLPCKHSCJUNN2JVN?articleID=199500718.

217 they've relocated a huge portion of their technical support operations: J. Barlow and C. Møller, *A Complaint Is a Gift,* 2nd ed. (San Francisco: Berrett-Koehler Publishers, 2008), 40.

222 "Do it right the first time!": John A. Goodman, "Manage complaints to enhance loyalty," *Quality Progress,* 2006, 28–34; and H. Liao, "Do It Right This Time: The Role of Employee Service Recovery Performance in Customer-Perceived Justice and Customer Loyalty After Service Failures," *Journal of Applied Psychology* 92 (2007): 475–89.

222 eight steps companies should follow: Barlow and Møller, *Complaint Is a Gift.*

223 they create what Goodman calls "customer delight": J. A. Goodman, S. Newman, and C. Grimm, "The ROI of Delight," *Customer Relationship Management* 8 (2003): 12; and John A. Goodman, *Strategic Customer Service: Managing the customer experience to increase positive word of mouth, build loyalty and maximize profits* (New York: AMACOM, American Management Association, 2009).

227 call-center employee handles an average of ten hostile calls a day: A. A. Grandey, D. Dickter, and S. Hock-Peng, "The customer is not always right: Customer aggression and emotion regulation of service employees," *Journal of Organizational Behavior* 25, no. 3 (2004): 397–418.

230 display rules can add a huge layer of stress to an already challenging job: A. Grandey, "When 'the show must go on': Surface and deep acting as determinants of emotional exhaustion and peer-rated service delivery," *Academy of Management Journal* 46 (2003): 86–96.

230 The mental effort required to regulate their emotions: A. R. Hochschild, *The Managed Heart: Commercialization of Human Feeling* (Berkeley: University of California Press, 1983); and A. Grandey, "Emotion regulation in the workplace: A new way to conceptualize emotional labor," *Journal of Occupational Health Psychology* 5 (2000): 95–110.

230 They typically use one of two methods: Grandey, "When 'the show must go on.' "

231 representatives with strict display rules feel more distressed: P. Totterdell and D. Holman, "Emotional regulation in customer service roles: Testing a model of emotional labor," *Journal of Occupational Health Psychology* 8, no. 1 (2003): 55–73.

233 Call-Yachol call center's Web site (English tab) is at www.callyachol.co.il.

Chapter 8: Squeaking as Social Activism

240 the company admitted, "we've boobed!": BBC News, "Victory for customers in bra war," news.bbc.co.uk/2/hi/uk_news/8039332.stm.

241 "I'm working on a Web site where girls": Updates about Ms. Williams's Web site and blog for women and adolescent girls can be found at www.missredsays.wordpress.com.

242 Matthew Holley: Background on Matthew and the Holleys and information on the foundation the Holleys set up to keep alive Matthew's desire to inspire youth can be found at www.matthewholleyfoundation.com/1.html.

244 the Holley Provision: www.matthewholleyfoundation.com/11.html.

244 One study examined the role of self-efficacy: G. Makoul and M. Roloff, "The role of efficacy and outcome expectations in the decision to withhold relational complaints," *Communication Research* 25, no. 1 (1998): 5–29.

245 Life presents us with frequent opportunities to influence our communities: R. H. Warland, R. O. Herrmann, and D. E. Moore, "Consumer complaining and community involvement: An exploration of their theoretical and empirical linkages," *Journal of Consumer Affairs* 18, no. 1 (1984): 64–78.

248 Complimenting others and expressing appreciation ... boost the mood: See "gratitude" in M. E. P. Seligman, *Authentic Happiness: Using the new positive psychology to realize your potential for lasting fulfillment* (New York: Free Press, 2002).

249 Michael Bloomberg announced the million tree initiative: www.milliontreesnyc.org/html/home/home.shtml.

253 A common example of overrepresentation occurs in elections: For an example of voter turnout during an off-year election see www .wsws.org/articles/1999/nov1999/elec-n05.shtml.

257 But when decision makers hear complaints from three different people: K. R. B. Weaver et al., "Inferring the popularity of an opinion from its familiarity: A repetitive voice can sound like a chorus," *Journal of Personality and Social Psychology* 92, no. 5 (May 2007): 821–33.

258 *homework has little to do with achievement:* H. Cooper, J. C. Robinson, and E. A. Patall, "Does homework improve academic achievement? A synthesis of research, 1987–2003," *Review of Educational Research* 76, no. 1 (2006): 1–62; and A. Kohn, *The Homework Myth: Why Our Kids Get Too Much of a Bad Thing* (Cambridge, MA: Da Capo Press, 2006).

259 having regular family meals: M. E. Eisenberg et al., "Correlations between family meals and psychosocial well-being among adolescents," *Archives of Pediatric Adolescent Medicine* 158, no. 8 (2004): 792–96.

259 help with disordered-eating behaviors: M. W. Gilman et al., "Family dinner and disordered eating behaviors in a large cohort of adolescents," *Eating Disorders* 18 (2010): 10–24.

259 Sara Bennett: S. Bennett and N. Kalish, *The Case Against Homework: How Homework Is Hurting Our Children and What We Can Do About It* (New York: Crown, 2006).

260 Sara Bennett's informative Web site: For references, sample complaint letters, support, and assistance from other parents—www.stophomework.com.

261 four main issues that had a negative impact: J. A. Goodman and D. Ward, "Satisfied patients lower risk and improve the bottom line," *Patient Safety & Quality Healthcare,* March/April, 2008.

263 Father of Potty Parity: J. F. Banzhaf III, "Final frontier for the law?" *National Law Journal* 13 (April 1990).

263 Sandra Rawls's and Savannah Day's studies cited in K. H. Anthony and M. Dufrense, "Potty parity in perspective: Gender and family issues in planning and designing public restrooms,"

Journal of Planning Literature 21, no. 3 (2007): 267–94; and www.banzhaf.net.

264 legal complaints filed by the Father of Potty Parity himself: J. F. Banzhaf III against the University of Michigan, banzhaf.net/docs/ michigan.html.

Epilogue: Squeaking on Social Media

267 Stuart Elliott, "Milk Campaign Ended Amid Social Media Firestorm," *New York Times,* July 21, 2011. http://www.nytimes.com/2011/07/22/business/media/milk-campaign-withdrawn-amid-charges-of-sexism.html.

A Note On The Author

Guy Winch, Ph.D., received a doctorate in clinical psychology from New York University, completed a postdoctoral fellowship in family and couple therapy, and has been using complaints as a therapeutic tool in his psychotherapy practice for more than a decade. He also dabbles in stand-up comedy. This is his first book. He lives in New York City. Visit his Web site at http://guywinch.com.

47271414R00139

Made in the USA
Columbia, SC
30 December 2018